Miscommunication

To my wife and three children:
Morgan, Deborah, Lance, and Brooke

Miscommunication

C. David Mortensen

With Carter M. Ayres

SAGE Publications
International Educational and Professional Publisher
Thousand Oaks London New Delhi

For information address:

SAGE Publications, Inc.
2455 Teller Road
Thousand Oaks, California 91320
E-mail: order@sagepub.com

SAGE Publications Ltd.
6 Bonhill Street
London EC2A 4PU
United Kingdom

SAGE Publications India Pvt. Ltd.
M-32 Market
Greater Kailash I
New Delhi 110 048 India

Printed in the United States of America

Library of Congress Cataloging-in-Publication Data

Main entry under title:

Mortensen, C. David.
    Miscommunication / C. David Mortensen with
Carter M. Ayres.
        p. cm.
    Includes bibliographical references and index.
    ISBN 0-8039-7375-6 (cloth : alk paper).—ISBN 0-8039-7376-4
    (pbk: alk paper)
    1. Communication. I. Ayres, Carter M. II. Title.
P90.M66 1997   96-35714
302.2—dc20

    98 99 00 01 02 03 10 9 8 7 6 5 4 3 2

Acquiring Editor:	Margaret Seawell
Editorial Assistant:	Reneé Piernot
Production Editor:	Sanford Robinson
Production Assistant:	Karen Wiley
Typesetter/Designer:	Danielle Dillahunt
Cover Designer:	Ravi Balasuriya

Contents

Preface

Human interaction can be analyzed from any number of different angles. Our interest is primarily with the capacity and willingness of young adults to use complex linguistic skills to carry out a host of practical and pragmatic concerns in concert with the efforts of other people. We want to know how complex projects, activities, and routines of sense-making practice work or function when things go smoothly and everything turns out right. We also want to understand what happens when things go badly or get out of synch. At issue is the impact of the sheer *complexity* of forces and factors that make things turn out the way they do, for better or for worse. Such a recognition underscores the advantage of being in a good position to examine the nuts and bolts of what is said or done to acquire or preserve a tradition of high-quality performances. At issue is an important distinction between largely effective forms and faulty forms of face-to-face interaction. At the center of the drama is the core issue of how mutually accessible clusters or networks of individuals manage to move into or out of varying states, degrees, or gradations of difficulty and perplexity with one another.

The prevailing conditions may be more or less favorable to the shared pursuit or fulfillment of productive outcomes. We equate a favorable communicative atmosphere with the opportunity to construct a wide spectrum of agreements and understandings as the shared basis for an enduring working consensus. In contrast, largely unfavorable conditions are associated with a succession of highly protracted or deeply involving forms of misinterpretation that promote a wide spectrum of disagreements and misunderstandings. Our main objective is to assess the prospects for constructive change of those social settings that operate under mostly unfavorable conditions into those with better odds or options for acquiring, preserving, or sustaining a favorable range of opportunities for genuine human encounter. A long-range goal is to promote a greater measure of communicative literacy for every human being on the face of the globe.

The concept of *miscommunication* is very tricky to define. How can one describe (to someone else) what proves so difficult to figure out in the first place? One starting point is an initial presumption. Human beings are ordinarily quite sensitive to the larger issue of what transpires when things go well or badly. By this standard, acts or episodes of effective human encounter occur *whenever* someone (observer) interprets what someone else (participant) expresses in a clear, cogent, and coherent manner.

This is akin to demonstrating how the personal vocabulary/idiom of one person can be readily translated/interpreted/integrated into the vocabulary/idiom of any other. In other words, successful communication is a collective and collaborative achievement of the highest order. Hence the basic task is to work to improve the clarity and coherence of what we express or convey before other people. At issue are the basic dynamics at work within and across a wide spectrum of face-to-face interactions that somehow fall short (of some imposed standard) or miss the mark in a particularly telling or striking way. The study of miscommunication admits that sometimes things make no sense at all.

This book is organized around a basic set of themes. The essential progression is from abstract matters of theory to those of specific refinement and application. Relevant considerations are presented in three stages. First is a broad theoretical conception of the conditions that are necessary for various acts or episodes of miscommunication to occur. Second is the issue of how the theoretical conception of miscommunication in question applies to any number of salient conditions in which an array of agreements, disagreements, understandings, and misunderstandings come to light. Third is a concern with individual effort and shared struggle to improve the quality or substance of face-to-face interaction with fellow creatures like ourselves.

To these ends, the first four chapters present a broad theoretical conception of the subject of human miscommunication and the problematic use of words and gestures in public settings. Here we make a sharp distinction between the intrinsic features of observable conditions and the tacit consequences of such conditions being in place. In effect, the structure of intentional action leaves behind an imprint, a residue, or substratum of unintended or unforeseen consequences. Therefore, Chapters 1 through 4 focus on the negotiated coproduction of highly indistinct, inaccurate, unclear, or confused modes of (a) self-expression and (b) interpretive response.

Chapter 1 examines the impact of faulty implication on the form and content of shared performance. The concept of *implication* refers to any unspoken or unstated urge, desire, or intention that serves to color or skew the way we see specific and concrete things in the context of our subsequent encounters with other human beings. Here what is at stake is the composite impact of faulty (a) assumptions, (b) inferences, (c) expectations, (d) reflections, and the imposition of (e) extreme forms of attributional error in personal accounts of success or failure. It is useful, therefore, to examine the outer limits of *metacommunication*—in which the subject of communication is transformed into both the subject and the object of what takes place at the same time. To this end, Chapters 2, 3, and 4 examine the emergence of certain basic forms of (a) psychological or cognitive distortion in (1) the way in which individuals choose to express themselves and/or (2) the way in which other people interpret or take specific initiatives into account, (b) interpersonal disruption in the give-and-take or ebb-and-flow of conversation, and (c) linguistically based confusion over the definition and direction of subsequent actions. Taken together, a gradual or sudden buildup of a stockpile of faulty assumptions, cognitive distortions, interpersonal disruptions, and linguistic confusions serves to place an artificial and fabricated limit on the overall degree of our effectiveness as human interactants.

Chapters 5 and 6 make a case for the overarching theme. We contend that the routine (re)production of a steady stream of faulty implications, when combined with distorted, disrupted, or confused modes of shared activity, is likely to promote a climate of disagreement and misunderstanding among the respective parties. As a consequence, the emergence of either frequently repeated or highly pronounced acts or episodes of misinterpretation, misunderstanding, and miscommunication tends to weaken or erode our ability and willingness to maintain close ties with other people. The possibility of profound miscommunication is not to be ruled out at any point along the way. In light of these perplexing conditions, Chapter 7 invokes the dual concepts of *obtainable* and *realistic* standards to explore multiple possibilities for turning specific matters of personal liability into shared resources for mutual gain. The final objective is to improve the conditions in which we encounter one another on a daily basis.

A long list of acknowledgments is in order. It has been a privilege to be a professor of communication science, in the Department of Communication Arts, at the University of Wisconsin—Madison, for more than a quarter of the twentieth century. From the insight gained through personal contact with a total of some 20,000 students or more, it is possible, perhaps, to get a better glimmer of what is at stake within the framework of such a universal and inexhaustible form of living subject matter. A university-sponsored Human Subjects Committee offered steady guidance and direction to ensure the personal anonymity of those who participated in the study reported here. In addition, faculty members in communication science were a source of collective inspiration in a quest for more exacting and rigorous methods and standards of textual analysis, evaluation, and assessment. Linda Henzl maintained a joyful and receptive spirit while preparing an accurate computerized transcript of personal accounts. We are grateful to Sophie Craze, Margaret Seawell, and Renée Piernot at Sage, and Janet E. Brown for Sage, who did everything possible to fulfill the promise of the project from the initial phase to the final stage of production. In addition, several anonymous reviewers provided insightful, tough-minded, and penetrating comments about specific concerns with initial drafts.

CHAPTER 1

Implication

In the course of face-to-face interaction, we often withhold much of what we very much want to share with one another. Issues of personal and interpersonal importance may seem too difficult to discuss directly. For this reason, we tend to hint at the existence of such complex matters within the context of topics that are much easier to discuss. By doing so, we hope that others will notice these subtle implications, inquire further about them, and thereby strengthen our sense of connectedness with those around us. Whenever such optimal outcomes do not occur, others are left to develop alternative sets of working assumptions about the meanings of our indirect allusions and subtle hints. Faulty assumptions are often inaccurate, and tend to produce certain types of communicative difficulties that ultimately diminish, injure, or end relationships of vital importance. For this reason, effective and mutually supportive communication depends upon the capacity and willingness to discuss such tacit and covert matters in a fair and equitable manner. In this study, we equate a state of "weak" communication with the relative lack of skill or resolve to deal with questionable implications and inferences, and a condition of "strong" communication with the ability and willingness to discuss such tacit and covert matters in a clear and cogent manner. It is important to be *in a position* to discuss the impact of faulty implications in any case; at the very least, we can ensure that we are ready to share our problems and potential answers when others become able to do so as well.

The study of face-to-face interaction is fascinating precisely because it is so very complicated. The quality of our insight and understanding of other people, and of ourselves as well, acquires thematic definition through acts of complex elaboration and intricate detail. Personal knowledge of the larger process is quite imperfect, however, because no person has full access to what registers below the surface of other people's observations. Everyone strives, therefore, for a *generalized* conception of human understanding by constructing a set of inferences and implications—right or wrong—about the subtle meaning of what transpires.

It is impossible to describe or share relevant, salient, or important aspects of personal information without producing a steady stream of inferences and implications. Such a notion is important because it shows why the subject of human understanding is after all, by definition and of necessity, partial, incomplete, and error-prone. Several relevant components are entailed, as discussed in the *Oxford English Dictionary*. First is the notion of what it means to *implement,* or put to use. Unspoken implications are designed to be used like tools, equipment, or utensils. Each one is implemented in a distinctive and deliberate manner for a specified period of time. The activity is largely situation-bound and context-dependent. Therefore, what is gained or lost is not easily generalized across diverse types of social situations. Second is the element of *choice and decision.* Here what is suggested is the notion that one chooses to use something for a particular purpose or effect, namely, to satisfy or fulfill a given condition under mostly uncertain or unknown circumstances. Third is the *act of implicating,* which means to include as relevant, interesting, or involved in the manner of something that becomes intertwined or entangled in complex conditions. Fourth, there is the (hidden) presence of some *tacit, covert,* or *implicit* traces of sensory activation. Even simple actions may serve to evoke or stir up additional or secondary points of association along the way. What registers in one person's frame of reference may not be directly expressed or conveyed to anyone else. Finally, there is the suggestion of something *inexplicable,* not clearly stated, either vague and indefinite or somehow unknown or uncertain. In effect, each one is forced to deal with fuzzy and indistinct aspects of the larger process.

A key sign is a shift from the center of attention and sensitivity to the periphery of conscious awareness. Scharfstein (1993) describes a condition of ineffability in terms of the very shyness of words and gestures, their common tendency to vanish when one has the greatest need for them. At times, the shared context of human knowledge may be inadequate or insufficient to fulfill the full mandate of the need or desire for greater contact or depth of personal encounter. Here is where any given collection of interactants may evolve, suddenly or gradually, into a state of mutual impenetrability.

There is a wide spectrum of social conditions in which the linguistic idiom of any one person will not, and does not, translate neatly into those adapted by anyone else who is accessible or close at hand (Grace, 1987). Individuals are prone to express themselves in a highly personal idiom that may not always be effortlessly translated into equivalent terms by anyone else. As to the shifting parameters of uncertainty and apprehension, Scharfstein (1993) writes,

> I do not know why the process of eliciting our views from ourselves takes so long or why, in effect, it never ends. The only general reason I can propose is that we are internally so complex and personal an environment for the creation of thoughts that the internal "attitudes" and "positions" cannot be stated quickly and cannot be fully stated at all; and furthermore, personal conditions change their nuances quickly and often, and with each change elicit an at least subtly different verbal response from the listener, so that the whole flow of ostensibly similar thoughts may take a distinctly different path each time.... This kind of knowing that one does not yet exactly know never changes. (p. 13)

When a great deal of activity takes place within a short period of time, inferences and implications are most likely to flourish and proliferate. Polanyi's (1967) study of the innovative qualities of the implicit or tacit dimension in human knowledge is quite instructive. His work supports the idea that *"we can know more than we can tell"* (p. 4) about the presence of one another. At issue is how far the outer limits of personal experience extend beyond the focus of immediate awareness or scope of conscious control. His argument stems from the premise that we do not have direct access to all of the internal processes that make it possible to express the very things we do.

Polanyi speaks of these mechanisms as "indwelling," that is, any purposeful mode of personal conduct where the driving force is a deep commitment to the conviction that there is something there to be discovered (p. 17). By this standard, even highly skilled perform-ances may be achieved without a complete account of what is entailed on the part of everyone who may be concerned. In effect, individuals do not maintain direct access to the collective resources that make it possible to express themselves before others.

Because we do not know all the complexities and complications that make it possible to engage in effective human communication in the first place, we cannot pretend to be able to understand other people completely—without flaw, error, mistake, or miscalculation. No personal idiom is infallible. There are no perfect translations, or flawless interpreters, of the human code.

This is similar to Giddens's (1994) basic claim. As the members of a complex and diverse society, we do not possess complete knowledge of ourselves, much less of anyone else. For one thing, our own lives are full of uncertainty, ambiguity, paradox, and contradiction. We are, from one standpoint, passive subjects constrained by natural forces (large scale) over which we have little personal control. Yet we are also coproducers of a sense of social order (small scale) over which we have a great deal of control. The basic contradictions—involving active and passive possibilities of initiation and response—confound individual effort to achieve clear and complete communication. Hu-man knowledge involves our dual nature as *products* of the natural world but *creators* of the social world. A given way of life is both inherited and acquired at the same time. As a consequence, everyone is forced to come to terms with a negotiated definition of the relation between self and other as both passive and active sources of interven-tion in human affairs.

A multiplicity of things are implicated. Mythos fills the air. Per-sonal perspectives keep changing yet the basic processes somehow remain much the same. Over time we may come to see ourselves at the center of our own physical surroundings (first person perspec-tive), as objects of other observers (second person perspective), and as distanced from others viewed as different from or separate from ourselves (third person perspectives). At stake is the position and place of each person in relation to the organization of the larger scheme of things.

Matters of personal identity remain somewhat uncertain or unknown. Even simple acts defy the outer limits of personal appeal to any conventional, commonsense, or causal explanation. I move my arm at will without having complete access to what makes it possible for me to do so. What I am capable of doing is greater than what I can say about the process of production. Anyone who is in a similar position may consider what makes it possible, and perhaps necessary, to search for the larger, implicit, hidden truth within (Polanyi, 1967, p. 25). On a larger scale, collective efforts must tolerate personal deficiencies of inquiry in "a society which has such shortcomings fatally involved in its workings" (p. 92). What we know, therefore, must remain somewhat inarticulate. Yet, despite the limits of identification, definition, and description of personal knowledge, we somehow maintain the effort to create a social order in life, engage in constructive or communal actions, and thereby strive to preserve or sustain a coherent sense of worldview.

The process of mutual discovery moves from the center to the periphery of conscious awareness. At the outer limit is the renewed opportunity to fill in the blank spaces and the blind spots of each one's own version of the final equation. It is not necessary, therefore, to attempt to attend equally to every possible detail in the composite picture. Implicit learning enables one to grasp complex information without complete verbal knowledge of what transpires (Seger, 1994). One may remain unaware of (a) what transpires itself, as in subliminal perception, (b) what mental categories are being formed, as in stereotyping, and/or (c) what sorts of influences determine judgment or feeling, as in a misattribution of reason or cause (Bargh, 1994). The process of discovery involves a great deal of unconscious arousal (priming) of previously presented stimuli and provides a primitive evolutionary basis for explicit thought (Reber, 1992), cognitive development (Gelman, 1991), person perception, and decision making (Hill, Lewicki, Czyzewski, & Boss, 1989).

Because so much of what is gained from implicit learning is not fully accessible to conscious awareness, it is not possible to provide a full or, in many cases, any verbal account of what unfolds in such an inclusive and abstract way. Virtually anything that triggers implicit associations may be subject to influence that is quite incidental or undetectable (Higgins & Bargh, 1987; Kihlstrom, 1987; Kitayama, 1990; Niedenthal, 1989). This realization situates the focus of implicit learning right in the center of what eludes or limits the specific use of words and gestures as stable reference points for shared actions that operate at the periphery of conscious awareness (Haslam, 1994; Haslam & Fiske, 1992). It is an eternal puzzle. Human beings don't have privileged access to why they think, feel, and behave as they do; yet, without sufficiently developed expressive and responsive abilities, they can't tell one another why they are happy, angry, upset, disappointed, sad, or, in a variety of other ways, define, classify, and explain important matters in terms that make sense to other people.

The image of information being produced at a fast and furious pace undermines mystical notions of people having privileged access to the driving mechanisms of mind, body, and spirit. Instead, it explains why any group of individuals might not be able to access specific causes or good reasons why they should act the very way they do (Graesser, Singer, & Trabasso, 1994). The two domains of implicit and explicit forms of knowledge fit together insofar as one's own conception of things remains coherent at a local (situation-specific) and a global (generalized) level of interpretation. The line of division between the private and the public sphere is fluid and permeable.

The capacity and willingness to make sense together depends upon implicature because, as Scheff (1990) claims, (a) what individuals articulate to one another ordinarily leaves some aspects (of content and form) unarticulated; (b) for this reason, it is "almost impossible for the interactants to understand fully *what* they are talking about, at its various levels, or to understand the implications of the *form* their talk takes" (p. 27); and (c) what gets worked out in interpretation is imaginary effort to link explicit conditions with implicit inferences. Here Scheff appeals to Peirce's (1955) concept of *abduction* (rapid and expansive cycling between observation and imagination) as active effort to locate relevant patterns (reference) upon which many cognitive search operations are predicated.

A similar principle is echoed in Grice's (1989) notion that cognitive schemes incorporate elements of implication and implicature as they make explicit reference to words and gestures that are not themselves directly stated. Hinting is a case in point. Some types of nonconventional action may be mutually comprehended without any dependence on the meaning of spoken utterances (with little or no distinctive relevance). The tacit goal of cooperative action is to give out no more or no less verbal information than what is required on the basis of efficiency or efficacy. Hence, Grice's famous implications: Strive to express yourself honestly; avoid obscurity of expression, ambiguity; be brief; and be orderly. Violations of commonly held but unstated interpretive maxims invite further scrutiny or inspection. Due to contextual and background factors, as well as prior acquaintance with the basic logic of conversational games, it is not useful or relevant to spell everything out in minute detail.

As a corollary, many relevant things must be left unsaid. The necessity to understand the sheer sweep of personal articulations and their intended meanings is difficult enough. Very often the intended meaning of spoken actions does not register in the interpreted meaning. Members of close relationships, for example, may be under greater pressure to be quite sensitive to words and gestures and their underlying implications. In a fast-paced, culturally diverse society, human beings are quite limited in their ability to pick out other people's implications.

The tacit dimension of personal relevance is fully implicated in how well or badly individuals treat one another. We find ourselves daily in the company of those who may not help us to mobilize the energy and effort required to make our inferences and implications clear. There may even be a tacit threat of misuse or abuse. The subject of rhetoric, according to Richards (1965), should be "a study of misunderstanding and its remedies" in a vast and inexhaustive domain where "we have no measure with which to calculate the extent and degree of our hourly losses in communication" (p. 3). In effect, everyone is left to decide for himself or herself how good forms of communication may differ from bad.

There are skills to be mastered to be sure, but no one treatise can successfully apply them to all possible or plausible situations. Each language user is left to rummage between *clear* and *obscure* conceptions, and between *distinct* and *confused* viewpoints. A clear idea, according to Peirce (1955), is one that can be taken into account when it is met so that no other will be mistaken for it. *If* it fails this standard, it is said to be obscure (p. 23). Peirce invites everyone to get involved in the larger enterprise to develop greater clarity and less obscurity in human affairs. Here an act of miscommunication is the equivalent of walking around in a muddle or a daze.

The standard of expressive clarity holds for speaking and listening as well as for thinking and feeling. The ideal is to express ourselves so clearly and fluently that others will be able to grasp and comprehend our intention or meaning without great effort (S. Millar, 1993). Notice that it takes the combined effort of two or more to follow along with what is being said by one. Because the opposite of intelligibility is lack of clarity, or unintelligibility, we have an obtainable standard and a lower threshold for defining failure, that is, muffled voices, confusing talk, baffling remarks, stammering, and hesitation. Garbled speech can be noticed but not in a readily interpretable manner. Glossolalia and speaking in tongues—in the expectation of a miracle—are more extreme cases in point. Here it does not matter whether anyone gets the point or not. The ideal of a crystal-clear expression may be viewed as one way of ensuring mutual understanding as the overall goal of communication (Bartsch, 1987).

The ultimate test of personal clarity is whether any given act of self-expression can be accurately interpreted by another observer. The enterprise can be best described as a combination of luck, effort, and ability in a constantly shifting or unsettled equation (Sternberg & Kolligian, 1990). This suggests that what passes for innate talent is usually the result of intense and deliberate practice to become as fluent and articulate a person as possible (Ericsson, Krampe, & Tesch-Romer, 1993). Said another way, the ultimate test of conventional language is whether it can be used by any one individual as a mechanism to communicate with any other one. By this standard, "successful communication takes place when the hearer understands the speaker as the speaker intended" (Dummett, 1993, p. 180).

In short, implications complicate matters. What you see and hear is not always what you get. The meaning or specific relevance of what someone says or does is not to be taken as merely given or self-evident. Although we cannot help taking some things for granted, we may presume too much or too little—when framed from someone else's point of view. Of course, some types of overt actions are easier to grasp or comprehend while others turn out to be far more complex, intricate, and entangled. To notice something happening to someone else requires less, for instance, than it does to establish what it means to that particular person, or why it matters to any other observer as well. The flow of inference and implication makes personal statements much more than they may seem at first, and one is left to grasp whatever is possible with limited awareness and knowledge.

Relevant issues revolve around seven categories of implicit activity. First, personal *assumption* consists of tacit premises about the way things are—or might turn out to be. It is impossible not to presume, or take certain things for granted, because initial hunches are derived mainly from the working premises acquired from previous exchanges with other people. One implicates the current time or newly anticipated future with salient urges or dispositions carried over from the way that things used to be. One imposes upon what takes place now with what transpired before, in real or imagined form. Second, *inference* involves inductive leaps from one assumption to another, or from one premise, through a reasoning device, to a particular conclusion. Inferential movement involves systemic application of personal logic to a specific case in point. The important thing is whether one's own private calculations and musings are subject to reality-testing against the logical standards of anyone else. Third, *expectation* describes future-oriented meanings and decisions that establish minute (microlevel) connections between what transpires in the present tense (what transpires now) and the limits of the immediate future (what takes place next). What matters as relevant or salient is the overall degree to which we live up to the largely unstated or unspoken expectations of ourselves and others. Fourth, *reflection* discusses the ways in which one may give added meaning to what is said and done now based on what was said and done in past encounters. The composite makeup of tacit expectation and silent reflection preserves a sense of personal continuity within the larger flow of past, present, and future events.

Taken together, these implicit devices serve as self-correcting or self-monitoring guidelines. When used properly, the ability to know how and when to monitor questionable aspects of socialized activity is what enables us to make small-scale adjustments and accommodations in how we (a) present ourselves before others or (b) react to subsequent responses in turn. Fifth, *attribution* accounts for largely unspoken decisions that assign responsibility for specific outcomes, both success and failure, to self, other, situation, or basic principle as the main cause or reason things turn out the way they do. Here the goal is to minimize the use of extreme forms of attributional error in personal accounts of success and failure. Sixth, *metacommunication* refers broadly to communication about the process of communication that makes questions of inference and implication both the subject and the object of explicit deliberation. In effect, the effective use of such mechanisms makes it possible to correct the application of misleading implications in midcourse. Seventh, the search for *common ground* is described as shared effort to establish an initial base of operation. It is called a "search" or a "quest" because there are no quick fixes or tricks of the trade to lead anyone to an optimum state of consensus or mutual understanding of problematic circumstance. The total magnitude of misinterpretation, misinformation, and miscommunication is a composite function of how well (or poorly) each person works to correct or minimize the proliferation of faulty implications.

People often find it easier to manage and control the production of false and faulty sequences of inference and implication in those very circumstances where (a) solid agreements can be reached about the various motives, intentions, and interpretations of one another's actions and (b) adequate levels of mutual understanding can be maintained about the meaning and relevance of complex sequences of goal-directed action. As a consequence, it should be more difficult to sustain a long succession of high-quality performances in the absence of any working consensus about the personal meaning of whatever is said or done. Of considerable relevance is the broad issue of what causes people to go through such indistinct periods where they are suddenly unable or unwilling to make clear and coherent sense of present circumstances.

As a way to test the broad outlines of the theory of miscommunication envisioned here against the narrow confines of specific domains of practice and application, it has proven useful to ask a diverse range of people to reconstruct a selected list of prior interactions where certain types of social conditions have prevailed. Of immediate concern are the distinctions between favorable or unfavorable *circumstance* in relation to effective or faulty courses of personal *action*. A series of test cases for Chapters 1 through 6 are based on the personal accounts of 80 adults enrolled in undergraduate courses in communication arts at the University of Wisconsin—Madison. Each subject was asked to complete an "Interaction Profile." Instructions read as follows:

> Make a mental inventory of the people you encounter on a frequent basis. Now select the one person you would rank as having achieved the highest level of personal agreement of anyone on the list. Second,

select the one person you would rank as having achieved the strongest level of personal disagreement of anyone on the list. Third, select the one person you would rank as having achieved the highest level of personal understanding of anyone on the list. Fourth, select the one person you would rank as having achieved the strongest level of personal misunderstanding of anyone on the list. Notice that the same person may show up on one or more of the categories, i.e., a person who shared the highest level of agreement may be the same one you would rank as having established the strongest level of understanding as well. Provide a detailed account of the actual types of face-to-face interactions that have taken place in each of these different types of human interaction. Describe each category with as much detail as possible.

Respondents were encouraged to focus not so much on matters of physical appearance or personality and character traits but on the central issue of what had actually transpired during either a short episode or a long sequence of direct and/or mediated forms of personal encounter. Participation was strictly voluntary with assurance given that anonymity would be preserved by deleting any personal references. Participants signed release forms granting permission to include their personal accounts.

The link between theory and practice will be explored in several different spheres and clusters of identity and association. To this end, each chapter will begin with a review of recent findings in cognitive psychology and communication research. Each of these reviews provides a tentative theoretical frame of reference for the study of mutual effort in making sense of diverse acts of miscommunication where states of agreement and understanding, or disagreement and misunderstanding, prevail. We want to know, in the final analysis, how the participants choose to express themselves, or respond to others, particularly under duress or pressure, or where complex levels of exchange shift rapidly, either going from better to worse or from bad to good.

ASSUMPTION

Personal implications are an important but implied source of significance or relevance. If others don't understand our tacit implications, they are left to develop alternative personal assumptions (about us) rather than acquire a direct, immediate, and genuine understanding of what we are actually thinking, feeling, saying, and doing—unless, of course, we suddenly become brave and tell them directly what we actually want to say. Such working assumptions aren't necessarily bad, except to the degree that each participant tends to treat his or her initial hunches about others as somehow an intuitively self-evident source of definition and direction that applies across many diverse and varied forms of personal encounters. For this reason, our working assumptions serve as unstated suppositions with the power to affect the tone, depth, and direction of future events. For example, a person may feel in control, at peace, or even fulfilled when others appear to think well of him or her ("I'm likeable, and I have lots of friends"); just as surely, a person may suddenly feel out of control, anxious, and very concerned when others appear to think ill of him or her ("I know she doesn't like me—I can tell just by looking at her!").

There is considerable importance to what any one person may presume or take for granted about another. After all, human beings are not always able to make solid or well-founded assumptions about the general causes and specific reasons for questionable actions. Many unspoken hunches help to construct our worldviews for us, while others focus on specific issues and problems that we may want to solve.

The assumptions we make often seem to work well too. We answer our own questions, such as "What is George thinking?" by assuming something like the following: "Yes, I bet I know—George is glad to see me!" Additional evidence to the contrary—for example, George is frowning—is easily explained by the revised premise that "George is glad to see me, but something's wrong because he's frowning." Persistent thinkers will consider alternative possibilities to explain George's behavior. For example, "George is glad to see me, but he's pretending to be quite angry about something." Each assumptive slant is different, and any one may be either right or wrong, depending on George's actual state of mind at the time. In this way, our working premises lead us to supply the missing links of information about what George is thinking, feeling, saying, and doing.

Still, the possibility of personal bias, as with the use of rose-colored glasses, is everywhere one may want to look. No matter what is taken for granted, some degree of uncertainty and tentativeness will remain.

Human concerns do not go completely away. The work of self-assessment involves a considerable degree of attentiveness to unsettled aspects of personal engagement in an incomplete and unfinished process. Larger issues involve a great deal of attentiveness to unresolved matters of individual or mutual concern. What matters is whether our cherished assumptions turn out to be quite (a) positive or negative in outlook, (b) open or closed to further inspection, and (c) true or false as a consequence of their application or use.

Positive/Negative Slant

An unslanted premise is defined as neutral, nonapplicable, or mute. It makes no real difference one way or another. The orienting slant or skew of a given assumption is what disposes one toward certain types of social conditions and away from any plausible alternatives. When acting as such primitive steering mechanisms, positive assumptions tend to be generous and expansive. They help one to focus on the actual fulfillment of potentials, namely, what people are capable of and willing to achieve together. The common accent is placed on what is possible or sufficient about the existing supply of resources, capacities, and skills of each member to pursue and achieve a tradition of high-quality performances or, even more, engage in the spirited pursuit of optimum outcomes. Hence there is an enhanced willingness to subject one's own private calculations and musings against the unspoken personal standards of someone else.

In contrast, largely negative assumptions deflect short-term attention away from a larger sense of what is possible or necessary to achieve one's own ends. They may shift the object of attention away from the larger margin of opportunity for mutual achievement—what is available in abundance—to what is missing or in short supply. Often there is heightened sensitivity to the possibility or prospect of a degree of unfulfillment or some measure of loss. A narrow or rigid set of working premises is selectively attentive to threatening implications and pessimism about coping rather than capitalizing on assets.

In an interesting study, Langston (1994) examined processes underlying a given set of positive experiences. He distinguished between a condition of *coping* with negative events and *capitalizing* on positive events. At the (micro) level of noticeable differences, small aspects of self-enhancing acts are parlayed, one after another, into a series, producing a larger return from a single event. However, it is important to be (a) in control of (b) the expressive responses of others so that a consistent flow of positive events can be expected to accumulate over time. Multiple perspectives expand in a productive and fruitful direction. Two daily diary studies of undergraduates showed that "expressive responses and perceived control were associated with positive affect above and beyond the benefits due to the valence of the positive events themselves" (p. 1112). There is a widespread tendency for people to engage in reality negotiation by distancing themselves from negative feedback about themselves and increasing links with good associations. Such a model makes allowance for illusions that bias input (reality) to sustain a favorable or enhanced conception of personal identity (Roth, Snyder, & Pace, 1986). The general tendency is to maximize one's status in the eyes of self and other (R. Collins, 1975).

A state of flat affect, or low emotive expressiveness, is a key negative symptom of deficiency across a broad spectrum of positive and negative moods (Kring, Smith, & Neale, 1994). To make matters worse, negative assumptions often represent a degree of personal misinterpretation due more to imagination than to an accurate reflection of what others truly think and feel. Learned thought habits—very possibly unresolved issues from the past—play a central role in the development of negative working assumptions that keep one withdrawn and in limbo. Rather than helping us to resolve the core of our mutual concerns, intuitions and imaginations evaluate the total range of interpretive options in the skewed light of past, present, and anticipated experience and encourage us to choose problem-solving strategies that "just seem right," even though we may end up by withdrawing even further than before.

The decision to adopt a positive or a negative outlook can be quite important. In coping with tension and stress, it helps to think constructively—in a manner that solves everyday problems in living at a minimal cost in stress (Epstein, 1990; Epstein & Meier, 1989). In a stressful laboratory situation, poor constructive thinkers generated more negative affective and cognitive responses than did good constructive thinkers with less maladaptive modes of automatic thinking (Katz & Epstein, 1991). Self-enhancing viewpoints play a critical role in shaping the subsequent meaning and impact of stressful life events (Zautra & Wrabetz, 1991).

Closely related is a body of evidence suggesting that a collective tendency toward positive action facilitates the acquisition, development, and maintenance of mutually satisfying relationships (W. Jones, 1985; Long & Andrews, 1990). In this work, positive outlooks are associated with emotional warmth (*empathy*, that is, taking on the feelings of others) and perspective-taking ability (*accuracy*, that is, taking the other's view into account). The desire to be seen in a favorable light sets the stage for sustained and highly credible verification of each other's self-views. These findings do not mean that negative looks have no value. The literature on defensive pessimism shows that some people actually benefit from having negative expectations about future events where the outcome cannot be anticipated (Norem & Cantor, 1986; Showers, 1988, 1992).

Personal assumptions guide personal conduct and steer close relations in different temporal pathways. Essentially, these unspoken guides have the power to redefine and redirect our neural pathways and conscious trajectories toward one set of social outcomes and away from a larger range of alternatives, which encourage or constrain yet another set of working assumptions, and so on. Such simple mechanisms illustrate why thoughts "race," and why people "jump" to hasty conclusions. Their thoughts lunge forward as they bounce from implication to assumption to implication to assumption ad infinitum. There may be little critical judgment involved. Thoughts, often negative and ridiculous at best, suddenly race off in every direction like a steel ball crashing about inside a pinball machine. For this reason, personal assumptions may become the very "stuff" of a great deal of misinformation, miscommunication, hurt, and injury.

Typically, mutually determined outcomes produce some degree of misinformation, misinterpretation, or misunderstanding along the way. For this reason, a steady pileup of faulty assumptions can have negative consequences for us as well as others as objects of care and concern. To grasp such varied points of view, we have to be willing to see how our working premises conflict with theirs—not an easy task by any means. Usually, answers to such questions come more readily as we move toward a state of greater personal maturity and integration. Genuine understanding of other people, as well as of ourselves, occurs as we learn to see things from others' points of view as well as more deeply from our own. Eventually, we will see others as fallible like us,

and develop a deeper and more fulfilling sense of common ground
to explore with them.

Open/Closed to Inspection

Under conditions where the very possibility of interaction is
treated as an opportunity rather than a liability, it is usually an
advantage to treat one's working assumptions as worthy of further
inspection or consideration. We want to be aware of what we assume
so as to exert the greatest possible level of cognitive control over tacit
thoughts and their effects. The main alternative is to be controlled by
premises worthy of further inspection but that are thoughtlessly
accepted in a strictly fatalistic manner. Each time we presume that "this
is just the way things are and nothing more can be done about it," we
narrow our total range of options and cancel out a wider array of
alternatives that might otherwise be available.

A state of strong communication has been equated with the ability
to be as explicit and articulate as possible, and weak communication
with the inability or unwillingness to bring such tacit implications to
the surface in a manifest and observable form. Although it is largely
a personal advantage to be *in a position* to translate implicit notions
into explicit form, it is not, however, always advisable to do so. The
ever-present need to decide whether to disclose tacit cognitive operations remains a crucial one.

It is often a distinct disadvantage to keep things locked up inside
rather than taking the risk of letting them see the light of day; even
so, we know that remaining steadfastly or unconditionally open to the
immediate judgment of others is no panacea for human difficulties
either. Sometimes just "letting it all hang out" only makes things worse
rather than better. Unfortunately, those who are indiscriminately
open about intimate thoughts and feelings often alienate others
because they have not laid the necessary groundwork beforehand.

Self-disclosure is a totalistic concept. It is useful as a global measure of the efficacy of being more open than closed (Bochner, 1984).
Altman and Taylor (1973; D. Taylor & Altman, 1987) compare self-
disclosure with the act of peeling an onion. The surface, or outer layer,
consists of superficial areas of identification, that is, preferences,
tastes, style of clothing. Appearances are accessible to anyone who
cares to notice. Peel the outer layers and you penetrate into the deeper

levels of personal identity. Look beneath the surface and you discover social and political views, deeply ingrained habits, beliefs, values, and core notions of self-worth. Some layers are relatively easy to discover or disclose, while others remain locked within the deep recesses of personal secrets and repressed awareness. Here the *breadth* dimension refers to the total range of subject matter that is deemed worthy of inclusion. The *depth* dimension coincides with whatever aspects of personal information could not be obtained by anyone other than the one who initially disclosed them. Other relevant considerations include the duration of disclosure, the level of intimacy, and flexibility over time.

The model has been subject to revision, however, to take into account more of the dialectical tension between what is revealed or concealed from public view. We know that how much person A discloses to person B is not just a reflection of A's own makeup but an expression of how deeply involved person A is in B's own personal affairs (Petronio, 1991). In other words, self-disclosure is a relational characteristic. This makes the process of self-disclosure subject to a general rule of reciprocity—how much you reveal is contingent on how much others reveal in turn to you. Generally, people who reveal personal information about themselves (a) tend to be liked more than those who disclose at lower levels, (b) disclose more to those they initially like, and (c) are more satisfied as a result of such disclosure (N. Collins & Miller, 1994). Closely related is the link between emotional expressiveness and intimacy; highly self-expressive persons are in the most favorable position to achieve and sustain close ties with others (Monsour, 1992). Secure people have been shown to demonstrate more disclosure flexibility and topical reciprocity than do those who are either ambivalent or avoidant (Mikulincer & Nachshon, 1991). The link between self-disclosure and liking is moderated by such matters as the appropriateness of the disclosure, topic similarity, attributional tendencies, and depth versus breadth considerations (Bell & Daley, 1984; Dindia & Allen, 1992; L. Miller, 1990).

There are, however, countless exceptions to the rule of reciprocity—and this may be where much of the trouble begins. Under conditions of threat or stress, one may give in to the counterurge—to cover up rather than uncover. Moreover, what counts as the disclosure of personal information varies widely from individual to individual and setting to setting. Although interactants may share personal information in greater depth over time, it is still the case that direct, open, and highly disclosive communication occurs in a highly selective and strategic way.

For one thing, the process of self-disclosure is subject to all manner of revision and recalculation (VanLear, 1987, 1991). Even the question of how much to reveal is open to spirited debate. In the past, self-disclosure was often treated as a magic formula—the more the better (Chelune, 1979; Jourard, 1964). Recent findings place greater emphasis on the tension between risk and reward and how much the respective parties are prepared to handle (Weber & Harvey, 1994). Finally, openness may be associated with excessive levels of inquisitiveness, which are then subject to countermeasures—avoidance to reveal and willingness to conceal (Berger & Kellermann, 1989, 1994).

Personal decisions about disclosure interact with other choices over whether to respond to others directly or indirectly. The level of explicitness in message content plays an important part in the emotional response and critical judgments of persuasive efforts (Dillard, Kinney, & Cruz, 1996). Work on theories of politeness suggests a tendency for personal requests to be couched in indirect terms. Polite responses take into account both the literal and the indirect meanings of the speaker (H. Clark & Schunk, 1980). At issue is the blend of distinctive and idiosyncratic modes of self-expression with the multiple meanings at work on a more literal level. The form of request conveys pragmatically important cues about the social status of the respective parties, particularly in those situations where the "superior" source may take offense at an impolite request from an "inferior" or subordinate person (Kemper & Thissen, 1981). Personal concern for mutual interest is a reflection of openness and engagement in two-way as opposed to one-sided exchanges (Daves & Holland, 1989).

Several studies show how the style of implicit requests varies systematically across cultures. Kim and Wilson (1994) outline five types of considerations in monitoring relevant speech acts: (a) concern for clarity, that is, making one's intentions clear and explicit and the absence of hinting or obscurity; (b) imposing, that is, interfering with the hearer's autonomy or freedom of action; (c) consideration for the other's feelings, that is, obligation to help the hearer claim and sustain positive self-images; (d) minimizing the risk of disapproval for self, that is, saving positive face; and (e) effectiveness, that is, the achievement of a conversational goal. Results showed a high degree of consensus in the *relative* ordering of the first four dimensions among Korean and American subjects. On matters of effectiveness, however, Americans viewed the direct strategy as the most effective way of making a request whereas Koreans rated it as the least effective strategy (p. 227).

In another domain, the study of power struggles, gender differences play an important part. Falbo and Peplau (1980) report a tendency for men who view themselves as having more power in heterosexual relations to be more explicit, direct, and blunt when asking a woman to do something. In contrast, women have been shown to engage in more secret test strategies than did men in romantic relationships (Baxter & Wilmot, 1984). On matters of flirtation, the picture is complicated. Early work focused on directness as necessary for the judgment of flirtatious intent when compared with indirect, mediated, or ambiguous communication (Rowland, Crisler, & Cox, 1982). However, a more recent study by Abrahams (1994) locates flirtation along six descriptive dimensions: (a) sexually assertive, that is, who took the initiative; (b) overt, that is, clear and direct in intent, often using verbal and nonverbal cues simultaneously; (c) inviting, that is, suggesting the desire for further interaction, or hinting about intimacy; (d) playful, that is, fun and frivolous actions; (e) unconventional, that is, out of the ordinary and unique rather than normative and predictable; (f) nonverbal, that is, use of unspoken gestures. Men and women, it turns out, judged the flirtatiousness of depicted situations along these six dimensions in highly similar ways.

The movement toward closeness requires a delicate balance between hinting and greater explicitness. Hornstein (1985) focused on how a need for intimacy is conveyed during telephone conversations between pairs of female friends, acquaintances, and strangers. Results showed that friends used more implicit openings, covered a greater range of topics, asked more questions, and closed in more delicate and responsive ways. Conversely, avoidance strategies come into play. Belk and Snell (1988) examined situations of avoiding a request from a spouse when one doesn't especially want to do what the other party wants. Men and women were found to use similar avoidance strategies, depending on how much two-sided (bilateral) or one-sided (unilateral) action was associated either with compliant (acquiescent) or with noncompliant (resistant) styles of avoidance.

A similar picture emerges in various expressions of dissatisfaction with romantic ties. The work of Rusbult and Zembrody (1983) shows how variations in personal styles reflect different strategies for regulating implicit, silent tensions. Some entail active intervention to improve conditions, while others engage in passive waiting or even tolerate massive neglect and deterioration. Results show why some implicit-explicit pathways can be highly destructive and pessimistic while others are viewed as constructive, optimistic, active, and associated with larger efforts to discuss problems, to adapt active problem-solving strategies, and to produce more satisfying outcomes. Here acts of personal passivity were equated with acceptance of minor problems and expectations of improvement with little intervention. Neglectful persons, in contrast, ignored the other partner, behaved in a cruel or hostile manner, didn't care, engaged in types of behavior found to be ineffective in eliminating problems, and allowed conditions to worsen or fall apart. Across the board, considerations of constructiveness and destructiveness intersect with matters of activity or passivity.

In conflict-ridden conversations, similar patterns emerge. As a rule, people are quite sensitive to displays of assertiveness and withdrawal (Ruble & Thomas, 1976). As a consequence, distinctive conversational endings occur for many reasons, ranging from mutual agreement (contact is broken off simultaneously) to unilateral desire to terminate (without asking). In this context, Kellermann, Reynolds, and Chen (1991) report that nonresponsiveness—the failure or refusal to notice or acknowledge the other person or what has been said—is largely an inefficient strategy or procedure for putting things to rest. In sum, across a wide spectrum of shared activities, from initial greeting to the last word, small-scale transitions from implicit to explicit modes of self-expression have been found to play an important strategic role in settling outcomes.

True/False in Use

Behind every big claim to truth, many small aspects of identity and definition are taken into consideration. It is not always possible to know whether one's own premises of operation apply to someone else. A lot of things we suppose to be true may turn out to be quite false—when paired against the truth claims of anyone else. In light of all that is taken for granted, there is always the possibility that one is simply mistaken about one thing or another. Hence the very presumption of "seeing things clearly" refers to a state of taking one's immediate surroundings into full account where the main goal is not to presume too much or too little, by taking things in stride, keeping things in perspective, and neither missing out nor reading too much into little things. A careful reading of what takes place is surely an antidote to a constantly careless misreading of one's participation in the larger course of public events.

Deeply ingrained assumptions exert a subtle, indirect influence on matters of personal choice and decision. This makes their effects all but invisible and, therefore, all the harder to grasp and comprehend from the distanced standpoint of someone else's frame of reference. After all, working premises are not given or inherited features of the human landscape but are imprecise models that are fabricated on a tentative and provisional basis (Snyder, 1989). We *construct* our sacred assumptions as an architect might draw up the initial plans for a skyscraper. The original plans become antiquated as hundreds of needed modifications are made both to the plan and to the building itself as it moves toward completion. Furthermore, whatever we construct for ourselves may be deconstructed (open to further question) or even perhaps reconstructed (redesigned from the ground up) to help us find a more truthful and helpful way through the maze of appearance and reality.

So the critical matter is one of preparation and receptivity. It is often wise to be flexible and adaptive to the specific demand characteristics at work within the confines of the immediate situation. Although there is no surefire formula for what to say or leave unsaid, the most salient standard is dictated by the magnitude of human bond that has already been established. In other words, we must return over and over again to the ultimate issue of what we are willing and able to express to one another in considerable detail. Most important, we must identify and express what we have earned the right to elicit or convey at various stages, transitions, and junctures in personal history. Given these standards, we conclude that it is better to be in a position to engage in strong forms of face-to-face interaction—translating the implicit into explicit forms as it becomes important to do so—than to lack the resources or resolve to carry through with such intent. As always, we ourselves decide whether to acquire or relinquish the resolve to be open or closed at each step along the way.

Virtue in the Recognition of Faults

There is potential value in the tacit recognition that our own precious assumptions, hunches, and dispositional tendencies, upon further inspection, may turn out to be quite fallible, imperfect, incomplete, partial, contingent, tentative, provisional, inaccessible, or otherwise unavailable to someone else. Shared exposure to multiple frames of reference provides renewed opportunity to (a) face up to (uncover) or (b) refuse to face up to (cover up) signs of our own assumptive miscues. Indeed, it may be a source of relief to acknowledge that what we take for granted may turn out to be quite fallible, that is, liable to be mistaken, erroneous, or inaccurate. *Nullities* keep us from achieving a state of perfect, flawless, or total communication. For this reason, the word refers broadly to weaknesses, vulnerabilities, shortcomings, and deficiencies in language use.

The first nullity, according to Richardson (1991), is collective dependence on past experience as a personal guide in dealing with matters of great ambiguity and uncertainty in current circumstances. We are dependent on prior knowledge in ways that we cannot often help or escape. Because everyone carries around a distinctive legacy of memories acquired from a unique life history, and because the totality of history cannot be fully duplicated or replicated, we cannot and do not have complete knowledge of how others view things or attribute meaning to the historical events in their own lives. The second nullity has to do with the urgent consequences of living through a given sequence of choices based on the vagaries and vulnerabilities of past experience. Every time we choose a particular course of action, we pay a price for ignoring and precluding a larger array of newer, and potentially better, problem-solving methods or techniques. The price includes having to tolerate stressful outcomes, present and future, and strengthened but maladaptive decision-making habits that may lead to future difficulty.

These two nullities produce a significant amount of uneasiness or anxiety in our own dealings with other people. For example, we may call our own actions into question, and wonder whether we actually said or did the right thing in the right way at the right time. Furthermore, while interacting with others, there is a strong tendency to cover up our nullities, to pretend that we know what is actually going on. The risk of pretense begins from what is tacitly taken as self-evident and unworthy of further inspection, and may lead to even greater levels of anxiety and denial about problematic conditions later on.

So there may be considerable virtue in the recognition of personal faults. The correction of habitually imperfect courses of action may be modified to the extent that one is willing to confront deeply ingrained sources of doubt and uncertainty. Hope rests in the strength of the desire to "quell the babble of competing inner voices" (E. Jones & Gerald, 1967, p. 181). We struggle to redefine/rediscover what we mean to be/do with one another, as well as to redefine or update our respective representations of one another's conduct. In this way, we may absorb or reframe the troubling actions of significant others within a larger picture of what is truly important. For example, a study by Murray and Holmes (1993) shows how individuals construct storylike representations of their romantic partners to quell feelings of doubt and uncertainty engendered by their partners' faults. Respondents demonstrated an uncanny ability to weave "seemingly negative, contradictory elements into relationship-affirming narratives" (p. 713). Such reconstructions of virtue and fault are subject to dramatic alteration and reversal. In a spirit of tender mercy, the weaknesses, faults, and failures are recast into a more favorable light.

INFERENCE

Inferences permeate the hidden, tacit, or implied process through which one attempts to engage an observer. Observable and verifiable messages are allowed to carry unstated thoughts and feelings too indefinite or otherwise difficult to express to someone else in rather ordinary terms. As observable and tacit responses become entwined with one another, other important notions (on which a lot may be riding) may not be observed or experienced by the others with whom one tries to convey meaning. For example, I might say, "I have been thinking about my wife Jane . . ." Now it is up to you to know what I intended for you to grasp or comprehend. You may think about how I say the sentence, and try to determine what I meant. Do I seem to be happy or sad about my relationship with Jane?

The point is, you need to know what I am implying if you are to understand me from the standpoint of my own frame of reference.

You need to know what is happening with me because such unspoken sources of personal knowledge will help you respond in a way that I will think is accurate or otherwise appropriate. You certainly don't want to offend me by misunderstanding what my statement means—or, worse, by acting as if you don't care what it means. So, you reflect on what might or might not be of concern from your sense of my own standpoint. The range of possibilities may need to be widened or narrowed, depending on the impressions you are getting. You may also wonder why I have brought the topic up. Am I trying to tell you that Jane is off-limits? If so, you might listen for anger in my voice and watch for a glare in my eyes. Perhaps I am trying to tell you that I'm worried about her. If so, you might look for a perplexed expression on my face or for a look of sorrow in my eyes.

These signals are intended to imply something important about how I am feeling about Jane. Just as important, they are intended to tell you what you might say or ask next. If there is anger flashing in my eyes, it may be logical to assume that I am jealous; on the other hand, if my eyes begin to well up with tears, it may be logical to assume I am worried about her health or safety. To misjudge this, and therefore to make an inaccurate assumption, may invite ridicule or rejection, so you want your interpretive logic and subsequent acts of self-expression to be well-founded. After considering all available evidence, you decide on the second meaning and say, "Oh yes, and how is Jane these days?" In so doing, you express a general awareness of the tacit message that I attempt to express or convey; this, of course, encourages further dialogue and greater openness.

Inferences serve as the sort of guiding mechanisms that are quite dependent on matters of context, application, and use. Of general concern is how a given set of inferences can be integrated into a larger system of personal logic. The ancient study of rhetoric invokes the image of one who engages in giving good reasons for relevant conclusions before a public body. In this spirit, philosophers study inferences in the structure of formal arguments and the resolution of technical disputes. At issue is what propositional elements follow from others in a well-reasoned form where one thing leads to a tacit inference or implication of something else. In general terms, the skilled advocate shows how a claim or conclusion is supported by or follows from its own premises. Logical relations connect elements together in a set: *If* this is the case, *then* something else follows—all, some, or none. If I can follow you, and you can follow me, we both pass the test of *validity*. If we can do so consistently over time, we both pass the test of *reliability*. What is found to be valid and reliable is to be taken as solid or well founded. What is seen as invalid and unreliable may be discarded.

Unsound arguments raise questions about errors and mistakes in formal inference-making activity. Any complete book on fallacies covers widespread mishandling of (a) specific instances (movement from particulars to generalizations, or *induction*) and (b) general claims (movement from generalizations to particulars, or *deduction*). With respect to specific instances, we may view X and Y as similar or comparable when someone else sees them as different or otherwise noncomparable. With regard to general claims, however, we may agree about X and Y but not about what we can deduce from, or generalize from, them.

Here the arrangement or alignment of assumptions, premises, and claims may get one into trouble. On complex matters, there may be no ideal way to test a particular generalization through all possible combinations of probable cases. An advocate may be tempted, therefore, to make faulty generalizations, jump to conclusions, mistake cause for reason, try to prove something post hoc (after the fact), indulge in false analogies, confuse the part with the whole, misclassify or blur distinctions, or take refuge in word magic. Notice how each of these slipups deals with contested aspects of subject matter.

On a personal level, we can take contested subject matter out on one another. Criticism of evidence, reason, or claim can turn personal in a flash. One may be tempted to indulge in word magic or mind games to make the worse case seem all the better. Psychological fallacies involve linguistic tricks of the trade, including misuse of authority, guilt by association, personal attacks (ad hominem) plus all manner of rationalization, special pleading (having it both ways), cunning lip service, and biased misconstructions (wishful thinking).

In ordinary conversation, where concerns over propositional precision or consistency may be more relaxed, informal, and loosely constructed, acts of inference may become less rigorous, and their substance more complicated and less truthful. So instead of a linear path from two premises to a conclusion, our personal logic permits, maybe even encourages, the exploration of a wide range of loose clusters of questionable information (R. Anderson & Mortensen, 1967). Here the act of following along (with someone's reasoning) is more a function of what we know about the other person than acceptance of the validity of the arguments per se. As a result, conclusions tend to follow from incomplete information, where one must "fill in the blanks" to complete the picture and provide the missing information. Critical thinking takes a lot of work, with much critical and valuative deliberation about what stands up to public scrutiny and what falls short of the mark (Makau, 1990; A. Millar, 1991; Walton, 1990).

Sensitivity to inferences provides information that goes beyond what is explicitly stated so as to bridge gaps in logic (Hewes & Planalp, 1987), deal with complexity (Goetz, 1979), respond appropriately (Kemper, Estil, Otalvaro, & Schadler, 1985), or track the wider context of meaning, particularly where most of what is expressed is deeply embedded or left implicit (McKoon & Ratcliff, 1992; Semin & Marsman, 1994; Toolan, 1991). This highly integrative process is logically akin to the act of discovery—where intuitive mental operations delight and surprise and turn one's priorities upside down.

Inference-making skill provides a sense of cause and reason for the complexity and complication of personal idioms rife with implication and assumption (Trope, 1986, 1989). Kasof and Lee (1993) review evidence that implicit causality in language use appears to be universal. Because each interactant may infer different meanings from a given set of information or circumstance, alternative concepts of what is truthful, important, or relevant vary widely from person to person. The degree of bias or slant depends on the extent of actor-observer divergence, contrast between active and passive voices, and stylistic accents. The dynamic involving unstated differences occurs in rapid and automatic fashion (Fletcher, Rosanowski, & Fitness, 1994). Related work by Uleman and Moskowitz (1994) shows why salient inferences can occur without intention or awareness as the result of each one's unique history and perceptual set. In this way, a simple, observable message makes possible the transmission of the complex aspects of the larger standpoint that seem too difficult or entangled to discuss (all at once).

So far, our study of miscommunication has been based on two broad and sweeping claims. First, our own personal assumptions may be faulty. Second, our inferences and reasoning principles may be misapplied or otherwise mistaken. Faulty assumptions and mistaken inferences are a fact of life and have been a constant throughout the

course of human history. The next consideration is how poorly constructed assumptions, inferences, and implications result in expectations that limit or diminish the quality of future interaction.

EXPECTATION

It is virtually impossible to come into direct contact with another
person without making personal assumptions. One cannot *not* assume. Almost inevitably, it seems, we take certain things for granted.
These unstated premises may seem obvious, unaffected, even reasonable. Even so, we often assume that something is true about someone's
act or utterance simply because our working premises made sense to
us at the moment in question. Or we may presume that our initial
hunches apply in all cases, based on the growing body of evidence that
we have been gathering together over time. What we disclose or
conceal from public view is a reflection of the distinct makeup of our
own uniquely constituted type of assumptive slant. We suspect that
everyone else fashions his or her own assumptive and presumptive
world in a similarly invisible way.

Assumptions and expectations about intentions, strategies, and
outcomes are necessary for those aspects of personal conduct that
remain almost totally invisible; even so, one may need to reduce the
number of assumptive errors by disclosing the specific qualities of
unstated notions to others. When this occurs, another opportunity is
created to set the record straight and establish a more accurate frame
of reference. When one continues to conceal personal viewpoints
from others, however, there may be a tendency to focus on erroneous
assumptions, expect the worst, and remain quite unaware of what
others are actually feeling, thinking, saying, and doing. Of course,
others may also make the same kinds of incorrect assumptions, and
have similar mistaken expectations, about oneself. Only with concerted effort comes the promise of heightened credibility and legiti-
macy and the abandonment of guessing games that ultimately
cheapen one's own questionable notions and hunches. Intricate sets
of small (micro) decisions come down to a matter of timing, whether
the respective parties find themselves in or out of synch, aligned or
nonaligned, and prepared or unprepared for what transpires next.

Personal expectations may be formed out of the larger need to reduce uncertainty, satisfy curiosity, control the behavior of others, or pursue a course of action with greatest potential benefit or return (Berger & Calabrese, 1975; Hewes, 1995). The *need* to anticipate is measured as the likelihood of something taking place in a generalized or person-specific way (Greene, 1995). There is an implicit standard of preference between alternative options and pathways to goal attainment (Burgoon & Walther, 1990). As investments increase, so does the impact of any violation. Failure to live up to the expectations of self or other may have a severe impact on subsequent events. The poorer the fit between what one expects to find and what actually transpires, the greater the likelihood of a struggle to reconcile the magnitude of discrepancy. One may, of course, be pleasantly surprised by sudden deviations from what is ordinary, mundane, or utterly predictable (Burgoon & LePoire, 1993; LePoire & Burgoon, 1994). The tension between prescriptive and predictive urges registers at the level of implication and inference. At issue is what qualifies as worthy of being valued or denigrated before or after the fact.

In a previous study (Mortensen, 1994), several hundred individuals were asked to reconstruct the experience of trying to express oneself in complicated public settings where successful communication seems difficult or impossible to achieve. We learned that assumptions, inferences, expectations, and reflections fit together at the level of risk and change. Just as assumptions may be sound or faulty, well founded or mistaken, personal expectations may be satisfied or remain out of reach. Here the relevant standard is whether one measures up to the idealized expectations of self and other. Such working premises set the stage for much of what, why, and how each episode of interaction is subject to further effort at framing and reframing problematic issues.

REFLECTION

The power of reflection enables one to reconsider (a) high-quality and (b) low-quality performances to see what can be learned about the odds of improving the quality of future encounters with other people. One may learn from past mistakes so as not to repeat them mindlessly. Moreover, it is an advantage to be in a position to reflect back upon the quality of interaction for tacit orientation and guidance about what to expect now or next. This distinction between effective and faulty interaction is critical in this context because the former is couched mostly in terms of what we want to *acquire* or *sustain* while the latter focuses on what we want to *overcome* or *leave behind*. Essentially, we are making an effort to promote a climate in which a wide spectrum of agreements (on viewpoints) and understandings (of personal conduct) can be more solidly established.

Personal reflections often cluster around considerations of success or failure. Respondents in our study tend to reflect back upon prior interactions in two major ways, depending largely on whether the shared circumstances were favorable or unfavorable and whether the behavior in question was effective or faulty as a mode of operation. Several major themes can be located in respondents' answers along the following dimensions: (a) performance aspirations, (b) anticipated reactions, (c) process considerations, (d) immediate effects, (e) long-term gains, and (f) ideal conditions.

Respondents' reconstructed interactions help us to define the unspoken, lower-level thresholds of performance aspiration. Under favorable conditions, respondents tend to focus on a mutual urge to make things better. There is shared determination to reconcile individual differences and find solutions together. No one has the desire to strive for perfection—the goal is to understand how the other can feel and think in a certain way. It is important to know when to talk and when to leave sensitive issues alone. There is a widespread presumption that other people have the best of intentions and are to be given all possible chances to clarify before one jumps to any conclusions.

Under unfavorable conditions, there is more of the contrasting urge to appear all-knowing and accept nothing less than perfect agreement. Some find it possible to have completely acceptable conversations but at times each one seems to speak an entirely different language. Some respondents have very different goals and different ways to fit existing relations within those goals. The severity of disagreement may not be recognized until the troubled relationship is finally over.

These reconstructed interactions also help in anticipating the distinctive reactions of others to specific aspects of mutual concern. Respondents recall that, under favorable conditions, they have mostly safe assumptions about certain types of responses. Most of the interactants generally look forward to the chance to get together. They share similar goals but have different methods of achieving them. Hard work is required to improve the style of interaction and sense how the other is going to react. There is no fear of saying what is on one's mind because of the direct knowledge that others will surely understand. Sometimes it is possible to know how other people will react before they actually respond. It helps to be able to predict how someone will react to what others say and do.

Under unfavorable conditions, there are widespread complaints about each party having a completely different orientation to the world with no possibility of compromise. No one sees things in the same way; it feels like hitting a brick wall. Heated reactions arise where everybody thinks he or she is the only one who is right. No one seems to be able to get into a groove; polarized positions are not easy to resolve. Strong statements imply that one must take a stand one way or another. One may start to expect that others will disagree over many things because they have disagreed over one thing in particular.

There is also a tendency to wait for problems to get worse before engaging in harsh discussions in which one party leaves angry and walks away or shuts the other out; there tends to be little communication in general. Some people try to interpret messages incorrectly or to avoid contact and not communicate at all. Each one seems to be constantly stepping on the other's toes. Everything is taken the wrong way so that no one can predict how things will turn out. Misunderstandings on all sides are rarely mentioned out of fear of saying the wrong thing: Everyone gets upset, the issue is dropped, and people stick to superficial topics or matters known ahead of time to be OK.

These reconstructed interactions envision the prospects for improvement of current activities in strikingly different terms. Under favorable conditions, there is a tendency to compromise, a willingness to take turns, and the shared desire to keep things as equal as possible. Interaction flows smoothly and much goes without being said, that is, conversations just seem to click and stay free and easy. Personal problems can be solved when the desired outcome can be quickly changed and methods of conflict resolution abound. Some people take the time to spell things out and discuss differences until each one is comfortable with the outcome or resolution. When engaging in unwelcome actions, constructive people don't pretend that nothing has happened, but deal with sensitive issues right away.

Under unfavorable conditions, respondents complain of never-ending power struggles that leave no one satisfied. A major theme is that it is actually someone else's problem: People play devil's advocate and disagree in a contest of wills. Talk always ends up in disagreement when everyone takes an opposing view, which only makes everyone else want to argue further, and no one ever ends up changing other people's viewpoints. It is difficult to discuss matters with someone who makes everything seem so cut and dried, and to give in is to admit the other was right after all. Some try to edge one another out. Communication is often one-sided and mostly on someone else's terms, particularly where there is little effort to find a middle ground because neither party is willing to look at the other's viewpoint. There is frequent mention of ever-present tension in the air and constant pulling back and forth. The interactants may not grasp why they fail to see eye to eye on issues, despite heavily detailed reasons, because they don't actually listen to one another. There may be constant effort to prove the other wrong, which leads to yet another destructive cycle. Too much is read into unwelcome actions without reaching a satisfactory conclusion or resolution of contested issues.

The reconstructed interactions call attention to different types of personal concerns about the outcomes and effects of interacting in one way or another. Respondents recall that, under favorable conditions, the respective parties enhance each other's perspectives. There is much effort at mutual reinforcement. Specific agreements build on one another and eventually lead to stronger ties. There is a shared ability to turn disagreements into agreements and come away feeling very satisfied because success is due to equality and absence of severe power struggles. Each party helps the other out of rough spots. Some people make each other laugh and find the same things funny. Interaction is always rich, new, and exciting, and no one ever runs out of things to say. People can work through tense situations; opinions are discussed so much that ideas end up being fine-tuned and further clarified for self and other. A successful interaction means that people get a lot out of it; individuals need not let differences tear them apart but use them to pull together.

Under unfavorable conditions, respondents recall, it is often a struggle to gain a greater understanding of where another person stands on an issue. It is possible to fall into bad communicative habits because people get so used to each other; there is a need to take a break when conversation is over, particularly when someone leaves the room or walks away. There may be no further effort to communicate when people go for long periods of time without speaking to one another and then only in small doses. Some are prone to keep things superficial and cover up any implied sense of threat.

Absolute disagreement leads to total silence; the response is to shut up and keep your mouth closed. Everything goes in one ear and out the other with a lot of ambiguity and confusion on all sides. Severe misunderstandings often allow no room to step back. Nothing is ever figured out, people just listen to what is said without reacting very much. Sometimes it is just less stressful not to talk; forced interchange tends to be brief and superficial because people refuse to open themselves up to one another and take down the walls that have been erected to protect them. Individuals cease to express risky ideas because they have fallen into a habit of producing misunderstanding and can't find a quick way out; it may be better to stay silent than start another fight.

Reconstructed interactions also focus on considerations of long-term gain or loss. Under favorable conditions, there is a gain in satisfaction over time. The respective parties transcend problems from the past. There are stronger relations, deeper friendships, and avoidance of emotional shutdown. Strong bonds are not easily broken. For some, there is an increased sense of self-esteem and self-worth. Close relations work better than before: There is a supportive bond, a feeling of warmth and harmony, and people share things that they have never said before to anyone else. It takes time, effort, and most of all genuine caring and love for the other; the process of working out personal differences promotes a sense of security and trust.

Under unfavorable conditions, severe disputes often produce mutual decisions to close the system to avoid tension and irritation, and the magnitude of harm can be amazing. Some people refuse to fit into each other's ideals. Specific disagreements lead to larger conflicts that never get resolved; some people refuse to deal with or confront things and just let them go. Taboo subjects pile up: "Sorry, I can't discuss it with you now." Sometimes proving you are right is not worth the pain it could cause you and others. At other times, all it may take is to come at an issue from a different angle to finally see what the other person means. It is possible to work through sticky issues and understand one another better. People can clear up the confusion and find out where things went wrong so as not to make the same old mistakes over and over again.

The reconstructed interactions in this study also projected well into the future. Under favorable conditions, each party looks forward to prospective future interaction. There is much discussion of future plans. Some people stay in close contact when there is a strong desire for future interaction and hope of forgiveness in the end. They look for similarities and welcome differences; it can be like starting out fresh again with the chance to rediscover each other in a totally new light. The effect is to be more calm, free, and relaxed. When people refuse to get bogged down in trivial details, there is more time and energy left over to talk about important matters and concerns.

Under unfavorable conditions, the exchange of ideas, even when opposing, promotes common ground and provides an outlet for clashing thoughts. You can get into petty arguments and still joke around and have a good time. Best friends can haggle over little things and still talk at length about whatever matters most. Despite the risk of constant conflict, it is possible to overlook disputes and disagreements and concentrate on how the various participants became such good friends in the first place. Some people always seem to find a compromise or solution and move on.

Severe disagreements may heighten one's sensitivity to the fact that others will not, and should not, always agree. Sometimes things have to get so bad that people are forced to sit down and work things through—with a promise not to have to go through sensitive matters again. It is a mistake to believe that effective forms of communication are impossible to attain or always out of reach. Those who generate greater levels of misunderstanding might do so less frequently if only they would work harder to figure out what might go wrong. People don't have to produce the types of severe misunderstandings that cannot finally be overcome.

ATTRIBUTION

When sustained relations manufacture a great deal of inaccurate and negative implications, the central question is this: Who is responsible for the outcomes we produce together? Consider the possibilities in general form. First, we can attribute cause or reason to ourselves. Second, we can attribute cause or reason to other people. Third, we can focus on situational or contextual factors we all share in common. Fourth, we can transcend appeal to individual cause or reason and point to forces and factors that operate beyond the locus of personal control: "The devil made me do it," or "it's in the genes," or even "society is the real culprit." It is interesting how various individuals choose specific attributional tendencies from within the narrow confines of their prevailing worldview. Psychologists, for example, are prone to focus on individual units of behavior. Sociologists talk in terms of group conformity, structure, or systems. Communication researchers look at message sequences embedded in complex processes of mutual influence. Clergy point to the effects of evil and sin in the world. Critical theorists (feminist, Marxist) focus on acts of domination, oppression, subordination, marginalization, scapegoating, and victimization as injurious sources of influence. Taken together, social scientists have produced volumes on the subject of attributional biases from myriad differing viewpoints.

Attributions place information in a cause-and-effect sequence. Assumptions, inferences, expectations, and reflections work together to fill in gaps, relate action to standards of valuation, and shift the focus of attention or emphasis. All of these causal interpretations are abstract calculations and are subject to standards of accuracy or error. Miscalculations fall into patterns, often repeated in a serial manner. Blame for disagreements, for example, falls heavily on unstable situational causes and on the partner's stable, negative traits (Ickes, 1985).

Moreover, conflict is construed as coming more from outside interference than from internally produced distractions or personal discontent. This may be due to the larger dimensions of distortion, inaccuracy, and incongruent viewpoints found to highly differentiate between incompatible or unsatisfied relationships and satisfied, well-adjusted ones (Sillars, 1985). It is sobering to confront evidence that individuals generally assume the accuracy of their own conceptions of others, even in close but ambiguous relationships where signs of misinterpretation and inaccurate mind reading abound. Sillars (1985) cites recognition by family therapists that "spouses often refer to each other in terms so vague and overgeneralized that they aggravate marital conflict" (p. 284; Thomas, 1977).

The link between tacit miscalculation and overt incompatibility suggests that the risk of self-congratulation is privately assumed at the other person's expense. When relevant issues unfold beyond the locus of personal control, we tend to look outside of ourselves for causal explanations. We may be tempted to point to the human condition, nature, the social fabric, or various changes in the ecological landscape. When we locate cause and reason within the immediacy of the existing situation in which we find ourselves, we may be prone to engage in what is called the fundamental attributional error. This occurs when we exaggerate the importance of personalities and undervalue the impact of situational forces—cramped quarters, noisy setting, poor lighting, rigid seating arrangements, and so forth.

The "error" is as strong as the tendency to view others as causes of communicative difficulty, and to ignore or minimize the impact of the social setting or the environment itself. So the observer looks on the outside of what is going on with other people and tends to make inferences about their internal states—intentions, desires, and motives. At the same time, the objects of observation are prone to look not at themselves but toward their own external circumstances. In effect, if I stutter while speaking to you, I will probably look to my external circumstance for cause or reason; in the meantime, you are apt to see my disfluency as attributed to what is going on inside me.

The tendency to frame what goes right or wrong in terms of personalities, rather than situational factors, is most acute when the issue at hand comes down to assigning responsibility for success or failure to behavioral outcomes. Individuals tend to hold one another responsible for jointly produced outcomes in predictable ways. When things work out well, we want to assign credit where credit is due—with ourselves. Of course, when things turn out badly, we are prone to assign discredit where it belongs—with someone else. In other words, individuals are inclined to violate the "law of totality" and hold one another disproportionately responsible for unwelcome outcomes. "It's Harry who is always so irritating! Get him near people, and he ruins relationships so quickly it's appalling. He starts conversations in a negative direction, reduces meetings to arguments, and discusses politics just to get a rise out of people. Trust Harry to ruin a terrific party!" Notice the word magic at work here. The effects of the outside world go away. The physical setting is ignored. The personal conduct of everyone (except Harry) is ruled out as null and void. The frame of reference shifts like a zoom lens that could take in the entire setting but instead is adjusted to take in only a very tight shot of one individual's personality—as if he were living, functioning, and acting in a social vacuum.

In effect, personal accounts are actually miniature theories of accountability. What starts out as a generalized description of what takes place is also an explanation, and justification, of one's personal interest in seeing things from a particular angle or slant. Our respective versions are a matter of negotiation. On this point, Edwards and Potter (1993) write,

> Because these constructed descriptions and reports are embedded within the performance of situated actions and are interactively responded to by other participants on that basis, this means that attributional inferences are an integral part of communicative actions in which descriptions and versions of events are closely bound up with establishing their possible explanations. In situated talk, we suggest, explanation is not a neutral business of making the best sense of experience, with language serving to inform the investigator of how and what people think. Rather, it is part of a social process of reality construction in which participants have a rhetorical stake or position and orient to what each other says as similarly positioned and possibly contentious. (pp. 24-25)

In other words, it matters whether one's attributional logic can withstand public scrutiny. Bradbury and Fincham (1992) asked married partners to report the quality of interaction, to make attributions for marital difficulties, and to engage in problem-solving discussions. Results showed that spouses' maladaptive attributions were related to less effective problem-solving strategies. Poorly founded attributions were also related to high rates of negative behavior and, for wives, to the tendency to reciprocate negative partner behavior. Not a surprise, faulty attributions were associated with high levels of personal and marital distress. No wonder that reckless attributions are tough to take in such highly exaggerated form. Hurtful messages inflict invisible damage in the name of anger (other oriented) and guilt (self oriented) over reckless or careless action (Vangelisti, 1994).

Attributional mistakes can be minimized but not eliminated. Casual or automatic thinking increases the likelihood of errors and mistakes. Favorable conditions promote more in-depth information processing and fewer miscalculations (Fletcher, Rosanowski, Rhodes, & Lange, 1992). Those who are adept at dealing with complex attributional decisions generate fewer errors than those who are less accurate because they can deal effectively with simple issues, tasks, and problems (Fletcher, Reeder, & Bull, 1990; Gilbert, Pelham, & Krull, 1988). In effect, the best protection is the capacity and willingness to take other people seriously in negotiating matters of considerable complexity and complication.

METACOMMUNICATION

Consider what happens when we communicate about the process of communication. Personal conduct is sometimes confusing or mystifying because it conveys information about subject matter (report) and instructions for interpreting it (command) at the same time. The content is framed by *what* we express and our relational conception is implied by *how* we express it. Whenever we shift the focus from what we are doing (what is being talked about) to the way we are doing it (what we want others to make of it), we are, in effect, making meta-comments about the comments per se. This leads to the possibility of paradox: We can be in a state of constant communication—and yet be almost completely unable to communicate about how and what we are communicating. In a classic statement, Watzlawick, Beavin, and Jackson (1967) point out that this is a major problem in society. They argue that the ability to engage in appropriate forms, levels, and amounts of bilateral metacommunication is not only the essence of effective and successful acts of communication but is also "intimately linked to the enormous problem of awareness of self and other" (p. 53). Conversely, the lack of ability or willingness to understand such signs and cues promotes weak forms of face-to-face interaction because the very activity we are constructing is itself not subject to any further deliberation.

Ruesch and Bateson (1968; Ruesch, 1973) consider metacommunication from a standpoint of mental health and psychological development. Their basic premise is that the perception of having been perceived is a fact that deeply influences and changes human behavior. Successful communication between self and other implies overt correction by others as well as covert correction by self. Interaction flows like a system of checks and balances to preserve open-ended opportunity for the integration of mutual purpose. It has a circular character in which change, correction, and self-regulation are implied. Personal logic, in the form of a self-monitored code, functions to guide (and evaluate) the movement toward selective and strategic integration of shared circumstance. Hence the process of minimizing mistakes, errors, and miscalculations is itself a basic operation and a means to permit an unobserved observer to form inferences about the logical-valuative system of what is observed.

This is an extremely important notion; we can, as observers, gain partial access to the design logic of the personal conduct of one another. Hence the efficacy of face-to-face interaction will depend upon the goodness of fit between the implicative system that two persons have in common and upon the complexities and complications of the interpersonal system itself. Bateson (1972) points out that our conversations do have an outline—if only one could see the form clearly. It is important, therefore, to have a conceptual system that will force us to see expressive action as both an internally patterned entity and a part of the larger patterned universe. A healthy ecology for interaction requires a level of flexibility that can match the capacity of the environment to sustain a state of elaborated complexity with opportunity for slow change of even basic (hardwired) characteristics. This position is consistent with the pragmatic recognition that communicative action not only conveys information but at the same time makes certain demands on subsequent behavior. Everything we say and do has content; the way we frame such content is therefore a metacommunication.

Specific instances of metacommunicative activity may be used to expand the domain of reality-testing and minimize the perpetuation of errors and miscalculations. Personal efforts are best suited to make minor corrections in the alignment or synchrony of conversational activity. Metacommentary works best, however, when the balance of power is evenly distributed, that is, when there is no stacked deck. Metacomments work less well, if at all, in those elite social hierarchies (based on maxims of domination and subordination) where the very possibility of making comments about what transpires is ruled out implicitly and in advance. When powerful hidden agendas are in force, those in positions of high rank and institutional authority may see acts of metacommunication as a sign of disloyalty, discredit, or disqualification on the part of subordinates.

Moreover, such discrete acts of (meta)commentary work in two directions simultaneously: (a) to minimize or neutralize the threat of conflict escalation during episodes of faulty interaction and (b) to heighten a sense of cohesion and solidarity when things are going quite smoothly. It helps one become more acutely aware of what does or doesn't have any communicative value to anyone or everyone else. Given the risk that self-serving assumptions cause others, it becomes critically important to find alternative ways to foster a spirit of mutuality.

THE SEARCH FOR COMMON GROUND

What registers below the surface of public appearance is richly implicative. It is a domain full of presumption: an indistinct, intuitive wellspring of tacit inclinations about oneself, about significant others such as family and close friends, about coworkers and acquaintances— and about the immediate relationship between you and me, whoever we may be. The richness and intricacy of our respective viewpoints is as deep and varied as life itself. The limits of our own presumptions are as inclusive as the world in which we live. Our conceptions of one another are multifaceted, filled with incredible detail, and highly specific at the level of current mood and attitude. It is small wonder, then, whenever we move out of one social setting and into another, that we carry these dynamic assumptions—the substrata for the formulation of values, beliefs, and attitudes—along with us. We rely on these primitive orienting devices to help reveal the truth about the people and situations around us; they encourage us to move ahead, or warn us away, depending on how we interpret our interpersonal realities. For all of us, assumptions, inferences, expectations, reflections, and attributions, taken together, provide a reflexive basis for our encompassing sense of what is real.

So much richly implicative material registers in silence. The structural boundaries of interactive silence are fuzzy, multifaceted, and ambiguous (Jaworski, 1993). Anything so ubiquitous can cause trouble too. Conceptions of miscommunication follow from the mis-judgment of someone else's silence. The crucial dividing line is the boundary line between a noncommunicative atmosphere—the habit of keeping silent, leaving important things unsaid, acting inattentive, mute, or nonresponsive—and an open system—where accepting silence extends the right to talk to others. Conceptions of not enough and too much talk enter into the larger equation about modes of indirectness as subject to more varied interpretation and active cognitive search for a context in which relevance can be maximized. In the language of pseudocommunication (shallow silence), the speaker extends total control over the content and meanings of verbal activity to be taken without question. Oppressive silence creates tension with the urge to break through silence equated with protracted struggle to overcome signs of reticence, submissiveness, private silence, and inexpressiveness (Jaworski, 1993). The concept of *pseudointimacy* is characterized by a constant hesitation to get too close to another. There may also be a lack of motivation to seek intimacy (Bartholomew, 1990). Dramatic or mythological exaggerations of affection and support are common indicators (Wynne, Ryckhoff, Day, & Hirsch, 1958).

The study of problematic communication examines the power of silence in extreme or polarized contexts. When major conversational difficulties occur, we may struggle with both what is experienced silently and what the silence itself conveys to anyone else. We find that some interactants get caught up in private mental deliberation over what to leave out of the flow of conversation. After all, the whole truth may be too much to admit, particularly when prior interactions have gone poorly. There is a tendency to consider why some things (a) are better left unsaid or (b) would only scare others away. Oddly, unquestioned silence may provide comfort and protection from unwanted or unwelcome talk or chatter, particularly where one party does not feel safe or secure. Protracted silence may well be construed as a protective barrier for high-risk implications filled with unspoken evaluation and judgments placing someone in an unfavorable or discredited light. Moreover, silence causes presumption—mainly over the right to wait or postpone the transition from implicit, tacit levels to more explicit, overt modes of self-expression. Some wait for the right moment to bring up sensitive or touchy matters. A code of silence may be invoked as a sign of loyalty, either to be assumed willingly or imposed coercively. Heavy silence can be oppressive, as with feeling trapped because of an implicit sense that (a) there's nothing to say, (b) it has all been said before, or (c) saying it would not change a thing. Moving out of a state of communicative difficulty is often accompanied by appeasement—where the distribution of sound and silence is relocated, more fairly or evenly. At the eventual point of resolution, silence becomes a sanctuary. For once, there is no tension between individual intent and unforeseen consequences. Finally, where a spirit of expressive freedom prevails, silence instills a communal sense of wonder and awe.

Implications surface in the spiral of silence. Elizabeth Nöelle-Neumann (1984, 1991) regards public opinion as a *tangible force* that makes people toe the line and stay in their place. Here the urge to share relevant information is subject to pressure, constrained by a conservative psychology of communication: Keep your unpopular or untested views to yourself, particularly when in the minority or espousing unpopular causes. In other words, the decision to go public with private hunches and notions takes into account the prevailing mood or climate of opinion in the community at large. Moving up the spiral is akin to a relocation, from the periphery and the fringe to center stage, where every expressive actor takes into account what everyone else can voice in a safe and secure manner. In effect, what we express to one another is a collective reflection of what we can express without getting into too much trouble. It's not fun to have to take back and eat your own words. Conversely, moving down the spiral is a centrifugal force into isolation. The very threat of sanction is enough to deter most of the people most of the time from disclosing what would only meet with disapproval, rejection, or banishment from the surrounding speech community (p. 13).

So it is a simple fact of life that some of our deepest inferences and implications are often difficult to identify or distinguish clearly. They may have no observable referents, and for this reason we may fear looking foolish when we try to sort them out to refer to them explicitly. Highly embedded sets of inferences and implications can be tough to quantify, are seldom what they seem, and often stir up more demanding realities than we usually are able to explain with the force of conventional words or gestures alone. For these reasons, no one maintains complete or unconditional access to all that makes up his or her sense of personal reality, or to the effects it has on one's own behavior or that of others. The same holds for the degree of direct access to the implicative domains of others. The end result is constant vulnerability to basic and repetitive forms of miscommunication that are so typical of the human species.

Considerable linguistic skill is involved in raising personal issues that may be particularly difficult to bring up, let alone to discuss in any sustained and meaningful way. It is this area of personal knowledge that has been the central focus of recent work in the field (Bavelas, Black, Chovil, & Mullett, 1990; Coupland, Giles, & Wiemann, 1991; Mortensen, 1994). The dynamic process of how and why things are left unsaid—and the damaging impact on the lives of so many adolescents and young adults—demands that a constantly developing understanding of the dynamics of the unspoken remains critical to the mental health of individuals, groups, and families. It is also instrumental to the development of a peaceful and progressive society in general.

CHAPTER 2

Distortion

When communicative difficulties are kept to a minimum, it becomes progressively easier to express ourselves clearly and interpret others accurately. Much depends on whether complex sequences of personal action can be precisely integrated over time. A high level of cognitive integration promotes the underlying sense that one is able to keep things clearly in focus. In contrast, things begin to disintegrate or unravel insofar as internal distractions or external interferences come into play. The misuse or neglect of basic linguistic skills may be responsible for a slow deterioration in the scope of relevance or meaningfulness of what is said or done. If left unchecked, a steady pileup of cognitive distortions tends to support a linguistic atmosphere where increased levels of slippage and miscommunication are likely to occur. The signs are all-encompassing: biased motivation; misleading, misapplied, or misinterpreted information; fabrication, pretense; subterfuge; inaccurate, imprecise, and poorly calibrated forms of action; and shallow or superficial consideration of embedded relations between source and subject matter. As personal difficulties multiply, repeated distortion of what we say and mean may become pervasive and habitual. Under conditions of great stress or duress, it takes concerted effort to reduce or minimize a rising confluence of unclear acts of self-expression and/or misplaced interpretive response.

The first chapter showed how faulty implications shape the observable significance of personal conduct. Under certain conditions, personal attitudes and moods may be used to promote the cultivation of largely favorable conditions, efficient production, and high-quality performance. At other times, when many cognitive disorientations come into play, shared activity fosters unfavorable conditions, ineffective production, and low-quality performance. At issue is the working logic, the design system, of those mechanisms that undermine or subvert the quality of human interaction and personal well-being. A state of cognitive disorientation—where one is inattentive, insensitive, indifferent, or otherwise out of focus—encourages a stance of emotive distance, detached involvement, and biased accounts of what takes place. Someone may misread one's intent. Another may have an axe to grind. In effect, there is no surefire way to eliminate the risk of cognitive distortion in the slant and tone of language use.

The ability to promote complex agreement and mutual understanding is a great source of stability in human affairs. In sharp contrast are the largely destabilizing consequences associated with pronounced states of disagreement and/or misunderstanding. A great deal of emotional turbulence can be generated in a short span of time by the perpetuation of a strong tendency to haggle and wrangle endlessly over the definitions of terms. For comparative purposes, consider how the tone and texture of interaction changes depending on whether the participants agree, disagree, understand, or misunderstand one another's respective viewpoints in the following examples.

Agreement. K and L are film majors who agree on stylistic and cinematographic aspects of filmmaking. They watch three movies a week from the classical Hollywood period (1935-1960). Both are great fans of Humphrey Bogart, Lauren Bacall, and Marlon Brando. They are working on a short film about manic depression. Each episode is played back on K's bedroom VCR and each shot is analyzed in terms of pros and cons. They go over the details of lighting, shot angles, and soundtracks. They agree about the problems to be solved to make the film better. If they disagree, which is extremely rare, each one seeks compromise. Basically, K and L agree about everything for which they share the same passion.

Disagreement. B and W crossed the line the first time they met. They have totally opposed notions of what is important in life, how people deserve to be treated, what friendship means, and what mutual respect implies. Incompatible viewpoints reflect *extremely* different positions about virtually everything. Neither party makes an effort to give in to the other on any level. Routine interactions are mostly adversarial and combative—where one person comes out the winner, the other the loser. B and W engage in a never-ending power struggle designed to torment the weaker party. Even civilized talk results in barely concealed signs of hostility. The main problem is not a simple misunderstanding but a constant refusal to affirm anything about the validity of the other's positions. B and W finally close off contact to avoid tension and irritation. The mutual conclusion is that such fundamental differences cannot be overcome.

Understanding. T and V interact easily, spontaneously, and quite naturally. Personal intentions are conveyed with simple body language and few words. They laugh a lot about silly things that only they seem to think are funny. With such a deep, unspoken level of mutual understanding, the relationship seems very solid, a source of mutual stability, and a touchstone for moments of confusion or unrest. T and V share an uncanny sense of one another's reaction to any given type of social situation—at times, one almost "becomes" the other. Neither knows why they seem to be virtually the same.

Misunderstanding. W and G generate a lot of stress when they are together. Both misinterpret and twist almost everything that is said or done. The result is long, useless arguments about the meaning of something. W and G are easily distracted from concentrating on the topics that they actually do intend to share. Much of the time is taken up by angry, frustrated, tension-filled silence. It has come to the point that W doesn't say anything because of the knowledge that anything can be and will be used against W in a different form. Interaction seems pretty futile. No matter how hard W tries to make G understand what W means, nothing seems to work. If the central focus of communication is to be so often frustrated, future interaction would only cause more hurt and confusion on all sides.

Notice how the personal accounts of agreement and understanding underscore the completion and fulfillment of joint projects, proper attention to detail, willingness to compromise, tolerance of uncertainty, and the stability necessary to justify faith in the prospects for further discovery. In contrast, the personal accounts of conditions of disagreement and misunderstanding place the accents on elements of discontinuity, disruption, and unpredictability in response to mutual effort to devalue and disconfirm the possibility of the completion of current projects and routines. Read between the lines and notice how cognitive disorientations are commonly equated with a host of internal distractions and external interferences; disruptions in existing habits, projects, and routines; and heavily slanted bias. There are repeated references to moments of resistance and one-sided opposition, plus considerable tension and irritation over the refusal to listen. A surplus of mistakes and interpretive blunders abounds. Words are twisted out of shape.

These central themes in respondents' reconstructed interactions open up a set of core issues. What is at stake is related to a number of basic considerations: (a) *interference* with the fulfillment of current goals, objectives, and tasks; (b) *bias* in the interplay between inference-making activity and the larger pattern of explicit action, particularly in matters of misleading information and multiple errors in routine operations, that is, misuse, misapplication, or misappropriation of general principles to specific instances, producing either unwanted (internal) distraction or (external) disruption and repeated mistakes in the identification of sources, relations, and evaluations; (c) *miscalculation* by taking a wrong (or misguided) course of action; (d) *deception* and fabrication; and (e) movement into pretense and *pseudo-communication*—all for the sake of mere appearance.

INTERFERENCE

At times, things go smoothly and nothing gets in the way. At other times, things seem to work out badly, unravel, or go astray. Hence it matters greatly how one deals with outside interference in the fulfillment of complex aspirations, intentions, plans, strategies, and goals. In this regard, face-to-face interaction can be construed as a reality-testing ceremony in which highly elaborated conceptions are subject to a mix of *facilitative* and *subversive* influences (Mortensen, 1991). At all times, the respective definitions, conceptions, and explanations of the respective parties are to be taken as intrinsic aspects of the total situation. Each act of self-presentation is subject to successive reinterpretation from a changing set of reference points. Therefore, *what* gets presented by one is relative to *how* it is represented by everyone else.

A state of cognitive clarity is intrinsically valuable. It makes common sense to be as fluent, articulate, precise, sensitive, and accurate as possible. As a consequence, others are placed in a better position to grasp and comprehend what one may wish to convey to or elicit from them. What transpires beneath the surface will sustain and enrich what takes place above. There is a progressive sense of wholeness and synthesis where internal conditions are oriented to take minute changes in external circumstances into fine-tuned account. Such conditions are akin to the feeling of cold water rushing over a dam, the sound of a well-crafted bell, a 20/20 view of a star-filled sky, or the smell, sight, and sound of a crackling fireplace on a cold winter night.

Because it can be so frustrating to describe elusive forms of cognitive activity within ourselves, most of us feel some sense of relief when we can describe specific physical events, such as an accident. After all, they are relatively normal events that practically everyone has observed at one time or another. When we speak about car accidents, we know to include information about whose car was damaged, who caused the accident to occur, what others nearby did to help the drivers, whose insurance will pay for the damages, and so on. We are not surprised when there are as many versions of what took place as there are bystanders.

The main ideal is to operate at the highest possible level of visual and auditory acuity, and mental and spiritual sensitivity, within one's own power. This is a universal standard. Everyone can make the most of what is available. However, being human and fallible, we tend to view others in terms of our own unique thresholds of sensitivity and awareness. Cognitive distortion occurs whenever we do not see clearly or hear distinctly, or, on a more complex level, whenever we are neither touched deeply by the immediate presence of others nor moved to touch in return through the eloquence of our own thoughtfulness and insight. Likewise, it is helpful to have realistic notions about what even the most clear, complete, and accurate forms of interchange may accomplish. If we are fully functioning individuals, we are in touch with these processes and able to identify relevant issues of personal importance. If we are poorly functioning individuals, distortion results because we do not see things clearly, hear distinctly, speak fluently, touch gently, or move fluidly. The other might as well not be there at all because, after all, his or her own perspective on shared activity will make no real observable impact.

As interactants, we are not always in a position to see things clearly or distinctly. Deficiencies in visual acuity may diminish the vibrancy and luminosity of the world around us. Distractions make us prone to ignore salient aspects of others' lives, as if they did not exist, and they also make us prone to self-absorption and even selfishness. Without visual acuity, we miss the rich detail in facial expressions and body language of others. Even small losses of acuity can camouflage a subtle look of pain or a sudden blush of embarrassment. This can happen if the light strikes the periphery of our visual field rather than the center, or we are tired, or we have used alcohol or drugs, or we are wearing our old glasses instead of the new pair we need to pick up this afternoon. Visual detail makes a positive difference because we are able to understand the complexity of others at a more refined level of distinction and discrimination.

Sensitive observers are able to view others as unified wholes, as complete persons, rather than as isolated and often detached objects of observation. Poor observers, on the other hand, are far less able to sustain the level of attention and focus required to see things in a unified way. If one remains inattentive for very long, there will be less effort devoted to learning new things about others and more of the same old urge to keep seeing others as stereotyped fragments of personality that need to be forced into one's own perspective. Those with poor observational skills are ill prepared to participate in preparation for the emergence of high-quality performance.

By striving to become more aware of one's own interpretive slant, it is possible to be better prepared to "check out" the accuracy of what one thinks others are trying to express. Expressive tolerance involves seeing others not as strangers but as human beings who, like us, are struggling to comprehend how they make their presence felt in the human world. If we aren't willing to take the initiative to participate in the wider collective enterprise, our own personal relations may be fraught with error and revert back to painful and even strife-ridden interchanges with some successful and the rest failures—translated, this means where some people's truth is recognized and everyone else's truth is squashed.

BIAS

The concept of personal *bias* is often equated with prejudice in thought, word, or deed. When used in this loose way, it conjures up undesirable or unfavorable images of people with narrow, rigid, or demeaning views of others. Although acts of bigotry certainly reveal strong biases, the term has a more precise range of application in social science literature. A biased interpretation involves salient, often unconscious, distortion in the way things are construed, measured, or taken into account. It results from deviations in the way things are added up (overvalued) or left out (undervalued) of the composite equation. The metaphor of a "stacked deck" captures both the motivational and the cognitive aspects of questionable actions undertaken by those who insist on viewing things according to their own preexisting, even deeply ingrained, predilections.

There are three broad standards for defining the existence and severity of biased responses—actors, observers, and abstract principles. First is the standard of the actors themselves. A particular action on the part of individual A may be compared with A's own standards. For example, person A treats men and women in an unbiased manner, except when meeting members of the opposite sex for the first time. This is a standard of self-consistency, or accuracy, when the activity in question is compared with the way A usually behaves. As an alternative, the questionable action of A may be evaluated against the standards of those who observed it. Here the issue is not a matter of individual consistency over time but the degree of consensus between self and others at any point. Finally, the activity at issue may be evaluated against a principle or logical mechanism. For example, a group of experts may provide an operational definition of gender differences that is clearly applicable, even though the actor (A) or observers (B, C, D) remain unaware of its relevance.

The simultaneous application of multiple standards of evaluation complicates not only the definition of personal bias but the prospects for interpersonal resolution. When A views A's action as unbiased, and B, C, and D construe it quite differently, the likelihood for miscommunication increases, due not just to contested definition but to incompatible standards of evaluation as well. The same holds when experts appeal to scientific standards that laypeople do not know or acknowledge as applicable. By these standards, bias can be difficult to detect and even more arduous to control. Nor can the attendant issues be separated from the way people think about their mental lapses. In other words, personal beliefs about one's own cognitive activity strongly influence both the strategies used to minimize faulty conceptions and the success of short-term outcomes. Even if a person tries to guard against making unfair inferences, judgments, or evaluations, a number of potential difficulties stand in the way.

One impediment is the degree of access to our mental processes. Psychologists have debated this issue of how well we can think about the way that we construct our thoughts, however well or poorly formed. Despite unresolved aspects of the larger controversy, Wilson and Brekke (1994) find "the idea that people are unaware of a substantial amount of their mental processing has a firmer toehold in social and cognitive psychology than ever before" (p. 121; see also Jacoby, Lindsay, & Toth, 1992; Kihlstrom, 1987; Posner & Rothbart, 1989). Even if one is aware of some unwanted influence, it can be quite difficult to stop faulty inclinations from occurring once the process is set in motion (Bargh, 1989; Logan, 1989; Wegner, 1992). Emotional overreaction, for example, can be triggered outside of immediate awareness and persist long after one realizes that "I'm getting out of control." Moreover, even if the original basis for a particular conception is recognized as flawed or discredited, the causal logic or explanatory tendency may persist, leading to belief perseverance (C. Anderson, 1989).

To act as self-censor requires not only mental control over lapses but also minimum exposure to new information, or situational cues, that confirm or disconfirm the highly ingrained but mistaken tendency. Although some mental biases cannot be avoided, it may be possible to inhibit overt behavior or undue exposure to information or situations that have been very troubling or unsettling in the past (Devine, 1989; Gilbert, 1991, 1993). It is possible to avoid unwanted influences, Wilson and Brekke (1994) conclude, if the interactants in question successfully satisfy four conditions: (a) awareness of the unwanted process, (b) motivation to correct, (c) sensitivity to the direction and magnitude of bias, and (d) ability to monitor or control one's responses consistently over time (p. 122).

Not all cognitive biases are created equally. Some matter more, linger longer, or damage more severely than others (Jussim, 1991). So there is actually no point in striving for some mythical or unobtainable standard of sheer objectivity or rationality in our direct dealings with others. Interests dictate involvement. No technique or strategy is bias-free. Therefore, efforts to remain impartial do not ensure greater accuracy, or neutralize desire or passion, but often foster a numbing stance of indifference or detachment. So the point is not to eliminate biases but to come to terms with them. Of particular relevance are three types of defensive filters that become salient during complex episodes of interaction and slowly diminish our capacity to appreciate the intrinsic value of what transpires: (a) ideological distortions, (b) ethnocentric priorities, and (c) egocentric methods of assessment and evaluation.

Ideological Bias

Disagreement. J and P ride the same Badger Bus. When J rides the bus, J just tries to mind J's own business. On one occasion, however, P proceeded to sit down next to J and started making small talk right away. This didn't bother J because J didn't actually have to think about anything. Then P started to talk to J about religion and asked what J thought about the existence of God. P's next question caused the downfall of the conversation. P asked if J had accepted Jesus as her personal Savior, the Messiah. As J was a Jew, J's answer was no. Instead of dropping the subject, P tried to persuade J to believe exactly as P did by pulling out his Bible and reading quotes from the Old Testament with terms that many Jews find offensive. J told P that J thought it was great that P was deeply involved in religion but J just did not believe as P did—all of this with the unspoken expectation that P would drop the subject. P did not but pulled out a flyer from his Bible study class and told J that it was for all people to study the Word of the Lord. When the bus finally pulled into Madison, in silent reflection J concluded that religion is a touchy subject that strangers probably should avoid.

Misunderstanding. G and K have slowly lost touch over a long period of time. G is highly educated while K is not. When they attempt to talk about the importance of achieving a high level of education, a great deal of disagreement and misunderstanding is produced on both sides. It is difficult for K to understand the point of view of G. Consequently, G merely listens passively without responding much. With a growing sense of failure, direct contact starts to diminish. Eventually G and K get caught up in a vicious circle in which less frequent episodes of conversation lead to even more frequent outbreaks of disagreement and misunderstanding, which in turn promotes less personal contact. As a consequence, G and K try to ignore one another to avoid even more severe failures of understanding. For these reasons, G doesn't feel comfortable talking to K about anything; the possibility of talk is implicitly associated with yet another bitter fight. Sometimes it is better not to say anything at all than to say what will be badly misconstrued anyway.

A personal ideology may be viewed as a way of looking at the world that is largely closed to inspection from the outside. Because it is impossible to be *in* the world without acquiring a generalized conception *of* one's place in the larger scheme of things, a highly personalized and improvised sense of the way things are (or should, might, could be) is automatically acquired along the way. By implication, some aspects of one's collective vision may be discarded or discredited. Everyone who learns how to converse with others becomes a theoretical as well as a practical entity. Ideology operates through language, and language, as a medium of exchange, is "partially constituted of what, in our society, is 'real' " (J. Thompson, 1987, p. 523).

The use of complex language qualifies as ideological insofar as it is used to create public justification for the privileges and perks of certain groups, institutions, or individuals in the social hierarchy. The work of Grundy and Weinstein (1974) equates the inflated and justificational use of language with (a) those who participate in the defense of established norms and rules, (b) those in positions of conflict who attempt to expand the scope of their own privileges and prerogatives,

and (c) those who try to strengthen their collective resolve by engaging in social conflicts aimed at obtaining a greater share of existing
resources.

The adverse effects of a false ideology depend on whose interests
are at stake. When groups discuss internal matters of close personal
interest, the context of debate and deliberation may be kept somewhat
free of conscious bias and distorting influences. It is more difficult to
maintain a democratic and egalitarian climate, however, when the
focus of attention shifts to the concerns of outsiders who have no say
in what transpires. Corson (1993) examined discourse in meetings of
school administrators and community representatives. When discussing internal organizational concerns, participants were able to remain
fair-minded in judging the sincerity, truthfulness, justifiability, and
meaningfulness of problem-solving efforts. When the agenda was
shifted to the concerns of an out-group with no direct patronage on
the board, distortions in communication and small injustices became
common as out-group interests were greatly compromised. Suddenly,
member comments became less and less evenhanded; arguments,
rebuttal, and challenge increased; main alternatives were dismissed as
unworkable; negative points piled up, which had a bandwagon effect
of opposition to outsiders' requests; severe prejudice smoothed the
way for ideological argument; and "a number of key verbal and
prosodic contributions *scaffold*[ed] the discourse in such a way as to
make the possibility of opposition seem unwise or risky, and to encourage collusion in a conspiracy of distorted communication into which
those around the table are drawn" (p. 177).

A personal ideology can be used as a vision to be imposed on
others. The massive imposition is coercive and defensive in aspiration.
Moreover, it is a slanted vision that tolerates existing social inequities
and remains utterly indifferent to the deprivations of outsiders. Most
important, underlying premises and working assumptions are covered
up, taken for granted, and excluded from deliberation. Participants
take refuge in one-way discourse ("It's true because I say so") rather
than two-way dialogue.

Ethnocentric Bias

Disagreement. F and S lost one another long ago. During S's
childhood and young adult years, F was an extremely prejudiced

person. F was never careful about what he said and used offensive terms for minority groups. They lived in a small, conservative, sheltered town. It used to bother S but he never lost sleep over it. However, once S got into an ethnically diverse university, he finally got up the nerve to point out that what F had been saying all along was dead wrong. So S tried to teach F the facts that he gained in a short period of time. It didn't seem to do much good and the two lost contact for a while. Oddly, a great deal of faulty communication can take place over just the issue in question.

Misunderstanding. Y and U live together but don't quarrel over words because of ever-present tension in the air. Each one lives a completely different lifestyle and every small thing seems to be in conflict. Because neither party can voice anger openly, both seem to bottle up hard feelings. U is from another culture and Y becomes annoyed with U's loud chatter when U is on the phone or in the next room with a friend. U speaks Spanish; Y is not a racist, but after a while, being around what you don't understand can begin to get to you. The sound of someone speaking a foreign language is more of a distraction than if basic English were being spoken. When the two talk, Y has to enunciate clearly, speak more slowly, and concentrate to understand U much of the time. When you have that kind of strain day-to-day, your own communicative difficulties are likely to increase.

Ideological discourse is prone to personal errors associated with inadequate feedback and intolerance of reality-testing from as many viewpoints as there are participants or spectators. Where monologue triumphs over dialogue, individuals will undermine the search for collective truth, cut off options, and reduce alternatives. The pure ideologue pretends to be talking *with* others but only as a means of hearing the sounds of his or her own voice. The coercive mix of pretense and contempt toward others hides the weighted value and vested interests of those who insist on giving commands without accepting them in return (Bentley, 1926). The underlying intent of such pervasive distortion is to cloak one's real motives in idealized form to gain deference for them (R. Collins, 1985).

Ideological biases are closely linked with the problem of ethnocentrism. There seems to be a universal cultural inclination to view one's own group as "the center of everything" and to measure and rate all others in reference to it (Sumner, 1906, p. 13). At issue is "a tendency to be unaware of the biases due to one's own make-up and the culture of one's own group and to judge and interact with outsiders on the basis of those biases" (Reynolds, Falger, & Vine, 1987, p. xvi). Because everyone is ethnocentric to some degree, the matter is best viewed on a continuum, ranging from little, some, or a great deal of exaggeration in matters of deference (praise) toward insiders and suspicion (blame) toward outsiders (Levinson, 1994). At issue is variation of a basic attribution error in supposing our own values to be universally relevant and applicable to everyone else rather than the other way around.

Double standards are not necessarily injurious or harmful. Sharp in-group/out-group distinctions promote heightened identification with one's own kind. Pearce (1989) uses competitive sporting events as a case in point. Rivalry between "us" and "them" can be downright intoxicating. The University of Wisconsin, for example, is notorious for the fanatical devotion of the student body to national sporting events. With an undergraduate class of 40,000 members, up to 50,000 devoted fans can be counted on to travel 3,000 miles to attend a Rose Bowl game. The out-of-state visitors, who outnumber the locals five to one, fill the stadium in a sea of red and white. The roar of the crowd ("Go Big Red") is deafening. Beer and bratwurst are consumed in record numbers. The party goes round the clock. Fans snake dance through the streets, arm in arm, in a hypnotic chant with T-shirts featuring a menacing badger and free condoms to boot ("Get Lucky Bucky"). It's good for business, TV exposure, tourism, ad and travel agencies. Pity poor UCLA. "There ain't no place like this place." Victory brings tears of joy. Spirits are lifted—no harm, no foul; so far so good.

Not all grand displays of ethnocentrism are quite so innocuous. Much depends on how much *psychological* distance is placed between ourselves and others. The magnitude of division between "us" and "them" is crucial. At low levels of distinction, a measure of local favoritism will still accommodate a larger sense of equality. This is called *cultural relativism*. It reinforces recognition that the actions of others must be understood in the context of *their* values and beliefs.

As relativism in perspective taking diminishes, and ethnocentrism increases, dualisms and schisms legitimate a stance of indifference to or avoidance or disparagement of outsiders. Trouble begins with ethnocentric speech that is in the service of pejorative (negative) expressions about the out-group such as name calling, inaccurate predictions and explanations for the behavior of other groups, and systematic insensitivity to the effects of one's actions on others (Pearce, 1989). It has been well-documented that out-group members are construed as more similar to each other than are in-group members (Judd & Park, 1988; E. Smith & Zarate, 1992). Moreover, out-group judgments are prone to low levels of sensitivity, crude stereotyping, and overgeneralizations (Judd, Ryan, & Park, 1991). In effect, a great deal of potentially valuable information is lost when individual distinctions are lumped together in one general category.

Highly ethnocentric codes are divisive. They promote excessive reliance on first person perspectives (self as source, other as object), make far too many (unstated, untested) assumptions, encourage scapegoating (affection toward insiders, hostility toward outsiders), instill loyalty (for your own kind) in exchange for protection from outside intervention, and exaggerate the value of two-valued classifications (friend/foe). Distortion results from biased forms of misclassification and false or mythical categorization. Such tendencies tend to be self-fulfilling by inhibiting attraction or blocking off communication. On this point, Van der Dennen (1987) writes,

> Without interaction, it is impossible for people to discover that they are basically similar to each other in their values, beliefs, concerns, and experience. In addition, without communication between people or groups, it is easy for autistic spirals of hostility to develop and for people to obtain disconfirming information that might lead to mutual understanding and better relations. (p. 30)

It is not clear what ethnocentric fabrications achieve or at what cost. Dunbar (1987) points out that we are dealing with complex attitudes and sentiments that do not have uniform effects on behavior but instead are open to considerable cultural manipulation. The crucial issue is whether the unpleasant aspects of human inclinations are pushed to the extremes of prejudice and bigotry or are diffused and inhibited.

Egocentric Bias

Disagreement. C and D have conflicting ideas about how to deal with other people and both know that neither one is ever going to change. C knows the way D feels close relations should be handled, and D knows how C feels. It's different from a simple misunderstanding because C thinks they actually do understand but they are so different and constantly diverging. C doesn't know if they have ever agreed about any one issue or situation. In fact, it seems as if they expect to disagree on everything and maybe even thrive on it. Neither wants to agree to any one thing out of a fear of being seen as the loser who must give in and admit the other is right. There is tension because both are aware of what usually occurs. C just waits for D's first snide remark and then has a pit bull way of verbally attacking practically any remark just to put D in D's place. When speaking to D, C tends to blurt out opinions that C would hold back if speaking to anyone else.

Misunderstanding. L and E's interactions always seem to go the same way—very predictably. L is a man who *always* thinks that he is *right*. L considers what L says to be the right and truthful standard by which everyone else is to be judged (while E doesn't). This is where the entire misunderstanding comes into play. E believes that everyone is entitled to his or her opinion and should be able to discuss disputed matters in a congenial and open manner. When L and E discuss anything, E always lets L explain his opinion and feelings. After L has finished with his argument and E doesn't agree with what L has said, it is finally E's turn to explain. Unfortunately, E receives dirty looks, sighs, and comments such as "you're wrong." E doesn't understand why L doesn't let E explain himself. The misunderstanding has led to enormous problems in communication. Basically there is no direct contact and there hasn't been for well over a year because E has grown tired of hearing that he is always the one who is wrong.

Egocentric bias is pervasive. In Western cultures, we place a great deal of faith in the inherent separateness of people. The stress on independence gives rise to a view of the person as a bounded, unique, more or less integrated motivational and cognitive universe, a dynamic center of awareness, emotion, judgment, and action organized into a distinctive whole and set contrastingly both against other such wholes and against a social and natural background. (Geertz, 1975, p. 48)

A strong sense of individuality accentuates awareness of self as an active agent, a producer of one's actions. It heightens the need to be in control, and to express one's own thoughts and feelings to others, while being

relatively less conscious of the need to receive the thoughts, feelings, and actions of others. Such acts are often intrinsically rewarding because they elicit pleasant, ego-focused emotions (e.g., pride) and also reduce unpleasant ones (e.g., frustration). Furthermore, the acts of standing out, themselves, form an important basis of self-esteem. (Markus & Kitayama, 1991, p. 246)

Egocentric assumptions are associated with inflated estimates of the degree to which others think or act in the same way as oneself. Consequently, alternative possibilities are easier to discount or rule out (Marks & Duval, 1991; Marks & Miller, 1987). As egocentrism increases, so does the overestimation of shared perspectives (Fenigstein & Abrams, 1993; Orive, 1988). Clearly, it matters how decisively the boundaries between self and other are drawn because the sharpness of the distinction gives shape to the potential for greater depth of personal engagement.

Egocentrism is associated with the enormous problem of narcissism and a host of self-enhancing biases. There is a widespread presumption that people are motivated to maintain and enhance their own self-esteem. Self-serving motives are useful in recasting impressions and recollections to produce a more flattering image (Deaux, 1992; Fiske & Taylor, 1991; Reis, 1994). S. Taylor and J. Brown (1988) discuss evidence of pervasive and enduring distortions of the self-concept in three separate domains: unrealistically positive self-evaluations, illusions of control, and unrealistic optimism (for a review, see Colvin & Block, 1994a, 1994b, and rejoinder from S. Taylor & Brown, 1994). According to criteria specified by the American Psychiatric Association (*Diagnostic and Statistical Manual of Mental*

Disorders, third edition), the defining attributes of a narcissistic personality include "a grandiose sense of self-importance" and a tendency to "exaggerate their accomplishments and talents, and expect to be noticed as 'special' even without appropriate achievement" (pp. 349-350).

Tendencies toward self-enhancement are pronounced in ego-involving contexts of social appraisal where failure would be threatening (Emmons, 1987; Raskin, Novacek, & Hogan, 1991a, 1991b). A study by John and Robins (1994) examined accuracy and bias in self-evaluations of performance in a group discussion task. A comparison of self, peer, and staff evaluation showed that the perceptions of self were less accurate than evaluations of others when the task was ego involving. Although 60% of the subjects overestimated their performance in the group discussion, a sizable minority of 38% underestimated theirs. As predicted, individual differences in the self-enhancement bias were found to be systematic and psychologically meaningful. The link was strongest with narcissism, a stable and generalized tendency to see oneself in an unrealistically positive way. These results are consistent with related evidence that discrepancies between actual and ideal conceptions of self are associated with characteristic moods and vulnerability to emotional distress. Actual-ideal discrepancies are correlated with dysphoria whereas actual-ought incongruities are linked with anxiety (Higgins, 1987; Higgins & Bargh, 1992; Kihistrom & Klein, 1994).

Narcissistic conversation is striking, sometimes almost comical, in profile. It involves far more than talking about oneself to the exclusion of showing appropriate concern for others. Nor can the prevailing features be whittled down to facile labels—vain, shallow, vicarious, gratuitous, or self-absorbed. It is important to keep in mind that personal traits are expressions of the prevailing forces at work in the surrounding culture. In a review of salient literature, Vangelisti, Knapp, and Daly (1990) identified four leading characteristics: (a) the use of inflated language as a means of covering up a negative self-image; (b) a willingness to exploit or seduce others as a means of seeking power and control; (c) exhibitionism, that is, putting on a good show, staying in the spotlight, coveting the opportunity to be the center of attention; and (d) avoidance of intimate relationships. The same study used written questionnaires and role-playing interactions to construct a topology of relevant behaviors. Conversational narcissism was found to entail considerable boasting, "one-upping" others' disclosures, "shifting" the focus back to oneself, overuse of "I" statements, and displaying impatience when others speak.

Summary

A common theme runs through the issues—ideological, ethnocentric, and egocentric—of cognitive bias. When we are tempted to identify other people as the so-called cause of our own communicative maladies, it is useful to remind ourselves that they are also the ultimate source of the solution. In this case, as Freud so insightfully observed, the curse cannot be easily separated from the cure. The trouble with highly narcissistic people is that they are afraid of getting too close to others. Cognitive biases are reflections of personal defenses against the promise and risk of establishing closer ties with others. Nonetheless, highly independent construals of self can be modified into more fully integrated notions of interdependence. In the words of Markus and Kitayama (1991), the experience of genuine interdependence

> entails seeing oneself as part of an encompassing social relationship and recognizing that one's behavior is determined, contingent on, and, to a large extent organized by what the actor perceives to be the thoughts, feelings, and actions of *others* in the relationship. (p. 227)

MISCALCULATION

Disagreement. M and T are polar opposites. M is a pessimist while T is an optimist. They get along well until sensitive personal issues arise. M makes a comment that she truly believes but also knows T will disagree with, and that gets the debate going. Then T will argue with M while making points and M will give a rebuttal. They go in circles trying to convince the other, who in fact does not hear a word. When M does listen to T's arguments, it only makes M oppose T even more. They are always in a debate; there is never an end or a victor.

Misunderstanding. G and P are so used to one another's frustrating views as to suffer an almost complete breakdown in communication. Because each one is unwilling to talk *with* the other, serious disagreements are a way of life. Usually G will wait for a problem to become worse before saying anything about it. Each dispute ends with one party getting angry and walking away or shutting the other person out. Serious personal problems (money, family, friends) are never brought up until they reach the maximum level and any potential solution has passed long ago. For example, this past winter, P had planned to visit his brother in Houston in the fall. By August, P was depressed because he really wanted to go but didn't have the money. So when P finally mentioned the dilemma, G said, "Well you had six months to save for this trip so what are you complaining about?" P replied, "I know! I know! I screwed up but I shouldn't have said a word. Forget I even mentioned it." This is how all disagreements go.

It is useful to think of interpretive actions in terms of definitions, classifications, and explanations. The question of *definition* specifies what counts as data or evidence for what transpires. *Classification* assigns rank and priority to relations between elements and to relations within larger dimensions and domains of flux and change. *Explanation* certifies or justifies the reasonableness or credibility of the constructive process. At all times there is movement beyond what is taken into immediate account as given. In effect, to interpret is to measure, estimate, or calculate the significance or relevance of everything one uses to take existing circumstances into account. It is a mistake, therefore, to reduce such a fantastically complex set of operations to a localized matter of *social perception* because genetic factors—transmitted from one generation to another—establish the outer parameters of performance that, along with acquired sensibilities, form a synthetic and integrated sense of what separates fact from fiction. This approach is predicated on a view of human reality as linguistically constructed.

Calculation and explanation work together. Personal accounts follow an economy of explanation (McLaughlin, Cody, & Read, 1992). Human beings are storytellers who seek to make sense of things by recasting mundane encounters into mythical events with heroic or tragic overtones (McAdams, 1993). A personal narrative unfolds in the manner of a morality play. It is moving and convincing at the level of a subtext where efforts at successful communication are identified with the (heroic) resolution of difficulty while those of failure take on tragic overtones. Powerful urges serve purposes that range from a search for "a path of enlightenment" to a "perpetuation of false consciousness" (McClure, 1992, p. 79). Multiple appeals to common sense guide personal behavior and subsequent accounts of the cause and reason for whatever action has taken place (Furnham, 1992). Excuses and rationalizations pile up after the fact (Weiner, 1992). At stake is the struggle to construct a coherent account in which everything "fits together" (Bennett, 1992; Read, 1992). Account evaluation is played out against the test of "background expectations" (Scott & Lyman, 1968).

Presumably human beings have a strong stake in the soundness of their cognitive calculations. The skillful use of complex language is highly advantageous. It facilitates constructive thinking (Katz & Epstein, 1991), better adaptation to changing, unforeseen circumstances (J. Anderson, 1991), cognitive growth (van Geert, 1991), high quality of life (Burling, 1986), and higher odds of survival (Handworker, 1989). Conversely, misuse or abuse of something so powerful and mysterious can be quite hazardous to one's health and well-being. The leverage afforded by a strong track record of solid or well-founded calculations still entails a possibility of miscalculation.

There is a great deal of current academic debate over the relative accuracy of human judgments. At one end of the spectrum are the intellectual pessimists who are inclined to document a litany of shortcomings, foolishness, and folly. At the other are the optimists who prefer to demonstrate the ability to steer the course and see things clearly. The former try to come to terms with low-quality performance—error and inaccuracy—while the latter have a vested interest in high-quality activity—accuracy and mistake-free conceptions. We turn now to a brief outline of the central themes on both sides of this important controversy.

Skepticism points to conditions where people's conceptions are poorly calibrated with nontrivial consequences. Errors, mistakes, lapses, and self-serving miscalculations are likely to go unnoticed at the very point where it becomes most difficult to recognize them (Wilson & Brekke, 1994). There may be no observable symptoms that anything has gone wrong. What operates outside of conscious awareness, namely, in automatic procedures, is not easily "fixable" (Bargh, 1989). In addition, motivational or cognitive resolve may be lacking to go back through complex thought processing to tease apart bits and pieces of invalid information and to correct them for any unwanted effect (Schul & Burnstein, 1985). Faith in one's ability to control misplaced beliefs is undermined where adherence to false propositions proves irresistible, that is, with slick, deceptive advertising (Gilbert, 1991, 1993).

Pervasive, enduring, and systematic departures from reality orientations stem from a basic motive toward self-enhancement. John and Robins (1994) point to psychological discussions of illusionary self-enhancement "as if it were a general law of human behavior applicable to all normal psychologically healthy individuals" (p. 208). They point to S. Taylor's (1989) conclusion that "normal thought is marked not by accuracy but by positive self-enhancing illusion" (p. 7). Similar themes are repeated in the suggestion of Paulhus and Reid (1991) that "the healthy person is prone to self-deceptivity" (p. 307) and Greenwald and Pratkanis (1984) in the assertion that self-enhancing biases *pervade* the "self-knowledge of the average normal adult of (at least) North American culture" (except for depressed individuals) (p. 139).

Much has been made of self-serving appraisals in the "above average" effect. When asked for a candid appraisal of their own capacities and performances in relation to those of others, people predominantly consider themselves to be above average. This form of self-inflation has been demonstrated in the domain of driving ability (Svenson, 1981), ethics (Baumhart, 1968), health (Weinstein, 1980, 1982), and managerial skills (Larwood & Whittaker, 1977). A notorious case in point comes from a survey of 1 million high school students (1976-1977). When the College Board asked them to rate themselves in relation to their peers, 70% judged themselves as above average in leadership ability whereas only 2% saw themselves as below average. In judgments of the ability to get along well with others, all students rated themselves as at least average, 60% placed themselves in the top 10%, and 25% placed themselves in the top 1% (as cited in Dunning, Meyerowitz, & Holzberg, 1989). Professors are not exempt. In one study, 94% of all college professors claimed to do above average work (Cross, 1977). These findings are typical of a flood of books and experiments devoted entirely to an exhausting and often gleeful documentation of a veritable litany of shortcomings and foibles in human judgment, evaluation, and appraisal. If taken at face value, it would be difficult to explain why things work as well as they do.

Fortunately, the majority of people can read an eye chart clearly, make trains run on time, and sustain quite reasonable, civilized conversations with others.

Documentable errors and miscalculations should be taken seriously if for no other reason than not to repeat them mindlessly or unnecessarily. We describe the fine line between poorly calibrated and finely tuned performance so as to better understand the magnitude of difference. Face-to-face interaction does not have to be error-free or flawless to qualify as efficacious or intrinsically valuable. Excellence is not the same as perfection. To complete the larger picture, it is necessary to identify a range of conditions associated with accurate and exacting forms of interpretive action.

Accuracy motivation does matter. A number of requirements are entailed. It is not enough for people to automatically assume that their beliefs or judgments are accurate or that others' notions are inaccurate. The presumption or intention must be subject to external confirmation. Unsubstantiated expectations are often poorly conceived and generally unwarranted. If there is no willingness or inclination to test them out, neither is there any possibility of acknowledging that one is muddleheaded or simply mistaken. Whether it turns out that we are right *or* wrong is something we must earn, not merely presume, the right to claim. This makes the discovery of error to be valuable as a self-correcting mechanism. When people believe their behavior to be contingent on the responses of others, they should be motivated to monitor what transpires from multiple reference points (Kenny & DePaulo, 1993).

Accuracy motivation leads people to abandon unwarranted expectations (Neuberg & Fiske, 1987). It also diminishes the frequency and magnitude of attributional errors (D'Agostino & Fincher-Kiefer, 1992; Osborne & Gilbert, 1992; Pittman & D'Agostino, 1989). Moreover, it facilitates the ability to deal with complex information and to recall expectancy-inconsistent information more readily (Driscoll, Hamilton, & Sorrentino, 1991). Finally, accuracy motivation is associated with a skillful search for diagnostic information (Kruglanski & Mayseless, 1988), sound evaluation of persuasive messages on the basis of argument quality (Petty & Cacioppo, 1986), and avoidance of reliance on relatively superficial feedback (Borgida & Howard-Pitney, 1983). In effect, available information is processed systematically because of a desire for a full and comprehensive understanding of underlying implications (E. Thompson, Roman, Moskowitz, Chaiken, & Bargh, 1994). Kruglanski (1990) suggests that a "fear of invalidity" leads people to want to minimize premature judgments in thought; to construct complex, multidimensional judgments; and to generate a greater number of hypotheses about a conclusion before settling on a final impression.

Accuracy may be validated at two levels. Generalized accuracy takes into account the ability of people to understand how they are viewed by people as a group. Specific accuracy focuses on the responses of a particular person. The highest levels of accuracy accrue when varying types of situations or relationships match up with the context of deliberation with a significant other. When both types of confirmation are copresent, we are in the best possible position to demonstrate that we *do* know what we know to be the case and have earned the right to feel relatively certain about it.

Confidence in accuracy increases when individuals are allowed to function in a natural, as opposed to a laboratory, setting (Berry, 1990; Funder, 1987). Much of the cited evidence about poorly calibrated action has been garnered in situations where the presence of others is implied rather than actual (Malloy & Albright, 1990). Once the standard of evaluation moves into the arena of direct human contact, a greater sense of accountability is required. There is considerable truth to the old adage that you are only as good as you appear to be in the eyes of others. In effect, the standard of measurement is not what we think of ourselves but what we think about what others think about us. Studies of the accuracy of eyewitness accounts show that confidence is related to the ability of subjects to describe the decisions that led to their respective judgments (Dunning & Stern, 1994). Even the most confident individuals have only partial access to these automatic processes and are modestly successful in sorting out accurate from inaccurate identifications (Leippe, Manion, & Romanczyk, 1992).

Much of the proving takes place at the level of nonverbal behavior. Ambady and Rosenthal (1992) argue that expressive behaviors, particularly nonverbal cues, exhibit a remarkable degree of communicative power. Much of this unstated expressive activity is unintended, unconscious, and yet extremely effective. Even our most intimate expectancies and biases are conveyed through subtle, almost imperceptible, nonverbal cues that operate at the periphery or even beyond the thresholds of conscious awareness. The test of accuracy takes place, then, at a very specific level of thin slices of expressive behavior. Judgments and evaluations based on fleeting glimpses and brief observations can be quite accurate (Funder & Colvin, 1988; Kenny, 1994; Watson, 1989). Results imply that intuition and natural judgment are more reliable than one might expect (Ambady & Rosenthal, 1992; Berry, 1991). In fact, people rapidly and unwittingly convey a great deal of information about themselves to others within exceedingly short time frames (2 or 3 seconds).

Brief clips of behaviors have been shown to indicate subtle expectancies that are influential in shaping social outcomes (Harris & Rosenthal, 1985). Although ratings of personality by strangers have been shown to be surprisingly high (Paunonen, 1991), global measures of accuracy are highly correlated with degree of acquaintanceship (Anderson & Cole, 1990). As the aggregate amount of salient information increases, people learn to rely not only on specific aspects of what they observe but also on abstract knowledge of how significant others react to changing social circumstances (Sherman & Klein, 1994). Another advantage of extensive interaction is the tendency for beliefs about conversation to converge and become finely coordinated (Wilkes-Gibbs & Clark, 1992).

Two related issues warrant acknowledgment. The first pertains to the relative accuracy of prediction using different channels of communication. The nonverbal channel includes visual information (face, body, or face and body); the vocal channel involves intonation (just tone of voice); the verbal channel relies on the spoken word (speech and transcripts); and the audiovisual channel combines visual and verbal cues. Although the impact of these expressive modalities depends on the type and topic of conversation, the more controllable channel is verbal (speech), followed by face and the body; the least controllable modality is voice (Ambady & Rosenthal, 1992). When verbal and nonverbal information is inconsistent, the leakier, less controllable, nonverbal behaviors may reveal more true intent (Noller, 1985b).

The second issue pertains to personal skill in matters of facial recognition. A great deal of emotional activation is registered in the face. Unlike the body, which can be covered up with clothing or protective posture, the face is highly visible. Not a surprise, people are experts at face reading. Dunning and Stern (1994) provide a compelling explanation. Memories about external events provide a wealth of contextual information about time and place as well as matters of rich sensory detail (color, shape, texture, tone of objects). When people recognize highly familiar facial expressions, the perceptual detail of what is seen is a good match to the sensory information contained in memory. Hence recognition is instantaneous, seeming to pop out at the observer.

Paradoxically, because of reliance on rapid, automated cognitive operations, completed without conscious awareness, people are often unable to articulate the basis for their rapid-fire decision. This is an extremely important discovery, not only for understanding why individuals can get things right without being able to say how but also for the experiential basis for a lingering or vague sense of miscommunication, particularly a momentary lapse of being at a loss for words. Moreover, people rely on representations of faces that contain a good deal of *configural* information, that is, patterned cues about relations and proportions of facial features and general shape (Wells & Turtle, 1987). As a result, information about the totality of facial appearance is not easily articulated. Inaccurate identification, in contrast, often relies on more deliberate, explicit cognitive strategies for a decision. This is the equivalent to thinking too much, second-guessing, or faulty attempts at mind reading.

The key controversy in question is whether accurate face reading is driven by cultural knowledge or is universally acquired. On one side are those who claim that some emotions are universally recognized from facial expressions. The universality thesis is couched in the following types of conclusions. Ekman (1980) writes, "Definitive data are now available on the question of universality" (p. 93). "There are some facial expressions of emotion which are universal" (p. 137). Izard (1980) speaks of "impressive evidence for the innateness and universality of six of the fundamental emotions: enjoyment (happiness), distress (sadness), anger, disgust, surprise, and fear" (p. 201). "Since all human beings recognize these expressions and attribute to them the *same* experiential significance, it is reasonable to infer that they are genetically based or preprogrammed" (p. 185). Buck (1988) concludes that "certain displays appear and are correctly recognized in widely different cultures" (p. 351). Brown (1991) writes, "The conclusion seems inescapable. There are universal emotional expressions" (p. 26). Finally, Carlson and Hatfield (1992) refer to "compelling evidence that six basic emotions are expressed in much the same ways in all cultures" (p. 221).

Despite confident pronouncements, the pancultural thesis has been called into serious question. An alternative explanation concedes that basic facial expressions may be highly related but insists that the linguistic associations still vary widely across cultural boundaries. This is an important rejoinder because it suggests that what we see may be universally applicable while the concepts and labels of description differ in ways that are a reflection of local culture and habit. A statement by Russell (1994) points out that the premise of universality is a background assumption, a part of common sense, at least in Western culture, but not in other cultures. There are grounds for caution.

The ability to recognize basic emotional states is a socially acquired skill that can be expected to range widely both within and across cultures. Moreover, different observers can provide different labels for the same expression. Emotional language can be fuzzy or highly charged, can blur distinctions, or can be used in ambiguous ways; that is, both A and B recognize the facial expression of C to register *happiness* while the connotations of the term may not coincide. Even when the same label is used, the situation still may account for more overlap in judgment than the stimulus per se. What does it mean to say an emotion is *easily* recognized across culture? Defenders of the universal thesis counter that Russell has misinterpreted what *universality* means. Despite qualms about method and evidence, Ekman (1994) contends that "evidence from both literate and preliterate cultures is overwhelming in support of universals in facial expression" (p. 268). Likewise, Izard (1990, 1994) counters that affirmative evidence is independent of language variation. Although there may be no final resolution to this fascinating debate, the issues themselves are critically important. At the heart of the matter is whether personal miscalculations can be justified on the basis of psychological operations, situational factors, or failed opportunities to see beyond the outer limits of one's own cultural heritage.

DECEPTION

Disagreement. N and P are friends who have difficulty getting close to each other. When they try to do something to make things better, the interaction fails to live up to what each one had expected. This makes them both avoid interaction for a time. They constantly flutter back and forth. Both have crossed the line many times. Because neither can figure out where each one is located on the total spectrum of friendship, they rarely understand why a given sequence of interaction takes the course it does. N has no idea why P acts the way P does. Sometimes N will call P on it and will always be met with denial. Perhaps P has the same confusion about dealing with N but it is never mentioned or voiced in any way. The worst part is the constant guessing over how to act on a given day.

Misunderstanding. P and T have a tendency to cover up any sign of personal misunderstanding, often to the point where important issues can be concealed just as a matter of whim. When using misplaced words, acts of misinterpretation lead to further episodes of misunderstanding. It doesn't matter whether the fault is reciprocal or not. There is a special signal that lights up and reminds them of an impending conflict. The seriousness of the dispute depends on the situation. The longer they don't talk about it, the longer a problem can exist below the surface. On the other hand, staying quiet has a calming effect and lets each one think the matter through. This calm period also gives them more time to find out the truth; it also provides an opportunity to think things over and talk afterward. Finally, mutual tolerance of such misunderstandings can lead to better understanding in the future.

Deception differs from other forms of cognitive distortion—interference, bias, and miscalculation—in matters of deliberateness and tactical advantage. Instead of being an unwanted influence, personal deceit may be a path of least resistance, particularly when something is to be gained. In this section, we examine the dynamics of interaction when the ideal of maximum communicative value—clarity, fluency, and explicitness—is short-circuited or bypassed. Deceptive messages strive to produce the very results that truth telling tries to avoid—false impressions and erroneous assumptions (O'Hair & Cody, 1994). By these standards, personal deception constitutes a sphere of distortion by strategic design and conscious intent. The essence of deception, as Thompson (1986) points out, is to create a mismatch in perspectives about something in particular.

Language is a medium and a tool. Ordinary discourse would not have such great power to reveal who and what we are if it did not also provide an equally salient means to conceal and cover up. The search for truth, as Heidegger (1962) points out, is a process of discovery. When fully concrete, personal discourse allows something to be seen for what it is, as either true or false. The things of which one speaks

> must be taken out of their hiddenness; one must let them be seen as something unhidden; that is, they must be *discovered*. Similarly, "being false" amounts to deceiving in the sense of *covering up*: putting something in front of something (in such a way as to let it be seen) and thereby passing it off *as* something which it is *not*. (pp. 56-57)

Heidegger speaks of things as covered up in the passive sense of lying hidden, as yet undiscovered, or else being buried, where something once disclosed is allowed to deteriorate, perhaps still visible but only as a simulation or a disguise. This is a technically accurate conception of what is at stake in terms of deceptive language.

It is possible to express or convey something, to make a difference or have an impact, without sharing the whole intention of communication (Airenti, Bara, & Colombetti, 1993). Deception takes a great deal of skill. It is risky as well as tricky and proves more difficult to pull off successfully than one might suppose. Four broad types of interpersonal requirements must be satisfied. First are antecedents to deception, that is, who is motivated and who is susceptible. Second are compositional matters, the design features of strategic disguise. Third are countervailing efforts at detection. Fourth are implications of taking into account the negative aspects of discovery.

No motivation for personal deception is more compelling than the possibility of getting away with it. Temptation abounds. Lying is ubiquitous, everywhere to be found. There are a number of social occasions when acts of prevarication are socially acceptable, that is, to protect life (Bok, 1978), to advance the goals of scientific experiments (Sharpe, Adair, & Roese, 1992), to protect the feelings of others (Taylor, Gittes, O'Neal, & Brown, 1994), to avoid needlessly self-destructive forms of behavior (Staw, 1981), or to defend national security interests in time of war (Robinson, 1993). Life is complicated in a society where "lying is endemic" and "the line between a lie and the truth is just not as clear-cut as parents and public ways of dealing with dishonesty would have it" (Saxe, 1991, pp. 410, 414).

Deceptive motivation is broadly associated with problem-solving strategies in unfavorable situations (Merydith & Wallbrown, 1991). Deceit affords a functional way of adapting to the conflicting demands of complex tasks (Bond & Robinson, 1988). The decision to deceive is calculated in strategic terms. In one equation, the person runs through four decisions: (a) Truthful activity will not accomplish the desired effect; (b) deceptive action will produce the desired response; (c) deceptive action would go undetected; and (d) if detected, deceit would not result in too much punishment (Booth-Butterfield & Booth-Butterfield, 1987). Not everyone is equally well qualified. Odds favor those people who are outgoing, highly expressive, and energetic over those who are quite anxious or apprehensive (DePaulo, Blank, Swaim, & Hairfield, 1992).

A study by Riggio, Tucker, and Throckmorton (1987) gave 38 college undergraduates a number of standardized social skill instruments. Participants were videotaped while giving short, persuasive messages under three conditions—truthful, deceptive, and neutral. A group of judges made ratings of the believability of each presentation. Results showed the expressive and socially tactful subjects were more successful deceivers. This finding was attributed to an honest demeanor bias in the socially skilled and a deceptive demeanor bias in the socially anxious. Likewise, when highly motivated to get away with their lies, more attractive speakers have a better chance of success than those judged to be less attractive (DePaulo, Kirkendol, Tang, & O'Brien, 1988).

Preparation and practice have been shown to enhance deceptive performance (DePaulo, LeMay, & Epstein, 1991). Planned lies are often more difficult to detect than spontaneous lies. Closely related are expectations for success (Levine & McCornack, 1992). In situations where persons think there is little chance of success, deceptions become easier to detect (DePaulo et al., 1991). Unfortunately, people tend to overestimate the accuracy of the evaluations they make of other people (deTurck, Harszlak, Bodhorn, & Texter, 1990). This is particularly the case with deception, where the gap between objective accuracy and confidence ranges between 10% and 20% (Zuckerman, DePaulo, & Rosenthal, 1981). Individual differences in truth and lie detection are quite modest (Bond, Kahler, & Paolicelli, 1985), while training efforts to improve people's skill in detection have not been very successful (Zuckerman, Koestner, & Alton, 1984).

The willingness to deceive others is related to the larger problem of self-deception, although the complex lines of connection are not always clear. If deception is a means of creating a false belief, one may not be fully conscious of the fuzzy boundaries separating the domain of fact from fiction. It is not always obvious how one can be so convincing to others without also appearing to be quite convincing to oneself. It is easy to make excuses, to rationalize one's actions for the sake of personal gain. Snyder and Higgins (1988) define excuse-making as

> the motivated process of shifting causal attributions for important negative personal outcomes from sources that are relatively more central to a person's sense of self to sources that are relatively less central, thereby resulting in subsequent benefits to one's image and sense of control. (pp. 237-238)

Such a conception shows why it can be difficult to disentangle the external audience from the internal audience. The less socially desirable component of two conflicting notions is often the easiest to hide from awareness. Unfavorable aspects of self-presentation are in greatest potential conflict with one's global sense of self-worth.

Excuse-making, therefore, slides easily into efforts at impression management, particularly when negative emotions are evoked. A study by Flett, Blankstein, Pliner, and Bator (1988) had a large group of undergraduates provide retrospective self-reports of the frequency, intensity, and duration of 14 positive and 14 negative emotional states. They also completed measures of impression management and self-deception that were found to be highly correlated with the aggregate amount of negative emotions, particularly those associated with anger. In effect, the need to present oneself favorably, in synch with prevailing social norms and standards, is closely associated with self-deception (Gudjonsson, 1990). By these standards, it is not surprising to find a connection between self-deception and such matters as illusions, delusions, escapism, wish-fulfillment, malingering, hidden agenda, motivated distortion, weird behavior, pretense ("not knowing"), and other forms of irrationality in everyday life (Bond, Omar, Pitre, & Lashley, 1992; Fleming & Darley, 1991; Jacobs, 1992).

Self-deception makes deceiving others easier. Manipulative use of language can assume almost magical qualities. At times, it is used as an instrument of cogent, sense-making practice. At other times, it enables one to revel in tricks, foolishness, nonsense, or what is taken as merely ludicrous. Evasive tactics serve hidden interests, deeply ingrained habits, and irrational styles of self-presentation. D. Jones (1989) equates self-deception with biased cognitive styles, motivated excuse strategies, and extremely "cold" belief formation. The *bias* in the style is disposed to selective interpretive actions bent on confirming personal beliefs about the relation of self and others to the world around us. Basic themes center on the need to disavow responsibility in the face of what goes wrong, and the urge to cling to reassuring myths instead. As Shean (1993) notes, "When we are blamed, we tend to present excuses that will block or mitigate blame or responsibility. These automatic and universal self-excusing strategies can become exaggerated and highly irrational when self-esteem is seriously threatened" (p. 50).

Types of deception run the gamut: falsifications, half-truths, and concealments (Metts & Chronis, 1986). A broader context includes fictions (i.e., exaggeration, tall tale, white lie, make-believe, irony, myth), playing (joke, tease, kid, trick, bluff, hoax), lies (dishonesty, fib, untruth, cheating), crimes (conspiracy, entrapment, spy, disguise, counterfeit, cover-up, forgery), masks (hypocrisy, two-facedness, back stabbing, evasion, masking, concealment), and "unlies" (distortion, mislead, false implication, misrepresent) (Hopper & Bell, 1984). Deception by active intervention employs a direct strategy, whereas deception by omission relies on passively allowing fabrications to continue (Chisholm & Freehan, 1977). Moreover, the action may be unilateral, as when perpetrated by one on another, or collaborative, as when two or more are implicated. Ordinary language lends itself to deceptive practices that blur the very distinction between truth and error (McCornack, Levine, Morrison, & Lapinski, 1996).

Among the various forms of interpersonal deceit, lying occurs most often. Lies fail, according to Ekman (1988), for any number of reasons, some of which have nothing to do with personal demeanor. Inadequate preparation and emotional interference are often implicated. In a study by Lippard (1988), 74 undergraduates recorded all instances of interpersonal deception over a 3-week period. Motivations for telling lies, which accounted for 81% of all entries, depended heavily on situational requirements. Most cited were efforts at controlling resources, self-protection, avoidance of conflict, protection of others, manipulations, excuses for failure, and joking. Underneath the surface were concerns about saving face, hurt feelings, and friendly requests.

The motivation to cover up increases in situations where there is a preponderance of negative emotions (Flett et al., 1988), violations of social expectations (Millar & Tesser, 1988), or effort to avoid stress or abuse (Hyman, 1989). In parent-child interaction, lying is viewed as a problematic behavior with little correspondence between saying and doing (Paniagua, 1989). Preservation of autonomy is also heavily implicated (Goleman, 1989). In organizational settings, deception functions as a means to influence supervisors (Deluga, 1991), minimize conflict over roles (Grover, 1993), and maximize advantage over those who are not well informed (Smith & Whitehead, 1993). Much depends on the stakes, of course—who has what to gain or lose. Opportunity means little in the absence of incentive.

By definition, a completely successful act of deception would conceal the secret and escape detection. Hence the urge may be nothing greater than the kick of seeing if one can get away with it. The ability to successfully deceive others may be viewed as an indispensable strategy to get what one wants (Burgoon & Buller, 1994). Falsified information is one of a number of strategic maneuvers designed to limit knowledge, abbreviate interaction, inhibit active responses, diminish directness and clarity, and disassociate from one's utterances (Burgoon, Buller, Guerro, Afifi, & Feldman, 1996).

Psychologists have yet to develop infallible lie-detection systems because, as Saxe (1991) notes, "individuals have too many options available to encode their thoughts for us to be able to probe what they choose to hide" (p. 411). Because efforts to deceive have been shown to promote arousal of the autonomic nervous system (Lykken, 1984), the crucial consideration is whether any increase in activation shows up at the level of observed behavior (Furedy & Ben-Shakhar, 1991). The discomfort and anxiety associated with deceptive communication has been linked with a number of nonverbal cues—more eye blinks, less eye contact, more hand gestures and feet/leg movement—as well as altered vocal behaviors—speech errors, pauses, longer response time, and shorter message duration (deTurck & Miller, 1985).

In the transition from truthful to deceptive actions, the distribution of content shifts as well. In a compliance-gaining task, Neuliep and Mattson (1990) asked respondents to write out exactly what they would say to get others to respond favorably across three situations. Subjects were instructed either to say exactly what they wanted or else to not tell the other person the real reason for the request. Truthful persuaders constructed messages involving positive and negative sanctions while deceptive persuaders composed messages based on rationale or explanation. Persons in truthful situations used more (a) promises for compliance, (b) recall of past obligations, (c) threats to engage in harmful actions for noncompliance, and (d) warning about negative consequences. Persons in the deceptive conditions offered reasons for compliance based mainly on distraction and rationalization without appeal to future consequences. These differences are consistent with a deceptive urge to get what one wants "right now" without taking long-term interests into account.

The ability of people to detect deception is often quite poor. Some reports show only slightly better performance than would be explained by chance alone (Kalbfleisch, 1992; Miller & Stiff, 1993). Such findings, however, occur mostly in noninteractive settings where people have been asked to distinguish between a "truthful" and "deceptive" message. Because deceptive messages involve the manipulation of highly sensitive information, it is important to study the subtle details of message composition in social contexts where receivers are not passive observers but have a more active stake in what transpires (Burgoon, Buller, Ebesu, & Rockwell, 1994). Fine-grained approaches suggest that deception is not a single type of event but a process in which certain elements are shaded through omission, concealment, distortion, equivocation, and diversionary tactics (Bavelas et al., 1990).

There is some comfort in knowing that proper training can improve accuracy in the detection of deceit (Ekman & O'Sullivan, 1991; Galin & Thorn, 1993). What is central is the level of personal involvement between sender and receiver and the activation of strategic adaptations on the part of both (Burgoon & Buller, 1994). Highly motivated deceivers are less likely to succeed when observers can see or hear their nonverbal cues (DePaulo et al., 1988). The more attention is paid to nonverbal cues, the less likely it is that deception will succeed (Ambady & Rosenthal, 1992; Poole & Craig, 1992).

Increased opportunity for two-way feedback also improves judgments of the veracity of communication (Zuckerman et al., 1984). Explicit behavioral training by deTurck et al. (1990) focused on six behavioral cues found in a previous study (deTurck & Miller, 1985) to be unique to deceptive situations. After five practice sessions, accuracy under trained conditions reached 77%, whereas under the untrained conditions, it was 63%. In a follow-up investigation, confidence in the detection of deceit was more realistic and accurate for those who received training as opposed to those who did not (deTurck & Miller, 1990).

The issue of training is associated with the degree of prior acquaintance. One might expect a general trend—the more you interact with someone, the better position you are in to discern the difference between truth and fabrication. The acquaintance process is, after all, a form of training. Hence there is reason to believe that intimacy and familiarity foster greater understanding of another person's attitudes and behaviors (Sillars, 1985). However, the effort to establish close ties with others also induces trust and belief in the veracity of other people's statements (G. R. Miller, Mongeau, & Sleight, 1986). Consequently, the mere belief that lies will not occur may subsequently distort the perception of others' actions. A number of studies demonstrate that while increased trust is a central means of establishing close bonds, it can decrease awareness of our partner's lies (McCornack & Parks, 1990). The issue of whether love is blind is complicated by the flip side of trust, namely, suspicion and the willingness to probe for soft spots in someone else's story. There is reason to believe that suspicion is as fundamental to the preservation of intimacy as is the sheer suspension of disbelief (McCornack & Levine, 1990). Unfortunately, suspicion may engender more suspicion in a self-fulfilling spiral.

A central question concerns when a "truth-bias" becomes overturned. When a *generalized* inclination to trust a partner is strong, there is a tendency to err on the side of blind faith regarding the veracity of whatever the other may say or do (Stiff, Kim, & Ramesh, 1992). Here negative situational cues are ignored or discounted in favor of a generalized truth-bias. When too many questionable actions pile up within a short time span, individuals will abandon their prevailing reluctance to doubt and adopt a "lie-bias." Folk wisdom suggests that far more effort is required to establish trust than to destroy it. If this is the case, a modest dose of suspicion can improve accuracy in the detection of deceit so long as it does not lead to a major disruption of a prevailing truth-bias. A study by McCornack and Levine (1990) found that individuals who were moderately suspicious about specific statements were able to judge the veracity of their partners' statements with close to 70% accuracy, which is substantially above chance. There is, however, a risk associated with probing. Increased scrutiny may cause deceivers to alter their behavior when they perceive suspicion on the part of others. Hence they adjust their self-presentations to make themselves appear more truthful and escape detection (Buller, Strzyzewski, & Comstock, 1991). There is considerable interplay between the skills of those who would fabricate for personal advantage and those who wish not to have the wool pulled over their eyes.

There are consequences to the discovery of deception. One possibility is the misinformation effect, in which people can come to believe that they saw things that never actually existed. False or misleading impressions can turn a lie into memory's truth. A person can readily become confused over what is true or false. There may be a tendency to remember things differently from the way they actually were. Once accepted, fabricated memories can be believed as strongly as genuine ones (Loftus, 1992). Misleading statements have been shown to impair memory and distort recall. Much of the time, however, the evidence is not quite so clear-cut, probably because of the enormous observable variation that separates covert and overt misrepresentations of information in which "omission of all relevant information serves as one anchor and explicit contradiction of truthful information as the other" (Metts, 1989, p. 160).

When fabrication is unmasked unequivocally as deceptive, pure and simple, the effects are generally quite negative (McCornack & Levine, 1990). This helps explain some of the risks of exposing lies, particularly when there is a sense of risk or danger (L. Taylor et al., 1994). There may be a great deal of uncertainty and emotional upheaval in the strength of relational commitments (Planalp & Honeycutt, 1985). Those who discover they have been lied to feel betrayed and show resentment, disappointment, suspicion, and wariness of new overtures (Bok, 1978). Similarly, Werth and Flaherty (1986) conducted interviews to find out what it feels like to deceive others or be the object of deceit. Several themes stood out. First, there was considerable self-deception by many recipients at the point of initial realization, mostly in the form of disbelief, pretense, and denial. Doublethink was common. Ramifications extended widely in global, all-encompassing experiences that pervaded every aspect of personal life. Recipients experienced intense, negative, conflicting emotions, an altered sense of reality, powerlessness, confusion, fear, anger, hurt, and lack of self-worth. Motivations for remaining in such troubled relations included the persistent hope of having misunderstood the deceiver's behavior, fear of losing connection, and strong urges to resolve paradoxical tensions between closeness and distance, attraction and separation.

PSEUDOCOMMUNICATION

Cognitive distortions have a cumulative impact. Up to a certain point, they may go undetected, make little difference, or cause no observable harm. Minimal levels of slippage in thought and feeling are part and parcel of the reality of everyday life. Successful encounters need not be flawless or error-free. Still, adaptation and flexibility to changing or demanding circumstance take face-to-face interaction only so far. After reaching the upper limits of tolerance, personal encounters may no longer support but rather subvert or undermine the very conditions that regulate the reproduction of the process. At critical junctures and transitions, the respective parties may be tempted to short-circuit mutual aspirations toward high-quality performance and give up or give in, follow the path of least resistance, go through the motions, or take the easy way out.

Pseudocommunication is one way of responding to a succession of poorly calibrated performances. It is not just a matter of one form of distortion or another getting out of hand. It is, instead, akin to the nagging sense that everything is unraveling, becoming unsettled, or operating beyond the limits of volitional control. The locus of personal difficulty may be attributed to extenuating circumstances, the actions of others, or outside and unwelcome interventions by second or third parties. If only other people would (a) stop doing what they are doing (violations of commission) or (b) start doing things differently (violations of omission), everything would be OK. In the meantime, it is time to play "let's pretend." The prefix *pseudo* is indicative of a sequence of exchanges based on false, pretentious, affected, or meaningless actions, usually for the sake of appearances. What follows are a series of prototypic scenarios taken from the personal reactions of undergraduates to a series of readings about fantasy bonds (Firestone, 1987), idle talk (Heidegger, 1962), collusion (Laing, Phillipson, & Lee, 1966), and pretense in impression management (Goffman, 1959).

The Snelling family lives in Semiole Forest, an upscale housing development in the affluent suburbs of Madison, Wisconsin. The huge contemporary home was designed by a famous architect who works in the tradition of Frank Lloyd Wright. It sits high on a hill, surrounded by oak trees, with a breathtaking, picture-perfect view of Lake Monona from every room in the house. The grounds are professionally landscaped. Everything is impeccable. Four children attend the most expensive private school in the state, Westwood Springs Academy. Mr. Snelling works 70 hours a week as head of a local ad agency, and Mrs. Snelling is a psychotherapist in a thriving private practice dealing with sexual dysfunctions in marriage. The family income of $250,000 makes it seem like the best of all possible worlds. All the kids in the neighborhood think the Snellings have it made. When visiting relatives, the parents are loving and speak glowingly about their wonderful life together. Everyone knows just what to say and how to say it. The children are striking in dress and demeanor. The parents present themselves to the rest of the family as blissfully happy. Yet the couple never seem to interact as such a couple should. Smiling and talking in even-toned voices, they seem content. However, they rarely show any mood other than a monotone of dull talk punctuated with lots of silence. They never raise their voices or show true feelings. Only one relative knows that it's all fake—a great job of acting to cover up several nasty family secrets, including a decade-old affair—compensation for lack of sex or love between husband and wife—alcohol and pharmaceutical drug addiction, clinical depression, and enough bad dreams to go around. No one outside the family knows the marriage will dissolve as soon as the children enter college.

A graduate student, Susan Maywood, had a female friend who loved to talk constantly about her new boyfriend, John. Whenever a group of female friends got together for a chat, everyone, including Susan, talked about anything that was on their minds. When the subject of men came up, all the women gave their ideas about the trials and tribulations of dealing with them, both the good and the bad. Yet Susan would describe endlessly how happy she was and how perfect her boyfriend was. She explained how romantic he was and how much in love they were and how their living situation has provided the perfect lifestyle. The reality was quite different. Susan and her "incredible hunk" fought constantly, but only when they were alone. She presented herself as very put together, and when he got together with his friends he did the same. The trouble was that they had no tolerance for being apart. Either one could decide to do something with other friends and it would result in intense feelings of jealousy, friction, and then a huge fight. If they were not constantly reassuring each other, they would erupt into another destructive dispute. Inside the walls of their apartment, Susan constantly sought affection and attention from John. Unfortunately, his eyes were glued to the TV after his having just downed a six-pack and smoked three bowls of pot. When Susan was at her wit's end, she screamed and cried until he felt the need to knock some sense into her. After that was over, Susan would open up a new bottle of vodka. On the few times when they went out together with other people, they made it seem that everything was wonderful and nothing ever went wrong. Up until the time he moved out and never came back, she insisted he was the best thing she'd ever had and wished her friends could be so lucky.

Ken Stewart's uncle was a proud Kansas farmer who eventually went broke. This past summer a group of relatives from Wisconsin traveled to a small town in Kansas for a family reunion. The uncle and his family showed up with a brand-new car and very nice clothes. The same man who recently had begged his northern relatives for loans on several occasions never said a word about his impending bankruptcy. Everyone knew he was poor but the subject of how he paid for his car never came up. The relatives simply smiled, told him he had a very nice car, and admired the clothes. They all knew he couldn't afford the stuff but no one said a word.

Holidays in general stimulate fantasy bonding. Everyone dresses up, makes a big meal, and, because of the variety of ages represented at the family gathering, maintains an appropriate level of interaction without paying disrespect to anyone's mother or saying something shocking in front of children. It's all very superficial. No one asks anything risky or controversial about anyone else. "How's school?" "What's new at work?" Everyone knows it is so shallow but no one seems to mind.

A college sophomore recalls: This past weekend I saw a nun I had as a teacher in grade school. She had been extremely demanding and insisted on maintaining a collective fantasy. She thought she was the best teacher in the school. Every student was expected to idolize her no matter what. Every night as we left class we had to say, "Goodnight Sister Margaret Mary, thank you for teaching us today." Students would gossip behind her back, ridicule and make fun, but no one ever questioned her need to feed the fantasy and never called it into question.

It would be foolish to strive for an overarching conception of pseudocommunication that applies to all of the people all of the time. The spectrum of opportunity is as open-ended as the number and type of social occasions where people are willing to play the game. Much of the activity in question is shallow and superficial and lacks in-depth exploration of potential reference, relevance, or meaning. The image of a flat rock skimming over the surface of the water comes to mind. Words and gestures can be passed along, as Heidegger (1962) observed, in the manner of idle chatter. He uses gossip as a model where people get caught up in what everyone else thinks without bothering to make the surface meanings their own. Firestone (1987) underscores the mechanical, almost mindless mode of exchange where people seek to protect themselves from the joy and hazards of getting too close to others. Circumstances run the gamut from extreme situations where people are difficult to deal with, or virtually impossible to accommodate or appease, to less compelling situations where anything goes.

Ordinary language can be notoriously imprecise, particularly when it comes to reading other people's hidden motives or secret intent. Sometimes the means and ends of the respective parties are mismatched, poorly aligned, or incommensurate with one another. Closely related are many disruptions, distractions, and interruptions in the flow and pace of existing habits, projects, or routines. Moreover, there tends to be a pileup of unfinished business and unresolved issues carried over from one situation to another. A great deal of emotional baggage can be quite difficult to unpack, particularly when carried around as a hidden burden or weight. When unloaded in a futile effort to settle things once and for all, it can only make matters worse. Finally, it can be most difficult, sometimes impossible, to measure the real effects of one's own behavior on others, or to know how to respond in kind.

The main motive is to maintain appearances. Secrets become collusive when the participants agree to agree far more than they are willing to admit to one another, much less to themselves. Loss of perspective occurs when each party gets caught up in the existing moment, unmindful of how immediate efforts at impression management distort the larger course of personal history. We may convey something to one another without being fully conscious of it ourselves. A false sense of reality entails, among other things, a fantasy of communication where the collective "phantasy *is* reality, and what is not their phantasy is not real" (Laing et al., 1966, p. 40).

In acts of pseudocommunication, conventional language is counterfeit, a measure of pretense, contrivance, and elusion. Here the interactants put themselves in false and untenable positions, often without knowing what to do or how to break out. Individual performances set the stage for gamelike strategies with what Goffman (1959) calls "a potentially infinite cycle of concealment, discovery, false revelation, and rediscovery" (p. 8). Such a system does not so much break down in the manner of severed telephone lines, it shifts aimlessly between the poles of success and failure. What is given accentuated, favored, or idealized treatment above the surface of public appearance serves to protect and conceal signs of disfavor and violated expectations below. On this point, Goffman (1959) writes,

> Whether an honest performer wishes to convey the truth or whether a dishonest performer wishes to convey a falsehood, both must take care to enliven their performances with appropriate expressions, exclude from their performances expressions that might discredit the impression being fostered, and take care lest the audience impute unintended meanings. Because of these shared dramatic contingencies, we can profitably study performances that are quite false in order to learn about ones that are quite honest. (p. 66)

To do so is to examine protracted struggle over whether to try and make things better or keep them from getting worse.

One thing seems reasonably certain. We will never run out of messy things to study. In the matter of misinformation, fabrication, camouflage, pretense, and cover-up, human beings must be quite good at perpetuating such poorly calibrated practices because there is far too much of it around. Endless cycles of distortion and disruption make face-to-face interchange far more tedious and obscure than it needs to be. A complete solution may be out of the question but a measure of relief for the benefit of all who are concerned is certainly possible.

CHAPTER 3

Disruption

Misaligned efforts to communicate, coupled with distortion in message content, frustrate the struggle to foster mutual understanding, and throw the transactional process into a dismaying state of disorder. Disruptive influences acquire a growing momentum of their own. Misgivings, disorientations, and psychological turbulence come to rule the day. Unresolved difficulties pile up. Stressful and urgent events come into play. Instability in turn-taking only makes matters worse. Negative affect prevails. Personal dissatisfaction increases imperceptibly. Disruptive violations are subject to a heavy measure of score-keeping. Misinformation and mutual misinterpretation abound. Unresolved issues are taken as a threat of dissolution. Observable implications include a measure of lessened openness and diminished spontaneity. Wounding implications include hurt and anxiety that become manifest as increased suspicion about the desires and motives of others. Under such conditions, individuals trust each other less and move further and more frequently apart. It often comes down to an issue of whether the broken pieces can be put back together again.

Faulty implications, cognitive distortions, and behavioral disruptions, taken together, interfere with shared efforts to achieve high-quality performance. It is possible to show how things fit together in thin slices and minute gradations of synchrony, alignment, and accommodation. Individuals, according to ecologists, have well-developed

84

mechanisms to identify and categorize what sorts of things fit together and what types of activities don't (Reynolds et al., 1987). The preservation of a mutual sense of "good fit" leads to a greater appreciation of the distinctive communicative value of what takes place. Favorable conditions are known to confer a broad range of benefits in matters of well-being and quality of life. These include, among other things, individual sensitivity to the expenditure of scarce resources, willingness to contribute good ideas, generalized faith in the pursuit of personal goals as worth the cost, and especially enhanced communication skills (Axelrod & Hamilton, 1981; Burnstein, Crandall, & Kitayama, 1994).

By these standards, unfavorable conditions would include any harsh, unsafe, degraded, unhealthy, or otherwise unsuitable environment for human interaction to take place. Discursive practices, after all, do not spring out of thin air. A rich confluence of behavioral and environmental factors must come together to preserve a state of harmony and accord. Diminished resolve to tolerate expressions of discord will eventually weaken the search for common ground. Moreover, severe distortions in thought and feeling may become deeply ingrained in protracted episodes of badly misinterpreted forms of action. Unwanted (internal) interference and (external) distraction only add to the bias, static, and noise in the open system. What is produced is often more imagined or fantasized than real.

Misgivings are an initial sign of disarray. Hidden misapprehensions carry forward to affect one's total range of choices and priorities. Essentially, we learn to use our private musings as a way to understand any particularly confusing or amorphous aspect of human behavior. Critical situations can be quite vexing to figure out, particularly when they operate beyond the outer limits of personal volition and conscious awareness. Life-threatening issues—particularly those that emanate from misuse or abuse by others—may lead the affected individuals to believe fleeting impressions left by adrenaline rather than the language of deliberation over solid fact. The words and images that spring up during the heat of the moment seem so vivid and real that one may not call their validity into question. It may even seen unthinkable to do so—as if it were a crime in itself to stop and think things through.

The validity of first impressions is severely tested at times of great urgency or duress. When one tries to express or convey some intense, vivid, or striking incident, some of the firsthand significance and highly charged meaning will be lost in subsequent translations to second and third parties. How can one person convey the myriad stockpiles of meanings, heavy emotional overtones, and full weight of personal experience that are incurred during an especially critical or urgent circumstance? Acts of physical and sexual violence, for example, cause an upsurge of emotional turbulence that must be encountered firsthand to grasp how such invasive acts can injure the body, confuse the mind, and dampen the spirit of the victim. The *redefinition* of one's behavior immediately after taking aggressive action imposes slight, tacit, covert alterations in the pattern of attribution to escape blame (Backman, 1988; R. Lamb & Lalljee, 1992).

It is easy to see how intolerable levels of psychological turbulence could come into play. Invasive actions such as rape (Janoff-Bulman, 1979), natural disasters (Burger & Palmer, 1992), death of a family member (Lehman, Wortman, & Williams, 1987), or a succession of serious illnesses (Pennebaker & Beall, 1986; S. Taylor, Wood, & Lichtman, 1983) threaten prior beliefs and entrenched behavioral patterns (Janoff-Bulman, 1992; S. Taylor, 1991). In addition, severe trauma causes mature people to reconstruct belief systems and design alternative types of causal explanations for life-altering events that are not easy to grasp or comprehend, much less explain to anyone else.

Chronic exposure to crowded living conditions is also likely to foster problematic circumstance, disrupt support networks, and cause residents to cope, in part, by withdrawing from one another (Baum & Paulus, 1987). Long-term chronic stress has insidious effects on the prevailing levels of social support (Lepore, Evans, & Schneider, 1991). Terminal physical illness, recurring mental illness, and acute bereavement are extreme chronic stressors that cause family members to withdraw support from ailing individuals—due to the sheer magnitude of debt and threat of overwhelming obligation (Wortman & Conway, 1985). The risks are striking. Lepore et al. (1991) state,

> If the victims do not recover from their loss or illness over time, or if their condition places continued or increasing demands on their support network, social bonds are likely to loosen and support is likely to deteriorate. The deterioration of support may, in turn, be aversive and increase psychological distress. (p. 900)

Conflict and violence, by nature, cause intense forms of cognitive disorientation in the way the respective victims view themselves (Mortensen, 1987). The social networks of violent offenders may be disorganized and chaotic, sometimes almost as a way of life (Howells, 1981). In hearing the news of invasive action, others react from a distanced standpoint that does not permit full appreciation of the sheer magnitude of the total burden. Under unusually strained or stressful circumstance, personal experience may become simply too complicated or convoluted to express or convey sensibly to others. If the firsthand account is later adjusted or altered to fit the framework of what others expect, a great deal of vivid material will be edited out of the composite picture. A previous study of symbolic violence demonstrates just how difficult it can be for victims of abuse to make clear sense of terrifying events in terms that others can grasp and understand secondhand (Mortensen, 1994). Significant disturbance in personal and social relationships, according to Duck and Gilmour (1981), "affects the well-being of the individual just as it can also be regarded in some contexts as symptomatic of individual disorder" (p. vii).

Due to the sheer inability to capture the impact of overpowering events, it is often necessary to rely on others to do the talking for us. When the sheer intensity and complexity of extreme personal experiences become too unwieldy to convey in ordinary, normative, or conventional terms, it is necessary to search for metaphors and analogies to bridge profound gaps in unshared history or guide joint movement into uncharted domains. Without a shared vision, events with such life-altering impact may remain too difficult to decipher or unpack. The problem of disruptiveness in human interchange can be examined at different levels of complication, ranging anywhere from large-scale (macro) interventions to those that unfold on a much smaller (micro) scale. Main issues involve (a) unmanageable circumstances, (b) relational instability, (c) conversational irregularity, (d) lack of reciprocity, (e) mutual misconstruction, and (f) the threat of dissolution.

UNMANAGEABLE CIRCUMSTANCE

K and X can't get along. Neither is willing to look at things from the other's point of view. Each one can go for long periods without saying a word. Conversation is a mix of chit chat and small talk. Due to so many contradictory beliefs about life in general, K and X just ignore basic issues and skim topics briefly. They never actually talk anymore. Because both know what powerful but unresolved issues exist beneath the surface, K and X simply refuse to confront or deal with anything, and just live their own way and leave it at that.

The process of living is a collective matter of unfinished business on a large scale. Unresolved difficulties are full of tiny contradictions, paradoxes, and inconsistencies that don't add up on a small scale. Unmanageable encounters, in this equation, foster a sense of too many things going on at once or far too much to handle all at once. Such conditions reflect a stance of indebtedness to prior instances where things did not work out well, were never resolved, and now linger in an emotional residue of inference and implication. At the base of everything are hidden issues over previous tensions that now serve to undermine a present-centered focus of constructive action. In simple terms, there can be (a) too much, (b) too little, or (c) just the right level of sensory activation for one's own good.

Personal exposure to excessive levels of complexity and complication may be associated with lived circumstances that become unmanageable or spin out of control. During extraordinary periods, our lives are literally too much with us. Metaphorically, we may think of the image of an individual with the weight of the world on his or her shoulders. When forced to deal with the imposition of unrealistic or unobtainable standards, the unresolved aspects of our private realities get dragged around in stressful or urgent scenarios from one public setting to another. This often leads to a sense of sharp discrepancy between what is and what ought, could, should, or would take place if only things were different, that is, more manageable or subject to a greater amount of personal volition and conscious control. Coping skills have been shown to function best when there is a clear sense that stressful or extreme events are controllable when dealt with directly as opposed to those viewed as uncontrollable and to be avoided (Valentiner, Holahan, & Moos, 1994). In contrast, the experience of uncontrollable events is associated with performance deficits on subsequent tasks (Zimmerman, 1990).

Personal standards may be unrealistic or set too high, as in the case of an average achiever growing up in a home with gifted family members. For others, it may be a matter of doing the very best you can only to discover that it is simply never good enough. This theme is critical to those who suffer with eating disorders, where there is an acute need to be perfect right down to the last detail of appearance and physical attractiveness. In addition, we found parents in highly devoted academic families who expect excellence from each child at all times as well as the ability to be well liked and admired by everyone else. Similarly, extremely religious families establish strict and exacting standards to be morally above reproach and witness to one's faith in every aspect of life. One describes this pressure as a need to be "on" at all times and never to be candid about doubts, insecurities, shortcomings, or disappointments. Another respondent refers to a pressure-cooker atmosphere where everyone must appear to be utterly flawless, sensitive, appropriate, and well mannered regardless of who or what may be present at the time. Such a search for moments of utter perfection can be unrelenting and unforgiving of the slightest miscalculation or slipup.

Note how personal expectations are double edged—an opportunity and a risk, to measure up or fail to make the grade. When highly improvised performances are measured against those obtainable standards that remain just out of reach, one is encouraged to strive to be at one's best and yet still remain tolerant of a host of personal nullities—deficiencies, weaknesses, and liabilities. Still, the fear of failure runs deep in those situations where it seems impossible to keep up with everything that is expected or tacitly required by everyone else. Violated expectations accompany the sense of not getting back as much as one gives. High achievers can be affected greatly when they come up short. One respondent feels that his entire life has been cursed with bad luck. No matter how hard he tries, he never gets back his due. Such individuals place so much pressure on themselves as to be vulnerable to a stance of fatalism and despair.

Another sign of an unmanageable circumstance shows up as soon as one tries to talk about a complex maze of unresolved issues all at once. There is a distinct sense that one's past holds one back from being fully present now. We use the metaphor of "invisible walls" to convey pervasive feelings of separation and distance from others. A good deal of emotional residue or psychological baggage may hold one back. There are diverse variations on a common set of themes: *Escapism* is the urge to run away and hide. *Disappointment* occurs over the failure to live up to the highly idealized expectations of others. *Alienation* is having no one else available to discuss the full magnitude of some unwelcome turn of major events in one's life. *Xenophobia* is fear of talking to strangers or those who are not well known and, by implication, who could not possibly understand. *Indifference* is the feeling that no one seems to care and everyone else seems far away—aloof and detached. *Malaise* is feeling somewhat disconnected. *Isolation* is feeling very different from and cut off from everyone else. *Shyness* is the vague sense that one is merely a spectator, an observer of vibrant action by others. *Loneliness* can be fleeting and transitory. The *void* is feeling full of so much emptiness. *Lies and illusions* involve being full of the sense that everything that matters from the past is left unresolved. There is also *withdrawal* into fictitious worlds, and *refusal* to permit the fulfillment of an expressive urge. All of these exclusionary states stem from the erection of impermeable boundaries between self and other in a narrative context.

A complicated style of life can be very difficult to talk about in a short space. We discovered, for example, that silence becomes quite powerful during pressing, urgent, or extraordinary sets of social circumstances. There is so much one could, might, or ought to say, to bring others up to date, that one may, after all, end up saying very little at all. Envisioned or imaginary conversations focus on such matters as why some things are better left unsaid or what types of utterances would only scare others away. Here the encompassing silence may become a protective barrier behind which one waits, feeling trapped inside, for an appropriate time to discover what to say and how to say it.

Finally, unmanageable circumstances are associated with a heightened and protracted sense of misinformation and miscommunication. Here what qualifies as having distinctive communicative value eventually becomes a sign of serious slippage, a mismatch in operative frames of reference, where patterns of initiation and response get out of alignment or stay quite out of synch. Here we found respondents who could not easily identify, define, or classify the swirl of sensations, perceptions, and ill-formed conceptions that were operative at the time. Most were excessively stimulated or agitated beyond a tolerable threshold. Much of what was reported was so indefinite or ill defined as to be inexplicable. When one has great difficulty making sense of a highly charged frame of reference to oneself, it becomes even more difficult to explain to anyone else.

Here we located a broad spectrum of relevant themes in respondents' reconstructed interactions: Individuals often construed frames of reference that defied clear definition or description. They generated a host of questions without answers. Many more felt constrained by an inadequate sense of expressive freedom. There were mythological conceptions of something being revealed (unclearly) on the inside but concealed (quite well) on the outside. Here the affected individuals saw themselves much like containers with water filling the inside that was not visible from the outside. Many were indecisive—not knowing exactly what to feel, think, say, or do. There were similar types of complaints by those individuals who couldn't express themselves to *anyone* who was present at the time. Many respondents harbored the presumption that they might have been able to share (the X factor) with other individuals who were absent from some problematic circumstance. There was also considerable anxiety—as in the case of not being able to find the right words or clear gestures—and considerable frustration over not knowing what to say or do next. Consequently, they had great difficulty being direct, explicit, and to the point. Instead, there was much misdirection, equivocation, and vagueness. Many got entangled in a puzzle box of contradiction and paradox. Some were left with a profound sense of having manufactured little more than nonsense or unintelligible episodes of turn-taking activity.

One final observation about such incoherent or inarticulate acts is in order. Many respondents were communicatively impatient. They picked the wrong time or place to discuss weighty personal matters with others. They also tried to impose themselves on those who were not instantly prepared to be attentive or receptive for a sufficient length of time to deal skillfully with the entangled and unresolved issues that were at hand. Often there was not enough shared history or common ground with which to proceed. Many people tried to cram too many details into too short a space, or else decided to resort to largely elliptical references—headlines, notes, and shorthand—where much of the encompassing context was missing or hastily supplied. The main discovery was that inaction or avoidance of face-to-face interaction may be better than episodes with mismatched people and poor or no communication at all.

At the other end of the spectrum are a host of very simple and uncomplicated circumstances. Here the profile of face-to-face interactions stands in sharp contrast to the overly burdensome interactions. As a rule, it is easy to define an uncomplicated set of personal circumstances. Greeting rituals and small talk serve useful functions as social lubricants and time-filling devices. Usually, there is a sufficient supply of preconstituted rules, roles, and norms to help one decide what to say and how to say it. Also, there is minimum risk and little danger of violating the core sensibilities of anyone else. More important, the various risks associated with protracted efforts to make sense of complicated personal matters are avoided altogether. Routine interactions help maintain order and deal with unfinished business one item at a time. Mature relations depend on diverse routines to preserve and conserve close connections (Canary & Stafford, 1993; Fincham, 1992).

The only liabilities have to do with the boredom and tedium associated with highly habituated and deeply ingrained forms of shared practice and verbal routine. People often take the easy way out or follow the path of least resistance. They make ordinary conversation a matter of expedience or convenience. They often tire of repeated episodes of face-to-face interaction that have become so predictable and routinized that one can virtually intuit what others will do or say next: So why pick up the phone or go through the bother of seeking people out? Such unstimulating and effortless episodes of face-to-face interaction solve one set of problems but, ironically, pose another—mainly the tug of boredom, indifference, and inertia. Boredom is a symptom of excessive certainty, the willingness to take things for granted, emotional deadness, and a prime fear; it is a major reason for the breakup of romantic couples (Cupach & Metts, 1986).

RELATIONAL INSTABILITY

Y and B express themselves in completely different ways. Recently B returned from across the hall and made a comment about how cold it was, and something about the popcorn they had just eaten. Then B saw some pictures on Y's desk and asked if they were from spring break and if B could see them. Y replied,

"Yes," in front of B, who started talking about her own pictures and quickly left the room. A couple of minutes later, B came back and decided that she wanted to show Y her pictures. Despite her being hard at work on a term paper, Y took the time to look and ask if B wanted Y to show hers. They talked for a couple of minutes. B did almost all the talking, because B always has to be talking, before abruptly leaving the room without so much as a word of good-bye. This is the way it always is—totally one-sided and strictly on B's terms.

The stability of face-to-face interaction matters a great deal in the long run (Nezlek, 1993). Personal and situational factors combine to form highly distinctive patterns. Sometimes unique behavior seems situation-specific and context-dependent whereas at others it remains highly predictable from one type of setting to another. Overall, the consistency of people's behavior is thought to be dependent on the organization and predictability of the generalized types of situations that they favor or choose for personal engagement (Magnusson & Endler, 1977). Behavior is somewhat erratic and unstable during initial stages of activity but settles down as soon as people have been in a situation long enough to achieve a stable *emotional stance* toward it (Stewart, 1982).

The stability of face-to-face interaction is associated with the resiliency of self-esteem. The central question is not whether self-esteem is high or low but whether it is stable or unstable over time. It does not take long for disruptive incidents to produce short-term changes in the affective tone of personal orientations toward stressful circumstances. In this equation, self-esteem may be high or low and stable or unstable. The concept of *stability* refers to the magnitude of fluctuations in momentary, situational, and contextually based conceptions of self-worth (Kernis, Cornell, Sun, Berry, & Harlow, 1993).

Relational instability has been associated with enhanced concern over one's self-picture, heightened sensitivity to valuative remarks, and excessive reliance on what others think. Among those with low self-esteem, instability is related to greater excuse-making following poor performances (Kernis, Grannemann, & Barclay, 1992), overgeneralization after failure (Kernis, Brockner, & Frankel, 1989), and fewer incidents of depression afterward. These findings are taken as evidence of resiliency and adaptive coping with threats to the preservation of orderly practice. Those with stable feelings of high self-esteem tend to react to positive events in an agreeable and self-enhancing manner but react to negative events with adverse signs of defensiveness and rejection (Kernis et al., 1993). In general, unstable feelings of self-worth are associated with heightened sensitivity and greater ego involvement in the course of day-to-day events. Hence an unstable environment has been shown to disrupt self-related feelings; of greatest risk are those forces and factors that pose a threat to the most positive and stable dimensions of what transpires.

Disruption is also associated with outbreaks of intense emotion. Unpleasant affect can have a particularly disruptive impact on the stability and continuity of face-to-face interaction. After all, when everyone stays relaxed and low key, it is easy to preserve the desire for continuity and consistency in the shape of things to come. It becomes much harder, of course, to maintain a coherent sense of social order in the face of constant emotional upheaval and highly charged outbursts. Negative information can be disruptive to an extreme degree. A study by Ruscher and Hammer (1994) provides a compelling explanation. First, extreme aspects of negative information are weighted heavily in impression formation and accorded increased attention (Fiske, 1980). Signs of threat and danger are difficult to ignore or even to discount. Second, newly acquired items of information call prior assumptions and expectations into question (Skowronski & Carlston, 1989). Third, favorable impressions are more easily disconfirmed than unfavorable traits and require relatively little effort to be disconfirmed (Rothbart & Park, 1986). Hence the disclosure of extreme and negative aspects of information and evaluation can override favorable initial impressions with relative ease (Sears, 1983).

Much depends on the level of prior acquaintance and the sheer breadth of personal engagement. Consistency during initial contacts is associated with a later capability to withstand unpleasant thoughts and feelings (Woike, Aronoff, Stollak, & Loraas, 1994). This ability to tolerate highly charged activity stems from greater coping skill, and adaptiveness, that "increases the individual's capacity to respond to an event more fully, whereas less adaptive regulatory structures lead to behaviors more likely to avoid or restrict the negative affect or discharge it through impulsive behaviors" (Aronoff, Stollak, & Woike, 1994, p. 105). Individuals with high or low ego adaptability were placed in dyads and asked to complete a series of stimulating tasks. As predicted, the more ego-adaptable subjects made greater contact with other people, became deeply engaged with the tasks, expressed themselves in varied and animated ways, and responded with greater intensity across a broader range of emotions than did the less adaptable members. Once again, the advantage rests with those who can express themselves as directly and explicitly as possible. The quest for high-quality performance, and the optimum course of life experience, lies in the capacity "to function more flexibly, more realistically, and more fully" (Aronoff, Stollak, & Woike, 1994, p. 113).

A preponderance of negative affect erodes the stability of close ties with others. A solid and substantial sense of connection with other people requires a healthy balance between positive and negative feelings. Studies of successful marriages indicate that periods of fighting and turmoil require a lot of love and passion as compensation for subversive episodes. Gottman (1994) argues for a "magic" ratio of five (positive) to one (negative) type of action. In effect, more positive than negative energy is required to sustain intimate relations over time. In the moment-by-moment sequences of interaction, husbands and wives in stable marriages "were balancing their negativity with a whopping amount of positivity, whereas those couples who were headed for divorce were doing little on the positive side to compensate for the growing negativity between them" (p. 58).

Closely related is solid evidence that marital satisfaction is positively related to reliance on constructive problem-solving strategies, mainly negotiation and compromise, and negatively related to the use of negative problem-solving methods, mostly coercion, withdrawal, and avoidance (Bowman, 1990; Christensen & Heavey, 1990; Kurdek, 1991). Generally speaking, open and explicit problem-solving strategies are positively associated with high levels of individual satisfaction with jointly produced outcomes (Metts & Cupach, 1990; Stafford & Canary, 1991). In effect, personal satisfaction is a mutual achievement, a reward for the ability to sustain a high level of interdependence with others.

Signs of stability or instability emerge in very thin slices indeed, a blink, smile, or grimace. It is significant that a global measure of *satisfaction* turns out to be a rather accurate reflection of the characteristic ways in which members respond to one another, moment by moment (Bullis, Clark, & Sline, 1993). Across a diverse set of relational conditions, the most widely applicable measure of satisfying interchanges remains the same, namely, more expressions of warmth and regard, and less of hostility and shame (Gottman & Krokoff, 1989). What produces the *sense* of satisfaction is a combination of rewarding events, mutual support, and shared interests (Argyle & Furnham, 1983). Basic concerns involve mutual agreement about core matters of intimacy, dominance, receptivity, composure, emotional distance, trust, and equality (Kelley & Burgoon, 1991).

Negative behaviors are particularly significant indicators of marital satisfaction. Negative actions have been shown to be more important signs of day-to-day satisfaction than positive behaviors, particularly in unstable marriages (Broderick & O'Leary, 1986). An increase in negative evaluations can promote a turning point in the course of relational history and signal a decrease in satisfaction (Bullis et al., 1993). Longitudinal studies show that negativity predicts diminished satisfaction over time (Gottman & Krokoff, 1989). In unstable marriages, distressed wives are more inclined than their husbands to act in a consistently negative manner toward the spouse (Notarius, Benson, Sloane, Vanzetti, & Hornyak, 1989). In general, the unequal matching between spouses is conducive to a considerable degree of marital unhappiness and instability (Newcomb & Bentler, 1981). Mutual expressions of dissimilarity lead to conflict and dissatisfaction, which in turn sets the stage for episodes of misery and instability. Once again, disorders of performance relate closely to disorders of satisfaction (Yaffe, 1981).

In a recent study, Huston and Vangelisti (1991) examined the interplay of affection, sexual interest, and negativity in the daily events of newly married couples who were followed for more than 2 years. Results showed that negativity was a strong indicator of satisfaction as early as 2 months into marriage. In unstable alliances, men tend to withdraw whereas women may become more hostile (Christensen & Heavey, 1990; Krokoff, 1987; Roberts & Krokoff, 1990). Men's negativity early in marriage, in particular, accounts for the decline in wives' satisfaction later on (Huston & Vangelisti, 1991). Overall, satisfaction is relatively stable in highly interdependent marriages. On this point, Huston and Vangelisti (1991) write,

> When husbands were initially satisfied, they were affectionate, and their wives maintained relatively high levels of affectional expression; when wives were less satisfied early in their marriage, both they and

their husbands were more negative, and their husbands became increasingly negative over time. These results provide some evidence for a self-fulfilling prophecy in marriage relations (Miller & Turnbull, 1986). The initial level of satisfaction may create an atmosphere in the marriage that encourages their spouse to behave in ways that reinforce their initial satisfaction. (p. 730)

Unstable relations are labor intensive. They are difficult to maintain, and take a lot of work simply to sustain or keep intact. Moreover, they are vulnerable and easily undermined. A high incidence of erratic or inconsistent episodes of behavior may not be anticipated or defended in advance. Loose relational definitions can be called into question at any time, particularly where there is lack of agreement about what to do or how to proceed (Wilmot, 1987). Inadequate mechanisms of regulation, as Dindia and Baxter (1987) point out, make it more difficult to keep disorganized relations in satisfactory condition or in good repair. When uncertain or apprehensive, the respective parties are likely to be pulled back and forth between an effort to make things better or to keep them from falling apart. The central tendency is to try to minimize reactive and negative urges rather than maximize proactive and positive efforts (Dindia & Baxter, 1987). The most anxious persons report less satisfaction, and more conflict and avoidance, than do secure types, who report high levels of satisfaction, intimacy, trust, and commitment in their relationships (Davis, Kirkpatrick, Levy, & O'Hearn, 1994).

The search for positivity as a means of personal satisfaction documents a process of gravitating toward those types of people who are best able to establish an atmosphere of commonality and mutual support. There is a tendency to seek out those who can quickly arrive at some overarching consensus on the limitations and boundaries of future interaction. Individuals seek out others as a matter of personal safety and as a means of protecting highly distinctive ways of seeing the world from either random or premeditated sources of unsettling influence and unwelcome change. Above all there is the need to preserve the delicate equilibrium that keeps our close ties with others safe and secure. A strong sense of commitment is positively associated with satisfaction with long-standing relationships (Acker & Davis, 1992; Griffin & Bartholomew, 1994).

Inevitably, the warnings we assign to the words and gestures of one another motivate us to speak and act on them. Personal logic, whether accurate or irrational, helps shape subsequent priorities and decisions. The stakes include a specific list of agreements or understandings; alternatively, they may include change in the fabric of generalized consensus that will affect the course of future interaction. Although there are limits on what may be shared, a working knowledge of the values, beliefs, and attitudes held in common allows the participants to understand one another's limits and boundaries; this is turn allows them to better accept one another as they are, and to express this caring in a supportive, compassionate, and selfless way. In our view, each individual fosters and nurtures this ideal state by working to reestablish a larger perspective in which limits and constraints are not amplified in isolation but are viewed in relation to the magnitude of unique opportunities.

CONVERSATIONAL IRREGULARITIES

T and C can't do anything right. They don't agree on anything. T views C as too inflexible. Many times T will want C to do something but C always says she can't because she is too busy. T claims that C should be more flexible. C doesn't agree because she thinks she *is* pretty flexible. Such disagreements lead to larger conflicts and arguments that leave both parties hurting each other's feelings because of the ingrained conflicts that do not get resolved. They usually don't understand each other's point of view mainly because they don't even try. They don't talk to each other as much as they might if they didn't disagree so much of the time. Now both T and C avoid contact as a means of preventing conflict from occurring. Because both worry about saying anything that might provoke further disagreement, T and C don't have as many conversations as they might otherwise. C feels unsafe because she doesn't have the freedom to say what she wants out of a larger fear that T will disagree strongly.

The process of give-and-take is dynamic and fluid. As conversation unfolds, each individual works to define, identify, and refine salient aspects of individuality and identity. At issue is the programmed logic of the turn-taking system itself. New frames of reference may seem strange and uncomfortable to one person if not to the other. One party may try to assume the upper hand because he or she is the professional and therefore presumably more knowledgeable. The other, on the other hand, may assume the same superior right, on other grounds, or may relinquish the right to be assertive altogether. In fair and democratic interchange, we would each expect roughly the same set of opportunities and constraints to simultaneously impinge on everyone. Clearly, the degree to which we are intolerant of the respective differences is critical not only to the present interaction but to the short- and long-term future as well.

The sequence of interruptions that begin to separate one person from the other gains strength to the extent that one or both parties continue to delay or neutralize the flow of encouraging speech and supportive gestures between one another. One or the other may take the upper hand and become derisive and moralistic by using his or her professional status as a pulpit from which to bully the other. In an attempt at self-defense, the other may denounce what he or she hears as null and void. As emotion overtakes thought, reason shuts down and conversation may deteriorate into acts of blaming, shouting, pushing, and even hitting. The trust that was initially in place seems misplaced and incomplete. What has been valuable to this point has been effectively interrupted and replaced with anxiety-producing and even confusing expressions of nonsense and irrationality. The concerns and issues that truly matter now remain unspoken.

Now, whenever the interactants come into direct contact, they feel that they must either speak or act to defend themselves. They still treasure the relationship but fear the other will interrupt various attempts at renewing the process of discourse and dialogue. Even the sight of the other across the lawn or courtyard has the ability to wipe out any attempt to verbalize the words or phrases that might touch on that original, confirming truth that defined their relationship and made it so pleasing and fulfilling. Anxiety enters one's consciousness like a needle, and injects negative images that galvanize the processes of self-defense; that in turn interrupts the potential for facilitating interchange once again. With time, even the remote possibility of unwelcome talk can shut down any chance for reconstructive communication before it has the chance to begin.

This generalized description underscores a central theme. Relational instability filters down to the minute details of conversational order. Face-to-face interaction is subject to any number of disruptions in form or content. When extreme and negative information is revealed, conversation shifts toward what is irregular, surprising, or out of balance with prior impressions (Nicotera, 1994). A study by Ruscher and Hammer (1994) examined how negative revelations (e.g., acknowledgment of a previously unknown stigma) disrupt the flow of ideas and lead to reappraisal and revision of prior impressions and unstated assumptions about the basis of common ground. When compared with undisrupted dyads, disrupted pairs quickly focused attention on the bridge-building effort, congruent information, and explicit discussion of how the stigma fit into the larger picture, with lots of mutual questions about it. By the end of a second conversation, the disrupted pairs had repaired some of the damage, but their overall impressions became more negative to accommodate the impact of such an extremely negative disclosure.

Some irregularities occur in the rhythms of speech. There is an important connection between the way individuals talk and what events are taken to mean. Rhythmic movement is a means of coordinating highly complicated forms of behavior *together.* Synchronous talk is highly animated, vivid, and rhythmic; it conveys a sense of attunement and precise integration of the turn-taking system. According to Cowley (1994), rhythmic patterns serve a number of critical functions in conversation. First, the synchrony of speaking and listening provides evidence of finely tuned coordination, often so close as to be below ordinary perceptual thresholds of recognition. Second, speech rhythms are a means of expressing enthusiasm and are viewed as such. Third, when each speaker displays sensitivity in response to the way the other is talking, there is a mutually sustained sense of the harmony of the moment. Finally, "patterning *across* utterances seems to be of paramount importance; for this reason individuals must be able to co-ordinate and be heard to be co-ordinating, the speech finely" (p. 372). If the "ability to participate fully in the life of one's fellows is inseparable from being able to speak and reply" (p. 373) in precise rhythmic patterns, it follows that any number of negative implications accrue from whatever interferes with the preservation of such finely tuned methods of synchronization.

Tolerance of verbal irregularity varies widely. Much depends on which types of pairings of initiation and response are to be viewed in complementary or antithetical terms. Of relevance is how each person's behavior constrains and elicits subsequent responses from others. From a democratic and egalitarian standpoint, a complementary state occurs "when the behavior of one participant elicits specific behavior from the other participant and is viewed as necessary for continued interaction" (Tracey, 1994, p. 864). In a case where every unit of A's behavior elicits and constrains B's sequence of response in a highly similar way, there would not be only a high *degree* of complementarily (in the patterns of initiative and response) but also a high *level* of predictability and consistency. In effect, the outline of conversation would not seem irregular or out of shape in any way due to the very ease and fluidity of turn-taking operations.

Signs of conversational irregularity become relevant at junctures where one unit of behavior (a) has no relevance for what follows, (b) merely duplicates what follows, or (c) prevents or prohibits one type of behavior from occurring. The ideal version may be undermined, therefore, by a whole host of mitigating circumstances—setting, status differences, time pressures, individual differences—that weaken the process of mutual influence or effort to keep it constant (Bluhm, Widiger, & Miele, 1990). For most people, the tension between constraint (minimizing alternatives) and expansion (maximizing alternatives) is a process that is subject to extensive change despite concerted effort to maintain a constant or narrow latitude of mutual regulation. A study by Tracey (1994) shows how the degree of complementary can be amplified, when antecedent behavior is friendly rather than hostile or dampened, depending mostly on how people feel about the succession of attempts to influence or resist the urge. The urge to be complementary has been associated with a high number of verbal exchanges and preference for less social distance rather than more (Nowicki & Manheim, 1991). The notion of complementarily does not hold up equally well in all situations. Hence it is a notion that applies to some of the people some of the time; there is no written guarantee.

LACK OF RECIPROCITY

D and Q are always at odds. D sees Q as opinionated—a person who feels the need to inflict his views on everyone else. Q makes strong statements that end in such a way as to imply that Q expects D to agree or disagree with Q's opinion. The following is an example: "I think they should take all the murderers and send them to the electric chair. That'd save us taxpayers a lot of money, wouldn't it?" This places D in a no-win situation. The option to agree would only promote the further expression of even more outrageous notions, and the decision to disagree would spark an intense debate. Q does not like to listen. D's spoken ideas/opinions are criticized, downgraded, or ridiculed. In extreme instances, D becomes the object of some very unfavorable comments. D assumes that Q is not sufficiently interested in what D has to say and D expresses this through critical statements, judgmental attitudes, failure to listen, and the urge to cut off someone's statement to interject one of his own. D changes the subject as a matter of whim (especially if D is losing the argument), stands or sits in a defiant manner (chin up, arms crossed on chest, leaning back), and dismisses Q's impatience by looking around at whatever else is going on, calling out to others while Q is talking, and making little eye contact. It is difficult to discuss anything with someone who is so full of absolute "cut-and-dried" statements, that is, "This is the way it is because that's the way I want it to be."

Individuals who have a vested interest in maintaining their sense of superiority over others are prone to use power struggles as a way of defending their questionable status. They may allow themselves to believe they have a right to defensively interrupt the other. When individuals turn themselves into authority figures, they may arrogantly assume their prerogative is to interrupt without being interrupted in turn.

The targets of their tirades, on the other hand, are expected to listen meekly and to control their own urges to become personally assertive. Essentially, they are expected to sit there and take it—for their own good, they may be told; in reality, they are expected to take it for the enhancement and satisfaction of the other. At stake is the overbearing individual's continued misuse of the strategic uses of talk and gesture to control the definition and direction of what transpires. The flow of words and gestures, when under the exclusive control of any one agent, is a seemingly safe but thoroughly flawed means of maintaining one person's inflated sense of influence and social importance.

Eventual divergence, rather than convergent lines of action, is the price that is paid for unilateral control of human relations. As it happens, close ties require mutual participation if they are to thrive. The outcome most directly associated with endless talk and overbearing discourse is protracted silence. One who talks virtually all the time consigns others to be silent for the same length of time; even more important, he consigns others to an inner turmoil of bottled-up thoughts, feelings, and impulses that form the core of a mounting sense of frustration and confusion in the person being held at bay by the other's continued monologue.

Life *is* a matter of give-and-take. The central question is the standard by which one measures the *cost* (expenditures) against the *gain* (return). Face-to-face interactions entail considerable effort to mobilize and implement accessible personal resources for some cause, rhythm, or reason. There is also an element of anticipation or expectation of some wider advantage or gain. It would be pointless to act otherwise. By these standards, what matters is the interplay between available resources (abundant/scarce) and collaborative effort to reallocate the distribution of those resources (more/less) for personal or collective ends.

Precise measurement presupposes the ability to calculate what things are worth (credit) or lacking (discredit) as sources of valuation. The opportunity for certification, or the risk of devaluation, may occur at three levels: material, economic, and symbolic. Material resources consist of any tangible object: land, dwelling, furniture, headset, art object, or computer. Economic resources involve barter over the conversion of any type of resource into some form of tangible monetary gain. Symbolic issues center on interpretive priorities and preferences for assigning rank and status to anything that matters more or less. Conversational resources consist of any property of one person that is made available to others as a means to satisfy some need or attain some goal. By this standard, one person's resource may be another person's liability.

Core resources cluster around matters of power, affection, and involvement. Each of these broad dimensions presupposes an investment of one's time, effort, and energy into shared activities to make things better or worse. Power is determined by how much influence one has. It is revealed in the ability to get what one wants (Boulding, 1990). The manifestation of power makes one strong while its relative absence makes one weak. The relevant standard is the difference between what makes one strong or weak (at the level of social inter-action).

Personal power is not distributed in a uniform way. Some people have a great deal of it while other people have practically none. The capacity to control, dominate, or alter people and events is what makes one powerful. The concept of power has been identified with three broad measures: (a) The person with the least to lose is the one with the greatest freedom to walk away. This component captures an essential aspect of power, that is, freedom from unwanted influence, or *autonomy*. (b) The person who talks the most has the greatest degree of social control (Kimble & Musgrove, 1988). This component takes into account the power of words and gestures to enable someone to dominate a conversation and prevent others from getting a word in edgewise (Blalock, 1989; Linkey & Firestone, 1990). (c) The one who gives the greatest number of commands has the highest degree of social standing or status (Collins, 1975). This stipulation is important because the sheer amount of talk may be less important than the ability to use talk to get others to do one's bidding. Here talking is a means of giving instructions and commands together with the power to sanction. Unfortunately, all three conceptions of power focus on individual traits more than on actual conduct during face-to-face interactions. Hence the collective base of power is equal to the potential for a state of interdependence to be sustained over time. Closely related is the ability to use words and gestures to minimize resistance and overcome obstacles.

The important point is to see power relations in dynamic terms. Considerations of power and affection work closely together. This means that the question of power cannot be separated from how individuals feel about it (Bradac, 1990; Bradac, Wiemann, & Schaefer, 1994). In fact, many social contexts evoke negative thoughts about control, such as relationships between peers who exhibit mutual dislike (Wiemann & Krueger, 1980), where individuals resist threats to their personal freedom (Gibbons, Bradac, & Busch, 1992; Gibbons, Busch, & Bradac, 1991), and where verbal disagreements prevail (D'Andrade & Wish, 1985). Conversely, positive thoughts about con-trol are linked with perceptions of high status (Bradac & Wisegarver, 1984). Persons with a high need for control are most likely to take active steps to control the flow of conversations, interrupt others frequently, and engage in acts of simultaneous talking (Burger, 1990). Moreover, powerful speaking styles are viewed as fluent, articulate, terse, direct, diversified, and effective while powerless speaking styles are associated with hesitation, uncertainty, and apprehension (Gibbons et al., 1991). Those in favorable power positions may employ more influence strategies because they perceive the right to do so (Roiger, 1993). The magnitude of inequality among group members has been shown to be a strong predictor of collective dissatisfaction with shared outcomes (Wall & Nolan, 1987). The muddle of negative and positive associations suggests how significantly issues of feeling and affection enter in to the larger equation of power dynamics.

To feel affection toward others is to like (weak measure) or love (strong measure) to be in their presence. To feel disaffection toward others is to dislike (weak measure) or hate (strong measure) to be in their presence. Positive regard can be measured in terms of personal satisfaction, degree of attraction, or infrequency of punishment. Conversely, negative responses are revealed in degree of dissatisfaction, avoidance, or willingness to coerce or impose adverse consequences. The distinction between positive and negative urges is not a matter of either-or. It is, instead, an issue of how complex urges mix and blend together, where aspects of like or love mingle with those of dislike and hate. Mature people *do* have to "deal not only with liking and loving but also with hate and dislike" in the same equation (Duck, 1994, p. 11). Finally, the meaning of power and affection are not only highly interdependent, they also covary with modifications and changes in the level and depth of personal involvement.

As involvement increases, people take things more and more seriously. The stakes go up. Change registers in the form of greater knowledge of one another, a stronger sense of commitment, better preparation for intimacy, and mutual desire for a completely developed and personalized relation (Duck, 1981, p. 6). Global depth of involvement is reflected in the number and range of topics and the frequency, depth, and diversity of sustained activities. Close personal involvement is envisioned as the fulfillment of greater intertwining of emotional life and the merging of private selves (Kurdek, 1987; Rusbult et al., 1993).

Conversational involvement requires a state of *responsiveness,* or mental alertness; *perceptiveness* in the design of appropriate attributions to the actions of self and other; and *attentiveness* to factors of relevance (Cegala, Savage, Brunner, & Conrad, 1982). In contrast, uninvolved participants are prone to be psychologically removed, preoccupied, distracted, uncertain, hesitant, or withdrawn. Evidence links involvement with the ability to maintain an immediate frame of reference, a focus on observable conditions, greater expressiveness, better interaction management, more altruism, and lack of social anxiety over negative responses from others (Coker & Burgoon, 1987).

The discussion of power, affection, and involvement is important to the larger problem of reciprocity. It is difficult enough to sustain a condition of reciprocity on just one basic dimension of resource distribution and mobilization. It is more demanding to satisfy a global sense of reciprocity on all three broad measures at once. In an ideal world, successful or high-quality performance would be equated with efforts to distribute the power as widely as possible, to encourage a surplus of positive affection as well as deep involvement in diverse ways for casual encounters as well as for close intimate ties.

As a baseline for comparison, we will start with the anatomy of close relationships with the highest degree of global reciprocity. The Relationship Closeness Inventory (RCI) by Berscheid, Snyder, and Omoto (1989) has received considerable attention. The RCI measures closeness in multidimensional terms consisting of the amount of time spent together (*frequency*), variety of encounters engaged in together (*diversity*), and degree of perceived influence over one another's decisions, activities, and plans (*strength*). These measures have been shown to predict whether romantic relationships stay intact. The findings also support a model of intimacy based on a process of escalating reciprocity of self-disclosures where individual feelings of one's "innermost self" can be validated, understood, and nurtured by the other (Reis & Shaver, 1988). A broad latitude of mutual involvement promotes a heightened sense of double reciprocity where the boundary lines of self and other blend together, coincide, or fuse (Aron, Aron, & Smollan, 1992). A powerful sense of *collectivity* pervades each person's own sense of *individual* identity.

A condition of genuine reciprocity is difficult to sustain. It takes two separate beings to construct a principle of reciprocity but only one member to violate it. So much depends on the affection dimension, whether those who like others are liked back. We know that reciprocity increases with the degree of acquaintance (Kenny, 1991,

1994; Kenny & DePaulo, 1993). However, because reciprocity effects are stronger in the domain of affect and liking, and weaker generally for other traits, there is no assurance of carryover from factors of attraction to other domains of involvement and interest. By these standards, we might expect less reciprocity over issues of power and involvement than over affection and liking.

Disruptive violations may prevent or inhibit ongoing activities, increase personal costs, or cause further tension or discomfort. The antecedent conditions may be produced in an almost mindless manner. The amount of affection in long-term, close relationships changes considerably from day to day. The same holds true for the level of tension, stress, strain, and conflict over opposing aims (Huston & Vangelisti, 1991). Individual preferences mingle with strength of liking someone else's preferences (Surra & Longstreth, 1990). Lack of reciprocity—being underbenefited or being overbenefited—is closely linked with the magnitude of negative affect (Buunk, Doosje, Jans, & Hopstaken, 1993). It is also associated with interaction between those of unequal status. These conditions may be linked with a fear of not being able to reciprocate (a) to the same degree or (b) in the same type of resource. Strict definitions of reciprocity are more important to some people than to others. So also is the relevance of the notion of equity itself.

Persons who operate out of *exchange* orientations calculate costs and rewards in response to specific benefits received in the past or expected in the future (Mills & Clark, 1994). Acceptance of a benefit incurs a debt or obligation to respond in kind. Persons who operate with a *communal* orientation count loss and gain in response to another person's welfare. The effort to match equally, according to Fiske (1992), "is a relational structure in which people can compare quantities and use the operations of addition and subtraction to assess imbalance (e.g., I did two favors for you and you did me one favor in return, so you owe me one") (p. 690). In contrast, effort to engage in communal sharing "is like a category or set, all of whose elements are equivalent (not differentiable with respect to a given property)" (p. 690). At issue is the core problem of reconciling very different ways of thinking about matters of separation and connection at the same time (Woike, 1994).

Those high in score-keeping are strongly oriented toward direct reciprocity. They expect immediate rewards and comparable forms of repayment in short order. Such persons expect to return favors promptly and feel uncomfortable when they are not in a position to do so. They keep track of individual contributions to activities for which there is a joint reward (M. Clark, 1984). They feel exploited when they help others in ways that are not specifically repaid (M. Clark & Waddell, 1985). The central tendency is widespread intolerance of temporary imbalances in the exchange process (Buunk & VanYperen, 1991). By contrast, those low in score-keeping favor communal orientations. Here the desire to give and receive benefits takes into account the needs and concerns of others. They do not keep track of individual contributions to tasks with joint rewards and do not feel exploited when their help is not repaid (M. Clark & Waddell, 1985). In a study by Clark, Ouellette, Powell, and Milberg (1987), those with strong communal orientations helped others significantly more than those with an exchange orientation. The former were more apt to keep track of others' needs even when they could not be of help (M. Clark, Mills, & Powell, 1986). These findings are consistent with evidence that the effects associated with lack of reciprocity can be moderated more easily where communal standards prevail (Buunk et al., 1993).

The debate over score-keeping leads to a central conclusion. Exchange logic may be fine for casual acquaintances and business dealings but a communal orientation provides more of a stabilizing factor in preserving close ties with others. Initial encounters may be regulated by exchange principles that weaken over time as partners move closer and adopt a more extensive framework of personal accountability (Erber & Tesser, 1994). The irony is that the more severely one attempts to calculate the razor-thin line between cost and reward in the short run, the more frequently and easily one will feel shortchanged in the long run. It is important to recognize that any method of counting resources against liabilities is imprecise and imperfect. Adding and subtracting from shifting lists of scorecards may not solve anything.

MUTUAL MISCONSTRUCTION

Q and Z are close friends who, despite severe disagreement, manage to spend a lot of time together and talk a great deal about many sorts of things. It seems as though it is in Q's nature to disagree with Z. They disagree over everything from music to taste in members of the opposite sex. Q is amazed that they spend as much time as they do together. They are almost always insulting one another, usually in a humorous, joking manner. As a matter of fact, most of the talk seems to lack seriousness and sincerity. It seems impossible for either Q or Z to be honest and share personal feelings and emotions with one another. Rarely do they discuss the relationship, and when they do it is after a huge disagreement or fight when Q is trying to resolve the conflict. They have no problem talking about other people, only about themselves and their own personal feelings and thoughts that are disclosed between them. Z tends to incorporate negativity with everything Q tries to do. Sometimes the relationship really frustrates Q. No matter how much Q tries to give Z a hard time about something, Z believes that the issue at hand is different from what Q does. Q always catches himself getting on Z's case and Z does the same to Q. What is most detrimental is that Z doesn't take anything Q says seriously, or else misinterprets Q's intentions. When Q compliments Z, he thinks Q is being sarcastic. It seems clear to Q that they don't understand one another, and if they can't, they actually have no chance to cope with the disputes that do arise.

Blind spots are instructive. They are a reminder of an old but important adage: What counts is not so much "the way things are" but how we take them to be. In other words, our interpretations of what is taking place are intrinsic aspects of what is actually taking place. We have a vested interest in construing things from a particular vantage point. The process is somewhat automatic but also selective and strategic as well (Kellermann, 1992). What is crucial is the basic recognition that what is true of one's own interpretive frame is, by definition, applicable to everyone else too. Every participant shares in basically the same task—making complex and elaborated sense of what transpires. Everyone must struggle to reconcile the multiplicity of perspectives, whether consensual or divergent in any public setting. Comparative analysis of the varied viewpoints takes place at several dimensions simultaneously. Kenny (1994) identifies the following basic considerations. (a) *Assimilation:* Does A see others as alike? (b)

Consensus: Is A seen the same way by others? (c) *Uniqueness:* Does A see X idiosyncratically? (d) *Reciprocity:* Do A and B see each other similarly? (e) *Target accuracy:* Is A's view of X correct? (f) *Assumed reciprocity:* Does A think others see A as A sees them? (g) *Meta-accuracy:* Does A know how A is seen? (h) *Assumed similarity:* Does A see others as A sees herself? (i) *Self-other agreement:* Do others see A as A sees herself?

The term *mutual misconstruction* applies to personal encounters where the respective parties have a hard time (re)translating the interpretations of self and other into a coherent vocabulary. A collective sense of misinterpretation may go unnoticed for a considerable period of time. Participants get into trouble by holding other people accountable for their own interpretive standards without seeing themselves as equally subject to the valuations of everyone else. There is a very distinct sense that the way I construe things is *the* model by which to judge the relevance of all other models. The imposition of self-reference on other, and resistance to other reference upon self, make it impossible to sort things out, to assign priority and preference, much less sovereignty, to the respective versions.

In addition, we don't have full access to what makes everyone else's viewpoint appear the way it does *to them*. The same principle holds for their bonded access to our own version. Hence tolerance for the multiplicity of contrasting viewpoints is a prerequisite for the achievement of a spirit of mutuality and an inclusive sense of identification—where everyone is taken seriously as intrinsically worthy of inclusion.

Unresolved aspects of prior interaction may perpetuate a condition of mutual misconstruction. Here there are several essential themes. There may be never-ending struggle over the right to leave the scene. Mental preparation may be useless. One discovers inner conflict between what one seeks to express and the disquieting sense of what the adverse outcomes might be. Written notes are too imprecise to decipher. Heavy workloads fall on those with opposed and polar viewpoints located at opposite ends of the spectrum of relevance and meaning. Added to the collective debt is a staunch refusal to deal with trials and tribulations without ever getting a chance to heal. Instead, each member withdraws into a hard shell of isolated existence, unable to break through to the other side. Life unfolds in an uneven mix of "yes" and "no." What matters is overcoming the many feelings bottled up inside through perseverance and faith that little faults and failures need not hold one back from achieving effective communication.

Such disruptions also show how powerful our mutual misconstructions can become. Here they are strong enough to be associated with lost love, forfeited opportunity, the dissolution of family ties, strained professional ties, diminished productivity, financial ruin, irrationality, reactivity, and, finally, the total collapse of well-functioning human beings. It takes considerable time to recover from such severe symbolic wounds and injuries.

THREAT OF DISSOLUTION

C and B are former roommates. C is able to see something from any point of view. This is a quality that C seems to have adopted to avoid arguments with people, but it also limits the potential amount of disagreement as well. The only exception to the rule is B. The way C deals with potential disagreement is total silence. If C absolutely disagrees with someone else, C usually doesn't argue. Rather, C shuts up and keeps her mouth shut. Hence protracted silence characterized a lot of the face-to-face interaction between C and B. When they did try to talk, it was very tense and brief. They said what they had to and then would shut up again. C and B were like night and day. B wanted to (sleep) nap all day and study or socialize all night. C worked at studies mostly during daylight hours and usually went to bed early. B was messy and C was quite clean. Neither liked to talk and neither (as a consequence) bothered to give any ground. Overall, day-to-day interaction consisted of hostile silence punctuated by disgusted sighs whenever the other was doing something bothersome.

Disruptive relations increase the risk of dissolution and termination, that is, the permanent dismemberment of an existing relationship, as opposed to turbulence or disorder that may or may not lead to dissolution (Duck, 1982, p. 2). The total enterprise evokes and conveys multiple conceptions of what is at stake. Duck (1982) speaks in terms of "pre-existing doom," "mechanical failure," "process loss," and "sudden death." Rodin (1982) stresses the dynamic interplay of inclusion and exclusion criteria for determining a "field of eligibles" based on criteria of liking with two exclusionary rules—dislike and disregard.

At issue is a domain where commitments weaken and obligations dissolve. Hill, Rubin, and Peplau (1976) found that romantic couples cited different interests as well as boredom and conflicting attitudes as reasons for breakups. Baxter (1986) collected almost 300 reasons for dissolution of romantic relationships and found that the need for autonomy; divergent attitudes, beliefs, and values; and lack of supportiveness were the most frequently cited reasons for splitting up. Owen (1993) studied metaphorical accounts of termination with references to up and down movements—things go down, hit bottom, or stay below some tolerable standard. Other metaphors appealed to organic considerations such as decay, death, injury, or illness. Finally, there were references to presence and absence. Here stress was placed on what was lacking and on emptiness, nonexistence, aloneness, or disappearance.

Explanations for relational deterioration and loss are full of excuse and blame. Cody (1982) examined self-reports of various reasons for relational disengagement and found three general types: (a) fault-finding, (b) refusals to compromise, and (c) constraints—someone wanting more than someone else could give. Metts and Cupach (1986) found that gender differences matter; when giving reasons for opposite-sex relational decay, women spoke about drifting apart, rule violations, and third-party involvement; men made most frequent reference to drifting apart, rule violation, and effects of critical events. Graziano and Musser (1982) refer to the "joining" and "parting" of the ways. Relational transgressions multiply. Minor offenses violate rules for appropriate conduct or are "more typically the unintended consequence of human fallibility" (Metts, 1994, pp. 237-238). The frequency, duration, and intensity of personal contacts diminish over time. Close ties with second and third parties narrow and contract.

Miller and Parks (1982) discuss several "communicative markers" of dissolving relationships: (a) decreased direct contact; (b) increased length of time between direct contacts; (c) increased uncertainty and difficulty in planning joint activities; (d) increased frequency of negative stress that may fan out to affect a person's general behavior in all of his or her other relationships; (e) increased frequency of negative comments about the partner and the overall relationship to those outside the relationship; (f) decreased physical proximity, rate and duration of touch, forward orientation, rate and duration of direct body orientations; (g) decreased rate of head, hand, and arm movements, rate and duration of smiling, mutual looks in the face; (h) decreased speaking qualities, such as pitch variation and discrepancy between participants' mean vocal intensity; (i) increased "non-ah" speech disfluency ratio; (j) decreased rate of speech; (k) decreased similarity of dress and object preferences as well as access to the other person's possessions; (l) decreased acquisition of joint possessions; and (m) increased rate of object manipulation during interaction.

It matters whether there is joint management of the threat of dissolution. McCall (1982) discusses the process of becoming unrelated in terms of the type of regulation that is involved. Deteriorated and mourning relations unfold as a lapse of loyalty and a fiction of solidarity is broken. The wound of deprivation signals some loss of benefits previously received. A person's own network of private associations are disrupted as well as his or her daily routines. There is grief—a mix of anger, bitterness, hurt, sadness, and self-pity—and, on the other side, some guilt, shame, self-doubt, and diminished self-esteem. Personal relationships are almost universally viewed in success/failure terms. The stigma of failure is a third wound. A secret wish to terminate the relationship destroys further idealization. What is at stake is "the person's silent thinking about the relationship—contemplating its place in the network of relationships, and deliberating as to how one feels and what one should do" (McCall, 1982, p. 221).

The cost of dissolving marital relations can be quite severe (Duck, 1991). A study by Gottman and Levenson (1992) examined marital processes closely associated with the threat of dissolution. Lack of mutual regulation was associated with severe marital problems, lower marital satisfaction, poorer health, more negative ratings of interactions, more negative emotional expression, less positive emotional expression, more stubbornness and withdrawal from interaction, greater defensiveness, greater (immediate) risk of marital dissolution, and higher incidence of consideration of dissolution and of actual separation.

The achievement of dissolution is a highly sensitive matter. The goal is to blend distinctive styles of directness and indirectness in discussions of deteriorated relations. Much depends on the tension between a unilateral or bilateral desire for withdrawal or avoidance (Baxter, 1984, 1985). Withdrawal is associated with avoidance, reduced depth of feeling, and less frequent contact. Pseudodeescalation involves a false declaration of interest in a greatly reduced scope of relations where the desire for a total exit is not made explicit. Cost escalation involves behavior that is too expensive for the other party to endure. Total disengagement may be accomplished without explicit acknowledgment of one's true aim. Fading away assumes some implicit understanding has ended. Also, there may be collusion to maintain the pretense of existing ties while striving for a condition of total noncontact. Directness involves an explicit declaration that the relationship is finished, with no chance for discussion or compromise. Another strategy is metacommunicative and entails discussion of the current state of deteriorated relations, acknowledgment of dissatisfaction, and a firm desire to exit while continuing to deal with unresolved problems. Once again, the link between the magnitude of disruption and the threat of dissolution is very strong.

The only surefire way to avoid the risk of mutual misconstruction is to avoid the risk of communication altogether. When necessary and inevitable slippages and miscalculations do occur, there is the possibility of learning from the mistakes of both parties and of applying the insight to future engagements. The knowledge and insight gained from previous acts of futility and failure may accumulate and, if seriously applied, establish the foundation for better interaction in the future. It is difficult to analyze and learn from one's faulty ways if one can't see past the immediate effects of pain, hurt, and injury. To be successful presupposes mutual recognition of the magnitude of difference between what works out well, poorly, or not at all. We are reminded of the incredible diversity of interpretations that are prevalent in an open system of communication. Of course, a measure of communicative success is the best teacher of all.

CHAPTER 4

Confusion

Confusion is internal and/or external chaos. Faulty implications, cognitive distortions, interpersonal disruptions, and complex signs of confusion and conflict promote a spirit or atmosphere of misinformation, misinterpretation, and miscommunication. Where there is considerable friction in the mix of expressive freedom and interpretive response, an atmosphere of uncertainty and commotion will prevail. The ineffective use, the misuse, and the abuse of ordinary language are fully implicated in signs of dislocation and conflict on all sides. As apprehension and complication increase, the accuracy of cognitive processing may be expected to decline as well. This in turn can lead to mutually meaningless (at best) and *alienating* (at worst) consequences. Strained and suffering relations bolster individual thresholds of discomfort and distress. Bilateral ambiguity traces the effects and outcomes of movement away from common ground and shared meaning. Mutual understanding diminishes. Nagging questions tug at those who are left to wonder about felt changes in such rapidly changing states of affairs. It takes a great deal of effort and struggle to understand complex matters in basic or simple terms— either the way it used to be or the way it might be if only framed from the stance of a radically new paradigm.

The first three chapters explored basic distinctions between effective and faulty forms of face-to-face interaction. Largely unchecked, ill-founded, or unwarranted assumptions, expectations, inferences,

115

implications, and attributions were shown to promote the emergence of weak and ineffectual forms of human communication. A simple and straightforward mode of interchange may turn out, upon reflection, to be quite messy and complex. Perplexing issues have a tendency to interrupt or disrupt the flow of shared activities, rituals, and routines. Hence a spectrum of personal concerns may be identified as closely aligned and synchronous or misaligned and quite out of synch. Distorted or misguided actions often work to subvert or undermine the larger effort to achieve coherent forms of sense-making practice.

The purpose of this chapter is to focus on the dynamics of commotion and confusion in face-to-face interaction. Of central interest are the small-scale changes and shifts in communicative tone that obscure our understanding of ourselves and of others. Vital signs are wavering of opinion, hesitation, doubt, or uncertainty as to one's ultimate course of action. At stake is any mode of shared activity capable of being grasped or comprehended in two or more distinct ways at once. Certain types of social exchange involve a double or dubious signification and equivocal expression—one that is questionable and obscure.

Confusing and bewildering actions increase the magnitude of disorder and upheaval in the lives of those who produce them. One may be prone to the liability of being confused over highly demanding and elaborated modes of exchange with other people. Moreover, others may appear disconcerted or perplexed to the point where the relative gradations of distinctions between elements are discarded or lost. The larger process may serve to ruin the clarity of thought or feeling—by distracting, perplexing, and bewildering—to mixing up or commingling.

During confusing moments, it may become virtually impossible to distinguish specific aspects of behavior from the larger pattern. To fail to discriminate between specific items is to erroneously regard them as identical or to mistake one for another. Such events may be characterized as a disorderly combination of just noticeable differences in the level of distinction and discrimination. What is left in question are complex and unresolved struggles over matters of definition, classification, and explanation of quite perplexing and bewildering modes of shared activity. The process unfolds without any claim to fixed or univocal meanings or appeal to a final authority.

There is something quite elusive about what bewilders. As a rule, the more obvious the confusion, the less one can say about it. What is so conspicuous is how a person's behavior can have so much relevance in the eyes of others without anyone in question being able to establish what is taking place. Confused behavior resists precise definition and classification. An exemplar is a set of instances in shared situations (A $\longleftrightarrow$ B) where A's view remains somewhat inexplicable to A, based on A's own frame of reference toward minute changes in external circumstance. In effect, person A manufactures, produces, and responds to the very conditions that elude A's efforts to make sense of some vital matter to someone else. What arises is a vague sense of linguistic complexity that magnifies the sheer *plurality* of sensations, feelings, and thoughts.

Confusions are acute when dealing with unusual or confusing urges that prove difficult to convey to anyone else on the strength of words and gestures alone. Such moments resemble what it would be like to look into a dark room and see only the outline of an unknown object and later tell a friend what it was that you saw. The friend will not go away with a clear idea of what you saw because you do not know yourself what you saw in such an indistinct setting. The lack of focus is captured in images of putting on a veil, letting smoke get in your eyes, walking into a mist, not being able to sleep at night, getting lost in a crowd, or not being able to find your way home. In effect, there is something missing from available testimony.

CONFLICT

While working in a bar, S and K are always at odds. Conversation is *never* civil. Talk is filled with profanities. They fail to agree over almost everything—politics, sports, music, or life in general. Even the act of looking at the other the wrong way can incite an outburst of anger. The odd thing is that S and K have never had a falling out that could explain such volatile feelings. S says, "Hi." K replies, "That shirt looks stupid on you." S retorts, "I didn't ask you, loser." The game never stops. Yet if someone would insult S or become abusive, K would come to S's defense. S was working at the bar late one night and a drunk customer came up and said,

"Hey, you have a really nice ass." Suddenly K grabbed the man by the collar, lifted him off the ground, and said, "Don't you ever talk to her like that again. Show her respect and apologize or I'll kick your ass right out of here." S was very happy that K cared enough to look out for her, even though they argue all the time. S finds herself defending K in *his* hassles and disputes as well.

Specific aspects of confused behavior are often quite difficult to interpret. Likewise, conflict in a much broader sense may be hard to transcend or overcome. Consequently, specific instances of friction, and broad currents of social conflict, often work together in quite interesting and fascinating ways. Confused activities involve elements of hesitation and indecisiveness over the pursuit of alternative pathways of shared action. Conflict, on the other hand, signifies resistance and interference with the fulfillment of individual goals and objectives. What emerges as a focal point of study is the complex interplay between highly uncertain or unclear pathways of decision and choice, and some resistance and interference on the part of others in the pursuit of those ends.

Any dynamic and complicated process will give rise to opposing or contradictory tendencies at one time or another. At the level of direct contact, one person may want to get closer (affiliate) while another seeks to move away (disaffiliate). The process of attachment has equally salient possibilities for detachment built in. The model represents the basic tension between connection (integration, interdependence) and separation (independence, autonomy). Within the larger process, considerations of power and influence generate various gradations of tension and stress over who is in control (dominance) and who is not (submission). There are also considerations of affection and feeling, plus matters of relevance and involvement, where one party wants to open up and explore (reveal) while another seeks to close down and ignore (conceal). These intersecting issues of power, affection, and involvement emerge as basic sources of dialectical tension in human affairs. A great deal of evidence has been gathered to show how tension, stress, and flux underlie human relations in the manner of an incomplete or unfinished negotiation (Baxter, 1990; Baxter & Dindia, 1990).

The literature on dialectical tensions documents a series of central claims. People who use words and gestures to convey meaning are presumed to make a series of small-scale adjustments and accommodations in response to signs of opposition from other people. Moment-by-moment fluctuations produce small-scale distinctions, which in turn give way to larger-scale transformations (Montgomery, 1993). Dialectical tensions are never totally eliminated or subject to final resolution. Similarly, relational definitions remain unsettled and provisional; such contradictory urges are mutually negating and simultaneously present (Baxter & Simon, 1993). Tensions regulate the scope of interpersonal boundaries as well (Montgomery, 1993). Relational well-being is preserved by allowing conflicting and contradictory urges to be sorted out at the same time. Dialectical strains unfold at the periphery of personal awareness, without conscious intent and at deliberate, focused, and strategic levels of purposeful action.

Extreme tensions are present whenever two tendencies overlap (unity) yet somehow mutually nullify one another (negation). Sometimes strongly contrasting viewpoints simply cancel one another out. Hence there is nothing intrinsically negative or positive about the neutralizing effects of any contradictory tendencies in human interchanges. The prevailing slant is a reflection of how the respective parties deal with the total array of choices and consequences at their own disposal. Deficient verbal skills have been shown to be highly correlated with verbal aggression and abuse (Infante, Chandler, & Rudd, 1989; Infante, Sabourin, Rudd, & Shannon, 1990). Similarly, abusive and nonabusive families handle dialectical tensions in different ways. Conflictual talk between members of abusive families was characterized as vague, imprecise, lacking in detail, oppositional, argumentative, complaining, angry, frustrated, and negatively (re)interpreted in bad endings with no clear sense of how to change the undesirable elements of everyday life (Sabourin & Stamp, 1995). Oppositional considerations come into play in multiple frames of reference that must take into account an elaborated configuration of behavioral features (Wojciszke, 1994).

The term *confusion* is widely applicable in an all-embracing way. A pure case of *miscommunication* or *problematic communication* would consist of diverse types of situations where the respective parties, when assessed against some (observable) standard, fail to grasp and comprehend the meaning, relevance, and significance of one another's actions. A test case is pure gibberish, babble, glossolalia, or other displays of sheer nonsense where even thin slices of action resist subsequent (reconstructive) effort at translation or interpretation. Specific instances include shared circumstance where (a) confused individuals foster (b) poorly defined relations with (c) a vague or obscure idiom or code. What transpires, whether by intent or accident, does not make a great deal of sense as the individuals in question consistently misread one another's intentions and strategies of goal-directed action.

Personal effort to confront or avoid shared confusion comes into play whenever someone or something is called into question and subject to further scrutiny, criticism, and the possibility of recrimination (Sternberg & Dobson, 1987). Destructive forms of verbal criticism are known to promote greater anger, tension, and resolve to handle future disagreements through resistance and avoidance with decreased likelihood of collaboration and compromise. Moreover, recriminating criticism lowers expectations of performance and self-efficacy (Baron, 1988). Poor criticism, in effect, promotes an atmosphere of conflict and confusion. Primary targets are deficient aspects of personality, disproportionate blame, and guilt induction over what goes wrong. The clash of verbal questioning, with claim weighted against counterclaim, often exhibits a recycling of stress and strain with heavy reliance on the same kinds of moves and tactics in successive turns at talk. Mutual regulation of escalatory tendencies by recycled maneuvers helps to even out and dilute the duration of verbal conflict and questioning manner (Canary, Cunningham, & Cody, 1988; Vuchinich, 1990).

The intensity of conflict is a matter of tacit agreement. It is a dialectical form of activity that involves considerable skill in negotiation mixed with automatic and reactive tendencies. As the respective parties move toward and away from a direct confrontation with salient aspects of opposition and exclusion, they generate a general strategy of action. At issue is the goodness of fit between issues of submission and dominance, concession and compromise, and those associated with a standoff, avoidance, or withdrawal. At the point of termination for most disputes, there are no winners and losers but as many versions of the final score as the number who kept count according to some private calculus of winning and losing (Vuchinich, 1990). Everyone calculates credit and debt in his or her own distinctive way without threat of a final accounting. By the same logic, the very inability to calculate things precisely is what keeps each party from realizing the full measure of irreconcilable differences.

It is useful to think of the intensity of dispute in relation to the sheer magnitude of what is at stake. Potential issues cluster around whatever humans value but find lacking, scarce, or uneven in access or supply. Grimshaw (1990) organizes personal issues around several basic considerations. Presumably there is a sense of attention to substantive issues seen as causes for participants' motivations. All conflictual talk involves some negotiation over personal identities, that is, what kinds of persons and what states-of-relations should come into play. At issue are skills in argument, in negotiation of multiple identities, and in instructions about the normative proprieties of talk. Much depends on the stakes in an evolving context. What is crucial is whether the individuals in question see themselves as speaking for themselves or for others. Such controversies have the potential to *expand* in focus, *change* in focus, or *spread* along preexisting boundaries of classes, categories, groups, friendship networks, and organizational affiliation. The disputants can win, lose, and draw in their own views, those of their opponents, and those of observers.

The connection between conflict and confusion cannot be narrowed down to a single formula. A number of studies document the futility of appeal to a single scale of weights to measure across a wide spectrum of possibilities. One representative study (Baxter, Wilmot, Simmons, & Swartz, 1993) shows how subtle and sensitive are the tones and textures of open-ended verbal conflict. What appears to be incompatible and/or a form of opposition may be easily vanquished by a playful enactment where surface features of serious conflict are exhibited just for the fun of it. More taxing are repetitive scenarios and heavily scripted modes of conflict devoted to one prevailing theme, much as in a broken record. Third-party interventions involve taking up sides or neutral interventions by outsiders to achieve resolution without bias toward either party. Indirect conflict involves the assumption of conflict without a word being spoken—as in the decision not to talk about it. Topic shifts ward off strain. Protracted conflicts are punctuated by heavy silence or withdrawal. The silent treatment signals something is wrong and the offender needs to take remedial action. Escalatory conflict goes through multiple stages in which the scope or intensity of interference increases over time. One-sided conflicts are enactments where someone utters a complaint or attempts to start a serious fight, but the other party fails to engage or respond in kind. Blowups and sarcastic conflict are characterized by a typically hostile or irritable spirit of uncooperativeness. Civil discussion and tacit conflict, in contrast, foster a spirit of cooperation in calm and rational discussions in which both parties state their positions clearly and in nonaccusatory ways. Cautious expressions are motivated by a desire to prevent further hurt or discontent in the other party. Here even the definition of *conflict* or *confusion* is up for grabs.

Styles of conflict resolution can vary widely (in one sense) and yet remain the same (consistent over time). Of central concern is the shape of the curve of escalation and deescalation along a baseline. The movement toward escalation registers in strained efforts to (a) stand one's ground and (b) still take the other person's interests into account. Moreover, the downward movement toward deescalation is marked by struggle to (c) encapsulate the conflict, (d) save face, and (e) forgive and forget. Personal styles of conflict resolution have been shown by Sternberg and Soriano (1984) to be fairly consistent across diverse types of social situations with stylistic emphasis on seven distinct modes of operation: physical action, economic action, waiting and seeing, accepting the situation, step-down, third-party intervention, and undermining someone's self-esteem and personal worth. Most individuals were quite consistent in their preferred modes of resolution both within and across different types of tasks, relations, and types of interference. Once again, the sheer diversity and complexity of personal interests and involvements virtually rule out any one grand strategy of operation.

AMBIGUITY

E and P are lovers who do not get along, and neither one can understand how or why. They get caught up in endless cycles of confusion and frustration. Either party will suddenly cut off conversation without understanding what went wrong. P does not like the way that E reacts to the things P says. Sometimes P accuses E of trying to put on an act to hide personal feelings.

Many times P expects E to do something, and when E doesn't follow through, P gets upset and reverts back to a previously destructive pattern of self-abuse. The high level of misunderstanding has led to mutual effort to keep the long-standing relation at a superficial level where neither is sure how to act or what to say, or knows why the other is saying or doing things that are in such serious question.

Personal conduct is ambiguous insofar as it is incapable of being grasped and comprehended in two or more distinct ways at once. Mixed messages are ambiguous by definition but in different ways. Even the simplest act (on the surface) can be construed from an alternative, even opposing frame of reference (below the surface). One may decide that something or someone else is acting in an ambiguous manner when questions of fact (what transpires) are left in doubt as unresolved or undecided (what lingers).

The degree of ambiguity in civil conversation—whether one is dealing with a simple misunderstanding or a complex morass of sticky implications—has a direct impact on the clarity and success of later actions. Simple ambiguity is a matter of whether something is to be defined, classified, or explained one way or another; for example, "Yes, I still went out drinking, even though I said that I would go home and study instead." Such apparent ambiguity disappears when an answer to the question at hand is a simple response such as *yes/no, on/off, up/down, you/me, us/them*. Heavily interpretive acts, as in reading a great deal into little things, however, are usually not necessary when only simple facts are under discussion (either you were studying or you were out drinking).

The more complex the issue at hand—in other words, the more difficult it is to make decisions strictly on a yes/no basis—the greater the likelihood that contrasting viewpoints and conflicting assertions will prevail. Where simple logic fails or does not apply, ongoing tolerance for opposing but equally plausible possibilities becomes a necessity. Indeed, complex ambiguity requires each party to be willing to consider multiple options and open-ended possibilities on an ongoing and indefinite basis. Still, the temptation to resolve complex issues (with a search for logical analysis and explicit frames of reference) often ends without reaching any satisfying means of resolution. In this way, complex forms of ambiguity can take one to a point of no return—a frustrating impasse where any further act of reflection or deliberation leads only to more emotional pain, anxiety, or abuse.

So far, the issue of personal ambiguity has been examined in terms of action, for example, as a product of something people *do* as a means to reach some goal. It may also be treated as a potential enemy of aspirations toward greater personal efficacy and communicative competence. Where manifest features of clarity, efficacy, and explicitness operate as standards by which to measure the communicative impact of what transpires, the overall level of ambiguity will diminish the magnitude of what is successfully expressed or conveyed from one source to any other.

One class of ambiguous acts stands in stark contrast to the standards of clarity and efficacy in matters of self-expression and interpretive response. Here are instances where the communicative abilities in question enable one to be crystal clear in giving precise expression to a broad spectrum of personal needs and desires but also with the power to decide to use ambiguity as a deliberate strategy or tactic. Such instances underscore the need to distinguish between acts of expressing oneself as clearly as possible (as a manifestation of a critical social *skill*) from the *decision* to muddy the water or not be as direct or forthcoming as one is capable of being in a given social context. This is why we took such care in the first chapter to distinguish between (a) being clear and transparent and (b) being in a position to be as clear and transparent as present circumstances permit.

It often pays to use linguistic ambiguity in strategic ways. There are any number of instances where optimum clarity is best deferred or postponed. Sometimes it does not pay to simply "tell it like it is." Instead, it is better to "keep them guessing" as long as possible. Joke-telling works best when only the joke-teller knows the punch line in advance. Humor plays tricks with ambiguity. A good joke begins with a description of some incongruent aspect of a situation followed by a sudden element of surprise. The whole point is to be fooled until the very end. Moreover, narratives and storytelling incorporate a great deal of drama and suspense. Suspension of disbelief holds us in our seats until we finally find out what happens in the end. Ludicrous displays of ambiguity work out well if they are sufficiently arresting to capture our attention and imagination, however briefly.

Flirtation thrives on delayed gratification. Once mutual intent is clearly established, flirtation ends (Sabine & Silver, 1982). In romantic relationships, not telling the partner what actually happened is often justified on the grounds of preventing needless pain and suffering (Metts, 1989). The use of abstract and nebulous symbols may be justified by the need to unify divergent groups, avoid destructive conflict, and suspend premature action (Spitzberg, 1993). Complex social rituals invite exploration and play in terms of just the right mix of clarity and ambiguity rather than the complete triumph of one end of the spectrum over the other.

Coping with ambiguity is not the same as resolving it. The relevant literature documents a number of basic considerations. Ambiguity is pervasive and far-reaching (Kenny & DePaulo, 1993). To some degree, the lack of unconditional clarity is simply the price of admission for the right to participate in the flux and change of shape of what's to come. Some people tolerate feelings of uncertainty and unpredictability much better than others. Those who are best prepared to deal with ambiguity and uncertainty are generally more tolerant of complex and elaborated forms of self-presentation than those who are less adaptable and flexible (Douglas, 1991). The safest course is to tolerate what can't be eliminated and to strive not to fabricate more than necessary.

The meaning of personal conduct is ambiguous in matters of defining competence and performance. Because the very definition of high-quality performance is unclear, people are free, as Dunning et al. (1989) claim,

> to use divergent criteria and to draw on the disparate types of behavioral evidence when evaluating themselves in comparison to their peers . . . people tend to use criteria and evidence, whether deliberately or inadvertently, that place them in an unduly positive light. (p. 1082)

Generally, the more ambivalent one's mind-set, the less likely it is that one will be in a position to take decisive action (King & Emmons, 1990).

Much depends on the degree of fit between whatever people observe and the global categories they use to classify and evaluate various attributes of relevance and meaning (Douglas, 1991). As levels of ambivalence and ambiguity increase, an individual tends to experience greater difficulty in knowing which items of observed activity (particulars) fit in best with which types of broad categories (generalizations). When this happens, there may be considerable or pronounced struggle to find a better match between situational factors and the application of various inferences about which categories of evaluation and judgment apply to any case in point (Trope, Cohen, & Alfieri, 1991). The search for resolution of highly polarized and contradictory impressions depends heavily on the particular range of feelings and emotions that prevail at the time (Lambert & Wedell, 1991). Overall, ambivalence over mixed emotions interferes with personal strivings and subjective well-being (King & Emmons, 1990). The magnitude of conflict and upheaval has been shown to be strongly associated with the degree of ambivalence that the participants feel toward their partners and the firmness with which they hold to their own positions and still maintain relational commitments (Fincham & Bradbury, 1989; Gryl, Stith, & Byrd, 1991). At the core of interference are unresolved tensions over the urge to use highly coordinated, interdependent, and integrative tactics as opposed to more individualistic strategies (Canary et al., 1988).

Of central importance is the ability and willingness to cope with ambiguity and ambivalence in ordinary terms. Sentence comprehension provides the baseline test. The meanings of words (and accompanying gestures) must be interpreted according to the context of the sentence, the central theme, and the coherence of the whole text itself (MacDonald, 1993, 1994). Hence even simple word (and image) recognition may require concerted effort, particularly where particulars are grasped and comprehended against the backdrop of (personal) intent and (interpersonal) alignment (Byrd, 1988; MacDonald, Pearlmutter, & Seidenberg, 1994). Therefore there may be a tactical advantage in late rather than premature closure; here decisions about what things mean are put off as long as possible as a means of taking into account greater spans of information and the most recently available impression.

It is at this point that the search for an accurate account must stop for a moment. Negotiations over (a) what to call things and (b) notions about the way things are give way to a more fundamental decision about the worth of the search for clarity and truth. Is it true that the other side will not give at all? Is one so committed to a certain way of viewing things that nothing anyone else says or does will change a thing? If so, the better alternative to further exposure to highly uncertain or anxious modes of exchange may be to accept the entire situation as unresolvable. Here the resolution of complex forms of ambiguity may be less important than the maintenance of one's own health and well-being. In this way, one may reject a fruitless search in a wilderness for a final answer that will never come.

EQUIVOCATION

X and J misread one another all the time. Recently X tried to explain the desire to pursue plan A. J couldn't see how plan A could be considered a proper use of time. X insisted that J follow plan A because X viewed plan A as necessary to make a living. J saw plan A as misplaced effort. What to one was a sign of initiative and determination was taken by the other as lazy and stupid. Over many years, X and J have struggled in a futile attempt to arrive at a clear definition of what is of central importance. Due to incompatible and largely contradictory ways of making sense of things, they settle for a superficial way of doing business. What one thinks is taken care of, the other ignores. Basically X and J don't listen to one another at all.

Confusion may also be understood as the result of what is stated equivocally as well as what is stated ambiguously. Where equivocation is concerned, ambiguity registers in some intrinsic features of expressive acts. People who are ambiguous give off equivocal cues of intent and purpose. It's a matter of stylistic confusion that results from the largely undecided and unsettled ways in which various individuals express themselves before others. One communicative style in particular is clearly implicated because it contributes directly to the amount of ambiguity in the course of daily events. The style is observable in the tension between what one says and what one means. Much ambiguity surrounds the question of why some teachers say they love to work with children but don't seem to enjoy the classroom.

When equivocation is pronounced, the respective parties may not know exactly where they stand—either in relation to one another or to the particular subject at hand. An imbalanced relation between what one says and what one does leads to heightened feelings of apprehension and uncertainty about the veracity of the information in question. It may also lead to a vague sense that the other person is being misleading and evasive by intent or deliberate design. With time, one becomes quite sure the other is wearing a verbal disguise, a coverup.

Acts of equivocation violate linguistic standards of clarity, directness, and precision. The major shift is from typically clear and straightforward modes of interchange to mainly unclear and nonstraightforward episodes. It is tempting to equate equivocation with faulty interaction per se; however, the issues are more complicated. A crucial consideration is whether vague activity is viewed as a liability or a resource. In a comparison of conflict styles in abusive and nonabusive family interactions, Sabourin and Stamp (1995) found that abusive actions and equivocal language were positively correlated. Nonabusive couples preserved a communicative atmosphere based on clear and richly detailed accounts of daily events. They also maintained a high level of interest, a great deal of physical movement, and active engagement. Abusive couples, in contrast, showed lack of detail in descriptions of daily events and expressed an overall lack of vitality, a stagnant quality. Moreover, abusive reactions narrow the scope of what is subject to discussion.

Although a good deal of questionable actions may be due to errors, lapses, slip-ups, and deficiencies in verbal and kinetic skill development, there are any number of circumstances where it pays not to be quite so effective or efficacious but to make one's faults a virtue in disguise. There is some irony in the willingness to acknowledge that the most effective thing to do is to be as clumsy and inarticulate as possible. Muddle through; let things go in one ear and out the other. Don't let them know you can hear every word. Pretend you can't follow along. Create the illusion you are at a loss for words and just don't know what to say. Hedge your bets. Why give away the store?

Face-to-face interaction may not reduce uncertainty or apprehension; in fact, it may well increase one's sensitivity to the magnitude of what one does not know or what others are not in a position to define or determine for themselves. A sense of confusion and uncertainty is often coupled with a state of indecisiveness over what to feel, think, say, or do in anticipation or response to what the expressed actions of others reveal or conceal from human view. When any one party is uncertain and indecisive at the same time, a vicious cycle may begin.

The more difficult it becomes to make sense to self and others, the less one may expect the interaction to make much sense to anyone else. One who does not know where to begin also risks making everything else come out wrong.

In a review of relevant literature, Chovil (1994) equates equivocation with several spheres of shared action: (a) messages that are systematically ambiguous, indirect, contradictory, or evasive; (b) disqualifications, that is, contradictions, inconsistencies, subject switches, tangentializations, incongruence, indifference, and imperviousness (Bavelas & Smith, 1982); (c) words and gestures that prove difficult to interpret due to double meanings or lack of any specific meaning (Eisenberg, 1984); (d) hedges, disclaimers, and disqualifications of responsibility for what one expresses, as in "I was only saying," "Now don't get me wrong," or "Don't take this in the wrong way" (Haley, 1959); (e) refusal to be pinned down or to respond to anything directly to prevent others from knowing the answer to the question (Dillon, 1990); (f) material taken out of context or topics changed in a sleight-of-hand (Washburn, 1969); and (g) unwelcome exposure to difficult situations where all direct types of responses would have negative consequences (Bavelas, 1983). "Equivocation is a solution to this difficult social dilemma; it is a way of avoiding any of the direct alternatives while at the same time enabling the speaker to respond to the situation" (Chovil, 1994, p. 115). A common thread is repeated exposure to difficult or problematic issues where there is no easy way out and no grand strategy for deciding what is "true" or "false" (Bavelas et al., 1990).

Equivocation is evasive. It is useful, therefore, as a means of avoidance and denial of confusion or conflict. A direct request can be neutralized by an indirect reply. When a direct command or instruction imposes negative or unfavorable consequences on the observer, an indirect response may constitute one's first line of defense. Taking evasive action is one way of avoiding the negative consequences of direct confrontation (Chovil, 1994). Highly reciprocated modes of evasion foster protracted displays of avoidance-avoidance conflict. The basic themes are to put off the day of reckoning, stall for time, deflect attention away from potential trouble spots and difficulties, let others interpret one's ambiguity any way they want, take refuge from being pinned down where the risk of avoidance is less than the threat of opportunity. Taking such an indefinite stance makes sense in a whole host of situations where the individuals in question are unsure of themselves but compelled to participate actively. In uncertain situations, it can be quite difficult to respond directly, reveal a lack of knowledge or skill, and face confirmation of one's limitations (Rummelhart, 1983).

VAGUENESS

R and T did not realize that they would end up with nothing in common. At the outset there was a lot of ambiguity and confusion (perhaps on both sides) because neither one had a deep or complete understanding to guide personal conduct through uncertain circumstance. When personal goals changed rapidly, things became more confusing—a snowball effect due to lack of interaction about the deterioration in the quality of the interaction. Direct contact was reduced to a few encounters. R can only speculate on the "truth" from the standpoint of R's feelings, beliefs, and observations. Genuine understanding was lacking on all sides and the poor quality pattern of exchange set up a haphazard and shaky relationship.

A vague style may be characterized as abstract, indistinct, lacking in details and particulars. In contrast, an obscure style may be characterized as remote, blurred, concealed, and somewhat mysterious. When taken together, the notions of vague and obscure may not be easy to explain in operational, normative, or conventional terms. One may observe something happen in plain sight and still not be able to define, classify, or explain it afterward to anyone else. It is not so clear, as Wojciszke (1994) notes, what it is in the behavior that promotes its equivocality. In a three-party situation, persons B and C may have equal and direct access, as observers, to the questionable actions by person A and still come up with quite different sorts of descriptive and valuative inferences (Higgins, 1989; Ross & Nisbett, 1990). Some actions may lack enough specificity to be classified into standard sets or elaborated types of highly embedded categories. Of added relevance is the risk of discrepant evaluations of any given item in question. Given (a) limited information-processing capacity (Ross & Nisbett,

1990), (b) unequal salience of different behavioral features (Borkenau, 1986), and (c) the tendency to rely only on a small subset of features to build up a behavioral construct, it may become more clear as to why so much personal behavior can be so obvious (in one sense) and so mystifying (in another).

It matters how well (or badly) people deal with feelings of uncertainty and hesitation. On this point, Weary and Edwards (1994) suggest,

> Most conceptualizations postulate that there is always some amount of uncertainty inherent in people's knowledge of their environment, but that they are motivated for survival purposes to develop cognitive representations of the world that are as accurate as possible; when people's subjective sense of accurate understanding becomes strained, there typically is an alternating response to the source of uncertainty and some action is taken to improve the state of knowledge. (p. 308)

As the level of uncertainty increases, individuals experience more variation, and more rapidly shifting frames of reference, of unequal duration and intensity (Vallacher, Nowak, & Kaufman, 1994).

Vague expressions are indecisive. They are useful where people are not yet ready to take a stand or make a commitment. The flight from specifics to abstraction makes it possible to say *something* without affirming or denying *anything* in particular. Conversely, preoccupation with specific details can obscure awareness of a larger pattern. Because obscure remarks are so difficult to interpret, reliance on such a noncommittal style of self-expression may be equated with lack of competence or deficit social skills. This is why evasive expressions bring discredit or disqualification to the speaker in the eyes of others (Wilder & Collins, 1994). Sillars and Wilmot (1994) equate a noncommittal style with unfocused questions (e.g., "What do you think?"), abstract or vague generalities (e.g., "Nothing in life that is worthwhile comes easily"), intellectualizing ("The deeper the issue, the more your sense of self is threatened"), topic shifts to what others think ("Mom always said that marriage is hard work"), procedural comments about the process of discussion ("You'll have to speak up so that I can hear you"), and other forms of vague or tangential reference. There is an element of paradox at work here. One can appear to be involved without actually being involved. Thus the use of vague or obscure references is a cautious way of dealing with uncertain, confusing, or conflictful situations.

Anxiety promotes vague urges. A central theme in respondents' reconstructed interactions is the sense of not being able to find the right words. Verbal anxiety undermines the fulfillment of expressive urges. It also interferes with the desire to be explicit, articulate, and discriminating. The process of making sense is integrative and constructive, while a state or condition of anxiety becomes disintegrative and deconstuctive of those same efforts. Whenever the respondents strive to account for what makes them anxious, they may be susceptible to Wittgenstein's dictum: What one cannot say, one must consign to silence. Anxiety is free-floating. It has no distinct point of beginning or specific location. It is roughly akin to numbness or vague aches and pains you feel all over, but the feelings left behind are not distinct enough to define or classify. Sometimes it takes little effort to assign names to things. The words fall off the tongue as automatically as the blinking of one's eyes. At other times, social conditions may not be favorable, or the requisite skills become inaccessible for no apparent reason. In each case, what is missing is the capacity or willingness to find modes of representation and reference that can be subjected to public scrutiny. Often there is concerned effort to speak up, all the while not knowing what to do or how to let go of unsettled burdens, worry, or doubt.

At the core of the issue is the basic need to restore a sense of causal understanding—what leads to what—and thereby restore interpretive and predictive control (Weary & Edwards, 1994). The need for closure is revealed in the "desire for a definite answer on some topic, any answer as opposed to confusion" (Webster & Kruglanski, 1993, cited by Weary & Edwards, 1994, p. 313). An acute sense of uncertainty about one's ability to understand one's position and place in the world has been linked with lower self-esteem and higher trait anxiety (Hartladge, Alloy, Vazques, & Dykman, 1993).

MISDIRECTION

T and D took a while to discover the full magnitude of their personal disagreements. Their initial interactions led T to view

D as a unique individual who was truly his own person—in positive and negative ways. Then T began to notice D's habits, actions, and attitudes as being quite unlike those of anyone else T had ever known. The following are cases in point: spontaneously singing opera in the library, remembering the smallest details, acting overtly concerned yet somehow aloof and strange. Over several months, the interactions slowly became so odd that it finally began to bother T. Suddenly D would say something so off that T wouldn't know how to react. T would raise his eyebrow in amazement and shake his head. Recently D expressed many things very carelessly simply to hurt T's feelings, and from then on the quality of interactions changed for the worse. Recently T found himself not being so cordial. Now T wouldn't say that he avoids D, but he doesn't make any effort to come into direct contact with D. Conversations have dwindled down to small talk. T doesn't have much to say and D seems to feel likewise.

When individuals come into direct contact, each one is in a position to observe the conduct of self/other firsthand from a distinct set of vantage points. At the same time, there is going to be considerable variation in the amount or degree of directness. The term *direct* refers to a style of self-expression that is "straight to the point." Things are to be taken literally and accepted at face value: What you see is what you get. What is said is what is meant and what is meant is what is said, as when taking people at their word. Opportunities are accepted more as a leap of faith than as well-founded belief.

The complementary opposite manner is more indirect. There is a tendency to hint at what one thinks and feels instead of expressing things outright. Similarly, one may prefer to guess about hidden thoughts and feelings in others rather than accept their explanations as reliable. Instead of taking people literally, they are to be construed in figurative, metaphorical, or allegorical terms. In cases of complex misdirection, the intent is not obvious or transparent but is purposefully more difficult to figure out. Sometimes the idiom may be playful or even ludicrous, as in "I was only kidding." Other times, there may be concerted effort to blur distinctions and ignore familiar signposts. One discovers the urge to divert and deflect attention away from conventional and normative ways of making sense of things.

There is, of course, a certain risk. If one person acts in a direct, straightforward and literal-minded way, while another decides to play, hint, and tease, the participants are going to operate on quite different wavelengths. Here the generated confusion is of a peculiar sort. Each member misreads the assumptions, intentions, and experiential frame of reference of the other on a consistent basis. What may be a laughing matter to one may be viewed as a bad joke to someone else. Such forms of personal misdirection are usually for one person's benefit but at someone else's expense. At issue is the magnitude of risk of violation and offense.

Simple forms of misdirection appear innocent; surely, one may reason, others are just "being themselves," and do not intend to do anyone any further harm by misguiding them. With time, one may discover that other people also choose different expressive frequencies for one person's benefit—and usually at the expense of the other. What matters in such situations is the degree to which the other feels offended or violated by the magnitude of misdirection taking place. A different viewpoint or perspective is one thing; a deliberate attempt to create a false impression or subterfuge is altogether different, and more serious.

PARADOX

B and D are rivals who make use of an avoidant system of communication. Both hardly ever talk to each other but both have absolutely no problem sharing deep personal feelings with other friends or relatives. It is a case of a brother and sister who don't understand what transpires because they hardly even know one another. For some reason, neither seems to feel sufficiently motivated to take the initiative and ask why the other avoids personal contact. B doesn't hold resentment toward D but still doesn't have any idea how she may feel about him deep down. For one thing, B is too scared to ask how his sister does feel because he knows he should have gone to her long ago and attempted to form some kind of bond. Because B is the big brother, he feels the relational distance is all his fault because he could have done something early on to change things. As the years have gone by, both have grown up, and neither says anything about their lives. It seems as if B doesn't even have a sister because she never says a word.

A paradox generates confusion in ways that make it hard to dispel. Consider the paradox of communication as a case in point. It is possible for individuals to presume to be engaged in a constant state of communication without any one person being able to say exactly what is conveyed (collectively). Such a condition has been recognized as a major problem in society (Watzlawick et al., 1967). Everyone assumes something is taking place—but there are as many angles and viewpoints as there are people involved. This kind of situation becomes the status quo precisely because individuals do not listen to find out what others are saying as completely and accurately as possible. Instead, they listen mainly to affirm their own unique viewpoints— whatever they may be. In other words, no one is actually trying to maintain access to the communicative standards of anyone else.

The puzzles that result from such circumstances are not easy to unravel. What individuals convey to one another may not be defined, examined, and understood, or acted upon, at the level at which it occurs. For this reason, what is recognized as having any distinctive communicative significance is more complicated than what any one participant or observer can grasp and comprehend. In effect, whatever qualifies as having shared relevance amounts to more than what any one participant or observer can say about it. Some facets of personal behavior may matter a great deal while others go unnoticed or are ignored. As a result, what we see and hear may or may not coincide with how others see and hear what transpires from another distinct position or angle.

As a corollary, what constitutes a paradox for one may not be so for anyone else. It all depends on whose standards apply to someone else. What person A asserts to be the case is something that person B may deny. What is included within the frame of reference of A may be precluded from that of B, C, or D. Either A or B may express himself in ways the other takes to be paradoxical. This occurs on a small scale each time a set of assertions, claims, or statements expressed by any one source is construed as contrary to what is received and accepted by any other. What is preconceived may not be reconciled with what is currently in the process of being formulated. In some sense, the past, present, and future of things just don't jell.

Paradox substitutes comparative logic of *both/and* for exclusive notions of *true/false* or *either/or.* Reasoning from consistent premises leads to a contradiction where you can talk out of both sides of your mouth at the same time. What fails to make common sense may use creative but unreasonable means to give, as Wilder and Collins (1994) state, "a profound glimpse of uncommon sense . . . by striking at the heart of the matter and suggesting that perhaps human behavior is characteristically and inimically contradictory, perplexing, and even perverse" (p. 85). Paradox, on the other hand, erodes faith in perfectionistic and utopian aspirations by calling attention to universal inefficiencies, intrinsic flaws, and misconstructive tendencies, with unforeseen or undesirable consequences (Coupland et al., 1991). One may experience paradox in the midst of what is trivial and mundane. In such a muddled and messy state of affairs, selective and strategic application of ordinary language makes it possible to go round in circles without ever once going directly from point A to point B. It is a domain without straight lines but with lots of waves and fuzzy oscillations.

A model of living paradox takes the form of a person who exhibits a perplexingly inconsistent way of life or persistently erratic trajectories of behavior. One may live a life that thrives on the very opportunity to pretend to be what one is not—to feign or imitate. To have to deal with an impossible person is a test case. One individual likens interacting with an impossible person to be like talking to a brick wall, where the other is not interested in what one strives to convey to him or her. The other person may have nothing to say in return. Another conjures up the image of those who are totally self-absorbed and have no concept of what it is to interact with someone else.

These main themes have a familiar ring. When individuals *must* tolerate one another, the state of relation may sink to the lowest common denominator. As such, direct contact is kept to a minimum, preserving the illusion that nothing worth noticing is happening anyway. Each one talks about self while tuning out the other. Any further use of words and gestures is considered futile because no one follows any unwritten rules; there is no eye contact, only mute facial expression, and little movement one way or another. The only point is not to make any point. Such impoverished interaction is taken as the justification for the perpetration of the very conditions responsible for the endless repetition of the faulty process. One may find that when around the impossible person, one tends to act impossible too. What is utterly impossible is to chart a course of any way out, the very presumption of the opportunity to find a way back to the possible, if not the plausible.

A paradoxical relation is two beings who become one and yet remain two. It is possible, after all, to *join together* and *break apart* at the same time. Such relations are replete with inconsistencies between surface appearance and in-depth experience. The respective parties tend to gravitate into two self-consistent but habitually incompatible frames of reference or courses of behavior. Inconsistent or unsuitable sets of circumstance are united into one complex assemblage. Any one thing may violate someone's pictures of how things should, could, or might otherwise be. Unexpected and impossible elements collide with one's current knowledge of the world. Radical paradox defines multiple states of relations as complete opposites where the presence or affirmation of the truth or reality of one is equivalent to the absence or denial of the other, because the two subdomains exhaust the universe of discourse. It is akin to the demand that one make sense of nonsense, of what is ludicrous in a self-validating pattern. The paradox of interaction comes full circle with whatever can evade the opportunity, either by short circuit, denial, or impasse.

The risk of paradox may not be eliminated, but it can be recognized at the level of its reproduction and reconstruction. What is required is the knowledge of how to neutralize or defuse the tendency to infuse paradoxical injunctions into the stream of conversational activity. These are instructions or commands imposed (as tacit standards) by one individual upon the personal conduct or range of options of any other individual. It is logically absurd to insist that something be obeyed that is virtually impossible to obey in total or unconditional terms. The injunction, "Be spontaneous," is a case where someone is placed in the untenable position of having to comply by responding in a way that must, by definition, not be forced or coerced to produce it. The imposition of a double bind is enforced where "you are damned if you do and damned if you don't" work your way out of the harsh demands. One can neither comment nor get out of the situation without risk of severe penalty.

A dilemma presents a peculiar form of paradox. It is found in conversations where people feel they are unwittingly being trapped by what transpires. Arguments and disputes often set up false choices and alternatives. Someone is confronted with oppositional forms of argument involving a choice between two (or more) alternatives, both equally unfavorable. One is cast into a position of doubt or perplexity, a difficult situation from which to extricate oneself. The most notorious instance is the prisoner's dilemma. It is a mixed-motive game with opposing incentives: one to cooperate, the other to compete. Two individuals must choose to cooperate or compete with one another with equal opportunity to cooperate or compete in a series of trials. To cooperate is to be exposed to the same fate as the other. To compete is to take advantage of what gives one a temporary edge. Here the strength of personal aspirations is tested against the magnitude of one's involvements and commitments to others.

At the level of collective action, incentives and achievements may not be well matched. The incentive to cooperate presupposes achievements that generate benefits for everyone in the group. The effort to moderate extremes becomes difficult or problematic insofar as self-interested individuals benefit even more from choosing not to cooperate (Weesie, 1994). The critical decision is whether to cooperate with individuals (whose immediate responses are uncertain or unknown) or else defect and fend for oneself. Here confusion registers in personal awareness of inequalities among a narrow range of options, incomplete information, and lack of correspondence, or disjunctures, in mutual response. Such simple but tricky games reveal how people allocate values, priorities, preferences, and resources in simulated situations with very little room to move. Fuzzy calculations of gain and loss give important clues about the behavior of people in "more complicated and sometimes indecipherable real-world environments" (Goetze, 1994, p. 84).

How individuals handle the tug of competitive and cooperative urges says a great deal about the active role the parties themselves play in the structure and process of such extreme forms of bipolar opposition (W. Smith, 1987). What happens is widespread effort to learn the structure of the game and adapt their behavior accordingly (Bornstein, Erev, & Goren, 1994). On a larger scale, Coombs (1987) outlines three variations on a central theme: (a) Conflict emerges out of being forced to choose between two options as a means to resolve opposing, incompatible goals; (b) conflict arises because individuals want different things but have to settle for the same thing; and (c) all other conflicts arise because individuals want the same thing and have to settle for different things (Coombs & Avrunin, 1988). Hard choices multiply under conditions of complication, complexity, and confusion over an uneven mix of options.

Compromising logic does not require a master plan or single, overarching strategy. However, if everyone pursues his or her own best interests exclusively, the collective as a whole will be worse off (Parks & Vu, 1994). The affiliative urge can act as a check on power motivation by "channeling concerns for control and influence into more personal, nurturant directions" (Peterson, Winter, & Doty, 1994, p. 721). The tendency of individuals to cooperate with an opponent increases when there is a chance for direct communication, and decreases when there is no such option. Without direct contact with one's adversary, competitive moves or outright withdrawal are more likely (Betz, 1991).

It pays to be nice. Go tit-for-tat. Respond in kind. Cooperate as long as your opponent cooperates. Compete as long as your opponent competes. TFT has been shown to be predictable, easy to recognize, does well with itself, and is fair but firm (Axelrod, 1984). There are limits to the applicability of the rule (Bendor, 1993). By being flexibly provocative, a strategy can ensure itself against being infinitely exploitable. Unfortunately, it would require very high-quality monitoring to sift through claim and counterclaim and distinguish between *nice and forgiving* and *harsh and unforgiving* for cooperative tactics to flourish and prosper. In a favorable climate, cooperative choices are more often maximized when cooperative overtures are reciprocated immediately than when they are delayed (Komorita, Hilty, & Parks, 1991).

On a larger scale, there is the possibility of third-party intervention. Professional mediators and arbitrators are trained to deal with people who get caught up in social dilemmas and can't get out. At stake is the effectiveness of mediation, the efficacy of a system of techniques, and the tentative usefulness of each tactic (Wall & Lynn, 1993). A minimum objective is improved communication sufficient to reduce the severity of the dispute. This is not always possible, particularly if the disputants have reached a hurting stalemate (Touval &

Zartman, 1989). Toughness on the part of the opposing parties—an
unwillingness to compromise—may sabotage the possibility for *any*
resolution. It is a dangerous game to play because if other parties also
insist on holding out, an impasse can be expected (Brams & Doherty,
1993). Mediators attempt to strike a power balance (Conlon & Fasolo,
1990), expand the agenda, explore agreements that yield high benefits to both sides (Bienenfeld, 1985), determine what points are
negotiable (Mayer, 1985), reframe the dispute (Sheppard, Blumenfield-
Jones, & Roth, 1989), exert pressure on other third parties, and
fine-tune any approaches that work well (Hiltrop, 1989).

Strong resistance makes negotiating flexibility crucial. Rigid and
tough bargaining must be redefined and redirected to deal with the
convergence of widely differing interests. Flexibility requires the willingness to forfeit gain to avoid either losses or deadlock (Druckman,
1993). Coercive tactics may be used to move a party off a position, or
onto a new position, or to save face. The strongest finding may seem
obvious. As the level of conflict increases, the likelihood of successful
mediation decreases (Hiltrop, 1989; W. Smith, 1987). Successful set-
tlements are most difficult to broker when one or both parties have
few resources (Pearson, Thoennes, & Vanderkooi, 1982). Resource
scarcity and power imbalances markedly reduce the total range of
options (Amy, 1983; Kressel & Pruitt, 1989). Also resistant are high-
level discord and intense disputes over principles and nondivisible
issues (Kressel & Pruitt, 1989). Low verbal interaction generally makes
matters worse (Wall & Lynn, 1993).

Compromising has been the object of extensive study. In a meta-
analysis of bargaining experiments reported over a 25-year period,
Druckman (1994) found the strongest effect sizes were obtained for
the mediator's own orientation, prior experience, time pressures, and
initial distance between positions. Most resistant to change are conditions where the respective parties do not expect future interaction,
where few issues are being contested and a deadline exists, where
competitive orientations are long-standing and/or face-saving pressures are strong, where *differences between positions* on important issues
are derived from long-held attitudes and/or linked to *contrasting
ideologies,* and where there are *tough or exploitative* opponents whose
intentions are easy to discern. These broad considerations shape
much of what is possible or ruled out.

It is tough to be placed in a situation where dialectical tensions between cooperative and competitive urges neither dissolve nor resolve to anyone's satisfaction. The struggle to come together and to pull apart may not be subject to moderation but merely the constant tug of being pushed or pulled, back and forth, in futile efforts at synthesis and integration. What is so unmanageable is the sheer plurality, diversity, complexity, and contradictory nature of what may take place very quickly. Paradoxical modes of face-to-face interaction are replete with traps, quandaries, magic tricks, and false options that unfold in the manner of a tug-of-war with far too much commotion and noise on all sides. Central issues revolve around endless cycles of confrontation with no sign of relief or resolution in sight.

Whenever there is tension, stress, or strain amidst conjoint effort to resolve some felt difficulty, either the difficulty is resolved or it is left unresolved. Insofar as the felt difficulties are resolved at the time and under the initial circumstances in which they arise, it is appropriate to characterize the process as a problem-solving exercise executed in the manner of a negotiated settlement. In an important study of the subject, Aldous and Ganey (1989) examine research on the factors that influence families' definition of behavior in problematic situations. Often there is only a vague sense that something is wrong before family members retrospectively define it as a problem. Sometimes problems do not lend themselves to a technical solution but must simply be lived through. Moreover, problems are often deeply "embedded" in the context of other concerns. Negative affect is common. So are signs of denial, avoidance, preoccupation with individual concerns, sketchy situational definitions, and discussion cover-ups, particularly when there is an uneven distribution of power. Finally, families, like other groups, continuously face extraordinary events with potentially significant negative consequences (Aldous & Ganey, 1989; Reid, 1985; Reiss, 1981). Hence issues become problematic insofar as they must be confronted repeatedly in the context of some institutionalized habit, ritual, or routine.

Conversational entanglements foster a sense of being trapped by the existing range of alternatives. In terms spelled out by Daly, Diesel, and Weber (1994), people have the sense that no matter what they do, they are bound to lose. Of course, if no one loses, no one wins either. In this sense, everyone is caught in the dilemma because no one can see out or beyond what appears to be the case right now. At issue is what it feels like to be placed in an awkward situation. Often there are negative feelings, as well as embarrassment and defensiveness, associated with not being able to extricate oneself from what transpires. A large number of undergraduate students enrolled in communication courses were asked to describe the sorts of conversational dilemmas they had faced during daily encounters with others. Eight clusters emerged: (a) situations where people were caught blatantly lying to others and were then confronted about it in a conversation; (b) situations where people desire to get what they want versus the obligation to attend to other people's needs by being polite or tactful; (c) moral issues, where people witness a wrongdoing or a violation of a rule by someone they like; (d) foot in mouth, where people either "let the cat out of the bag" by revealing secrets or what was to be kept quiet, or else are overheard saying something that was not intended for the listener; (e) inability to please, that is, no matter what people say or do, their words are not acceptable to another person; (f) ultimatums/pressure from others, where people are indeed able to please others but only by doing something that they do not want to do; (g) choosing sides, where people find themselves torn between two people they like, as in the case of unwelcome, third-party interventions in outside conflicts and disputes; and (h) the choice between being tactful and polite versus telling someone the truth, even if it hurts. Such conversational dilemmas become particularly difficult where extrication by avoidance (doing nothing) is almost impossible.

At issue are remedial strategies designed not so much to make things better but to keep them from getting worse (Newell & Stutman, 1988). Attempts to move off or beyond the "horns of a dilemma" are tests of one's competence in dealing with difficult people or impossible situations (Daly et al., 1994). On a larger scale, people devise specialized procedures for dealing with certain types of problematic actions and stay alert for conditions where bias, distortion, and disruption are likely to occur (Kramer, Pommerenke, & Newton, 1993). Specific strategies aim at early warning detection of ways to test the veracity of assertion and claim. People may be guided by quasiscientific methods for assessing all plausible interpretations for the same action (Hewes, 1995). Selective reinterpretation is assumed to correct and replace the bias with a more accurate version. At the core of the exercise is the sufficiency of reason to doubt or to accept things at face value.

CONTRADICTION

Y and R say one thing and mean another. R always speaks of men and how much they love her. This is difficult for Y because R's whole life seems to revolve around men. When Y tries to get the conversation on a different track, R speaks of how ugly R is—a complete contradiction of what was just said. Y has grown to think that what R needs is attention, which she shows by putting others down and bragging so much. One second, R will say how incredibly beautiful she is, and the next, she'll complain that she is so ugly. When Y tries to explain what is going on in Y's life, R will rip Y's ideas apart. Y gets the impression that R just doesn't seem to want to agree or understand anything that Y says or does.

There is a fine line between *paradox* and *contradiction*. The distinction is roughly between the appearance of irreconcilable differences and the contrast of mutually opposing terms. This makes it possible for interactants to pursue a paradoxical goal fraught with pitfalls and contradictions. Suppose the respective parties are perfectionistic in thought, word, and deed. They want their interpersonal encounters to live up to a mythical ideal. The quest may be viewed as a search for perfect harmony. The first sign is a relentless insistence on total order and control. There must be a place for everything and everything must be in its right place. Each person knows exactly what to say and how to act. No one is at a loss for words. A communal spirit is effortlessly obtained. Do the right thing. Follow the rules. Know your place. Wait your turn. Don't arrive too early and be sure to leave at just the right time. Rule out the possibility of mistakes and miscalculations. Take no liberty. Cause no offense. Insist on a flawless performance by the entire cast. No one sings out of turn, misses a beat, or gets out of line. Things work out fine each time.

The mythical search for perfection is full of contradiction, confusion, and illusion about human connections. There are no allowances for nullities—deficiencies, weaknesses, and vulnerabilities—or unknown matters of risk and change. Displays of words and gestures, however imperfect and imprecise, are used to deny the imperfection and imprecision of those who use them. The confusion takes the form of a conundrum; that is, fallible linguistic tools can lead to the production of infallible social products. When we insist on the imposition of unobtainable standards of performance, we leave ourselves open to a collective sense of inadequacy, shortcomings, and failure. The action of thinking, saying, and doing what is presumed to be beyond question or further inspection will not tolerate any expression of what is contrary or at variance with itself. This self-validating paradox has no alternative but to close in upon itself. The end point is limbo—where assertion rules out the possibility of denial.

The perfectionistic urge, the desire to transcend the risk of mistakes, errors, and miscalculations in favor of unquestioned forms of action, resonates in people who insist they are always right no matter what. A misguided urge leaves them in pursuit of the faulty premise that everyone else must be wrong. Every expressive act and subsequent interpretive response is/must/should be seen as utterly beyond reproach. Nothing is to be called into question or subject to scrutiny in indifferent spheres of operation where no questions are either called forth or allowed. In effect, the case is shut down. Captured by magical states of false innocence, such individuals are prone to attribute, project, or impose their own flawless conceptions of themselves onto others to (a) pick up the tab and (b) absorb the tacit impact of noxious pinpricks and invisible misdemeanors. Such conditions set up a corollary. Other people are expected to act in a lofty manner whenever in the presence of a person who presumes to do no wrong before others. The bubble bursts when pretence can no longer be sustained. Let anyone who presumes to be without mistake or error cast the first stone.

It is sheer folly to insist on flawless performance. Seductive utopian and perfectionistic visions ignore a good deal of what makes us human. They also make it harder to appeal to obtainable but sufficient and sustainable levels of achievement. Life *is* confusing precisely because it is so precious and precarious. Hence there is no final resolution, as Cupach (1994) notes, in domains where "social performances are botched, expectations are disconfirmed, identities are threatened, interactions are disrupted, and persons are held accountable" (p. 159). The promise of success means nothing apart from the risk of failure. Finding fault may mitigate the mindless repetition of error and mistake. Confusion and contradiction may be endemic and inevitable in social interaction (Cupach, 1994).

Because conflict and confusion are intrinsic features of everyday life, there is no use longing for friction-free conditions. There is simply "no assurance that communication will be certain or even relatively trouble-free" (Fish, 1989, p. 42). Even the best-laid descriptions, classifications, explanations, and predictions, as Maynard and Clayman (1991) state, "always leave something out, need fudging, or are replete with inconsistencies" (p. 397). Each one of us has, as Moore (1987) notes, "a perspectival conception of the world which we cannot rise above" (p. 20). Because "the possibility of description itself implies a point of view . . . this implies, in turn, niche oriented, imperfection, and partial representation" (A. Clark, 1984, p. 486). It is a fallacy, therefore, to think that "we can stand outside of what we observe, or observe, without distortion, what is alien to our experience" (Levenson, 1972, p. 8).

Confusion and conflict register in shared practices that remain open to further scrutiny. There is considerable exposure to distortion and disruption up and down the line. Hence the question of what transpires, when taken from any particular viewpoint, is not an "ultimately knowable object" (Dudley & Brown, 1981, p. 321). Although any physical setting may be fully shared, it is nonetheless subject to a principle of differential sensitivity (Knowles & Smith, 1984). Complex events will, as Fischer (1989) notes, "almost unavoidably, with some reasonable time span, eventuate in misunderstandings, misinterpretations, different conclusions, different cognitive adaptations and variations, and disparity of perception in certain domains" (p. 194).

There is power in concerted effort at retrospective clarification. Preliminary inquiry centers on the courage and resolve to talk about what went right or wrong in the past or anticipated future, as preparation for a better or brighter day. There are lessons to be learned about the experience of confusion and conflict, not only for their own sake but also as a means of constructing an alternative vision of one's position and place among others in the larger scheme of things. Personal accounts are likely to be invoked during periods where people are especially troubled, perplexed, or unsettled by some unwelcome element of stress or surprise, especially if it is unpleasant

(Weber, Harvey, & Orbuch, 1992). Working through loss is a potential gain where burden sharing implies burden bearing—right down to the last detail. At stake is the ability to talk silently and privately to oneself about *whatever* transpires in public settings, whether turning out well or badly, as a means of establishing a renewed sense of *hope* for the future and more enduring acts of *faith* reclaimed from the distant past (Weber et al., 1992). The goal is to minimize signs of misinterpretation and miscommunication at the earliest possible convenience.

CHAPTER 5

Agreement/ Disagreement

With disagreement, at this stage, disputes rule the day. Sometimes contentious individuals try out various methods of problem-solving activity to restore their relationship to its original condition. The participants may construe the stakes to be quite high. Everyone wants to succeed in such a complicated and entangled enterprise. However, each party may also watch silently and apprehensively for small signs of difficulty over large differences of opinion, despite the best of intentions. As divergent viewpoints increase, and convergent frames of reference decrease, certain individuals may attempt to share whatever perplexing problems or unresolved issues are salient at the time; however, such sharing may be construed as self-centered if each party is aware of the other as acting primarily in terms of self-directed orientations. Here a position of superiority/inferiority, rather than equality, has replaced the original goal of reestablishing a spirit of harmony and mutuality among the respective parties. At issue is whether the state of relations will ever be completely fair, supportive, or equal again. In addition, there may be no real cause or reason to restore a spirit of respect and understanding because subsequent personal attacks could well confirm the very worst fears of everyone who is involved. A corresponding urge is to construe the other as the main source of the problem, and so obviously in the wrong. The battle lines are drawn; when one steps over, the other rushes in, and each one is left to engage in self-inflated displays of one-sided blame and accusation.

The first four chapters identified several basic causes of miscommunication in human relations. Of central interest is what transpires when faulty implications, cognitive distortions, and interpersonal disruptions come together to promote the reproduction of highly confused or ambiguous modes of face-to-face interaction. At issue are a host of social situations where disagreements and disputes have adverse but largely unintended outcomes and consequences. Here is where an accumulation of unresolved issues can lead to greater levels of misinterpretation and misunderstanding later on. The main point is to see how the very tools we use to get ourselves into so many communicative difficulties are the same devices we must be prepared to *re*employ (or transform) to get ourselves out. In this equation, even minor disagreements can lead to major misunderstandings just as easily as petty misunderstandings can lead to severe disagreements. In other words, there is no linear, one-way pattern of causal order.

This chapter examines social conditions that promote a general climate of agreement or disagreement. We want to understand the mechanisms people use to cultivate a climate or atmosphere where a broad spectrum of agreements and understandings can be nurtured and sustained. There is considerable evidence to link high-quality interaction with the ability and willingness to agree about the way things are. Hence it is important to know what individuals miss or fail to take into account when disagreements and misunderstandings dominate the scene. Our method of inquiry relies on a comparative analysis of selected attributes and features of shared activity where levels of social skill dictate goals, strategies, tactics, and outcomes.

We conducted a series of a/b comparisons from the ground up. Preliminary analysis showed that basic distinctions between agreement and disagreement can be captured along eight dimensions of consideration: (a) the strength of relational ties, (b) multiple perspective taking ability, (c) compatibility of values, (d) similarity of interests, (e) depth of involvement, (f) quality of interaction, (g) equality of influence, and (h) future plans. What takes place in each dynamic sphere of action provides strategic indications of the causes, conditions, and outcomes of personal engagement in consensual or divergent forms of social action.

RELATIONAL TIES

It is useful to think about the organized features of human encounters in process-oriented terms. At one end of the spectrum are contacts between individuals who meet for the first time (zero history). Repeated encounters may lead to casual acquaintances, which may turn into deep friendships, love relations, or kinship ties. The movement from distant to close types of relational bonds can be organized around five broad categories: initial encounters, casual acquaintances, friendships, intimate relations, and kinship ties. By classifying individual accounts into one of these five general categories, an interesting profile emerges.

Agreements occurred across the entire spectrum of personal encounters. In contrast, disagreements often appeared where there was (a) less than an optimum degree of psychological freedom, (b) lack of equal treatment, or (c) frequent episodes of friction, strife, and tension. Moreover, personal disagreements reveal many shortsighted and misguided methods of mutual (mis)construction. The sharp contrast in profiles shows why agreement-making activity is so closely associated with the capacity and willingness to maintain strong ties with other people. A strong working consensus is critical in close, intimate, or kinship ties. Overall, friends and intimates were best able to establish a solid sense of common ground.

We discover how respondents who agree often grew up in similar neighborhoods, which tended to reinforce similar values and interests, how they became excited by their shared understandings, and how their differences were nonthreatening and even interesting to one another. Similarly, we look at ways in which respondents who disagree often have differing backgrounds, neighborhoods, values, and interests, and how they become frustrated by their often conflicting understandings of themselves and others in the world around them. From these comparisons, a central theme emerges in respondents' reconstructed interactions. Serious disagreements often develop from flawed efforts to maintain or increase one's sense of control over the entire course of interaction, while personal agreements are more closely associated with a spirit of receptivity and openness to new ways of thinking, feeling, behaving, and relating with others.

Agreement. K and H engage in conversations where each one uses sentence fragments or unique words because both are so familiar with the unstated context. Outsiders are not able to take much meaning from the insiders' code. Conversation flows without effort because so many thoughts and ideas are shared in common. Personal misunderstandings are uncommon but are usually resolved fairly quickly and with ease. They have been close friends for 8 years and know one another's communicative weaknesses and strengths very well. Individual differences do not hinder conversations greatly as each one is able to understand how to deal with a close friendship that is easy to maintain and still fulfills the needs of both parties.

Disagreement. F and O engage in talks that end up badly. F will say, "I can't discuss this with you because you are too closed-minded." O does not listen because F talks about the way things were in the past and why he did something a certain way back then. Next, when O tries to explain that what worked in the past won't necessarily work now, F retorts with the question, "Why it won't work now?" From that point, F and O get into a cycle of anger and resentment, even when O realizes where they are heading and tries to stop it. The process also works in reverse. O is sure each one thinks that he is doing everything to get his thoughts across, but O is simply looking at life from his point of view and F from his.

The personal accounts underscore a number of central themes. Those who establish solid working agreements described their relations as if they had lasted for decades. Similar backgrounds, upbringing, and opportunities fostered similar outlooks on life. They had a deep sense of the significance of shared childhood experiences, but the reason for its importance was difficult to define in specific terms. Some were together for so long that they had become a single entity. Blended identities emerged from compatible worldviews. Contact was frequent and predictable. A stockpile of prior agreements made it easier to discuss differences freely. When raising touchy issues, two-way reassurance made conversation more enjoyable. Routine matters flowed smoothly because the interactants didn't contradict or question one another at these times; instead, each felt that his or her thoughts and ideas were understood and well respected. For this reason, they knew they could talk with one another in a peaceful manner without fear of a dispute. When personal differences were not allowed to hinder the flow of conversation, fulfilling relations were most able to flourish and expand.

There was a certain joy in the mutual realization of close connection. When personal differences were shared in a nonthreatening way, genuine and lasting pleasure was most widespread. Specific arguments were more closely integrated into a working consensus that led to an even stronger sense of renewed connectedness. Many parties could discuss virtually everything because they did not need to become severely critical or judgmental of one another. What mattered to one mattered to the other. One respondent indicated that, with increasing age, he and his partner found they disagreed more often. After taking time to talk, each found it meaningful to explore an alternative viewpoint, to try out a new way of seeing things. In this case, a sense of blended identities evolved from the fact that they were willing to discuss their disagreement to see (a) if it was real or (b) if it was just the result of a simple act of miscommunication. If it was an instance of miscommunication, they laughed and forgot about it. If it was a genuine difference, they maintained an attitude of acceptance and respect for one another's perspectives. To them, this was far better than agreeing in an attempt to sidestep the issue; blind acceptance, they believed, was a sign of a relationship that wouldn't last, and they very much wanted to continue.

The disagreement section shows how it is possible to discount the potential for closeness and fail to establish a sense of common ground. Those who disagreed—either partially or completely—often treated one another as virtual strangers who had little or nothing in common. Severe personal blindness occurred among those who shared a common heritage, were coworker or neighbor, or had a history of intimacy as family member, lover, or friend. Of course, people everywhere—children, adolescents, and adults of all ages—experience the jarring effects of clashing opinions. For this reason, respondents presumed themselves to live in a turbulent world that would adversely affect close personal, family, and community ties. In unsettled territory, there was little reason to understand. It was easier to take a passive approach, become philosophical, or declare the situation lost. Another option was to be more active and direct and respond to shared difficulty with overt hostility.

There is another striking contrast. Those who agreed found it easy to identify more precisely what was taking place, and had little need to make further assumptions about the substance of interaction, but contentious individuals could not form a working consensus. Hence they felt forced to make assumptions about one another's motivations, intentions, attitudes, rightness or wrongness, what would happen next, and so on. Prevailing assumptions passed for truth in the minds of those who disagreed as a matter of whim. Comments about disagreements were rife with premises of questionable accuracy and validity that unduly emphasized gross differences and inaccurate portrayals of the actual problems that did exist. Selective disinformation had marginal value as a cover for what was hard to deny because it was taking place before one's very eyes.

Because questionable personal assumptions were constructed on the basis of a self-serving dialogue, rather than on realistic observations shared in sustained dialogue with others, those in routinely confused or conflicted relations were prone to become utterly convinced of the ultimate truth of their own perceptions, options, and decisions. Given the probability of severe disagreement as a constant presence, they were often tempted to generalize from specific assumptions to everything that might happen in the future. To prevent what they saw as "the worst that could happen," some were motivated to teach the other the error of his or her ways by explaining—and even harping on—*the truth* of her or his own assumptions. Usually, they justified such teaching because of yet another assumption—that what they were saying also was true. The harder they pushed *the truth,* however, the more they relied on exclusive perceptions of difference and distinction.

Another aspect of such teaching was a stance of righteous indignation. After all, what better basis was there on which to argue other than seemingly irrefutable evidence that one was completely right? Some rigidly held viewpoints must have seemed particularly clear and undeniably true when one considers the degree of stubbornness that often underlies such heavily weighted emotional assumptions. One respondent described such stubbornness within the context of an ongoing, and seemingly unavoidable, verbal battle. Such stiffness injured the self—as well as keeping others at a distance—when respondents directed their criticisms at themselves rather than others. Critical self-evaluation kept disagreement firmly entrenched in whatever transpired. The tragedy of righteous indignation is that, in reality, each person is trying to help resolve a difficult episode of serious or critical misunderstanding. Each one searches for a way to make what is so obvious to him or her equally visible to other people.

In this kind of situation, many respondents acted as if their very lives were at stake; they were constantly alert for the opportunity to gain verbal advantage. Each may have known that, rationally speaking, there was no point to such encounters; for example, they may have known their viewpoints were too divergent to be reconciled. Even so, they sparred with the tenacity of marines under fire. It was a grim game that may be compared with guerilla warfare. The other main options were inaction or withdrawal.

Some disagreements seemed destined to last forever. The accompanying negative assumptions drove people apart because they were painful to contemplate, to utter, and to hear. The residue of hurt and injury served to complicate issues to the point where some participants no longer tried to work together in the hope of transforming such a mass of disagreement into an equally abiding domain of agreement. It is not just a matter of the result of disagreements that randomly forced individuals apart. Many interactants *chose* to wall themselves off to avoid prolonged stress and strain.

Clearly, the ability to argue in a well-reasoned manner is an important measure of communicative competence. People are argumentative creatures who take issue with one another, not simply due to some imagined breakdown or lapse in civility but as a fundamental expression of the need to move things along, with persuasion, challenge, and defense of options (Antaki, 1994). Adversaries must maneuver through claim and counterclaim by pulling in and out of focus on specific frames of reference without losing sight of what is at stake. Because disagreements are so pervasive in society, people often care less about resolving differences than they do about actively defending or maintaining them.

Argumentative behavior does not *have* to be disruptive, even though it is often treated that way. The willingness to pay close attention to the exact words being spoken provides a stockpile of knowledge from which to build subsequent replies (Goodwin & Goodwin, 1987, 1990). Intricate coordination is particularly important during points of resolute opposition. When a *demand* is met with a *refusal,* either a disjunction is created or a point of contention is treated as part of the underlying coherence of a structure that remains intact. Opposition does not require objection to everything that *could* be disputed or refuted. Many points of contention can be discounted, ignored, tolerated, or ended simply by shifting the focus or slant of the topic, without resolution of any kind. Nor is it necessary, as occurred so frequently during severe disagreements, to quibble over minute detail so much that the process of confrontation grinds to a halt. Diversity and creativity in turn-taking and topic shifts help move things along. So the point is to not get stuck on small points of opposition construed as dichotomies or obstacles (Grimshaw, 1990; Lee & Peck, 1995).

COMMONALITY OF PERSPECTIVES

Chapter 1 underscored the importance of being in a position to establish an initial sense of common ground. Faulty implications are crucial factors and central themes in a wide spectrum of entanglements noted in respondents' answers. As common assumptions increase, the respective parties feel more assured that others will respond in a certain way. What holds at implicit levels of self-reference applies to explicit observation as well.

Agreement. Q and T: Q: Hey T, what's up? T: Just bought a new poetry book. Q: Oh yeah? Is it Jim Morrison? T: Yup. You think he concentrates too much on death? Q: Depends on whether or not you see death the way he does. T: Yeah, that's what I tell everybody; I think life itself is more painful than death would ever be. You go through so much more pain in the years spent living than the few seconds spent dying. Q: Exactly! Jim Morrison is trying to let everybody know that death takes away all the hurt that is felt while living.

Q and T are brothers who are very much alike. Their conversation seems as if they're talking to each other's own conscience. They can talk about anything and share the same views. Q and T skip all the small talk and proceed to the heart of the matter at hand, knowing already what's going to be said next. One will ask a question and the other will answer with the same response the first one would have suggested for himself.

Disagreement. Y and Z have opposite views of the world. Y is liberal and Z is conservative, which has the ingredients for interesting conversations. They usually start out with either one stating an opinion about something seen as a problem. When the other hears this statement, there is an instant reaction, usually a statement of the opposite opinion. The chain reaction provokes heated discussion where both parties think they are right. Although these discussions may lead to a greater understanding of each one's position, they rarely produce any type of agreement. Trying to change the other's opinions is like ramming one's head against a brick wall. This leads to much frustration and the need to take a break from intense conversations. However, the exchange of ideas, even when opposing, is a source of common ground and an outlet for divergent thoughts.

Underlying the threshold of personal agreement was a bedrock of working consensus upon which all else rested. What made so much agreement-oriented activity successful was the low level of friction— even when negotiating differences became a long and arduous process. More important, each member was able to maintain his or her sense of self without getting defensive. Each stuck to the job of maintaining the relationship as well as the task of making a point. In fact, many respondents worked together despite dissimilar viewpoints, and thereby discovered interesting truths about which of the various communicative strategies worked out either well or badly.

If something is bothersome, it is not necessary to pretend that nothing has happened. It is possible to let the other person know right away. By identifying communicative failures in this way, truth and openness aided the process of searching for mutual understanding. Clearly, some types of individual differences can make people seem more alike. Some claim that dynamic, problem-solving relationships like these were exciting. One was exploring. One was learning. Life together seemed like a miracle because of the foundation that was being mutually constructed.

On the side of disagreement, lack of commonality in perspective-taking ability was partly associated with the application of undesirable labels. It is possible to use labels as a mechanism to accent and highlight different views of the world. Moreover, misuse of labels may rule out the possibility of seeing things differently (in one sense) and similarly (in another) at the same time. The one who presumes to be able to read minds can be easily led astray. Some claimed to be able to read the inner motivations of other people. There was also a tendency to quit trying to comprehend the other person's reality in any detail. Where no one attempts to communicate at all, the unspoken assumption speaks for itself. The course of conversation may well degenerate into a verbal contest of wills that is all quite pointless.

It was not necessary for those with differing perspectives to allow close friendships to fall apart. Of course, there was a lot of stress and strain associated with sticking around so that the other could lay out his or her hidden agenda. Unpredictable interchanges could be upsetting, with a lot of emotional discomfort involved. Sometimes, however, some individuals could transcend such difficulty by maintaining the effort to understand what the other was trying to express. When it became evident that such productivity was not possible, and the focus of conversation reverted back to unresolved issues, avoidance of conflict seemed more desirable.

When individuals experienced considerable anxiety over the likelihood of yet another unresolvable outcome, they often withdrew from one another. They did this by assuming that they had little in common with the other person, and that avoiding one another made more sense. Unfortunately, there was a price to be attached to such short-circuited methods of problem solving. Essentially, the price involved the lingering but misplaced sense that genuine understanding would never become a personal reality.

For those who did not share common perspectives, personal differences were threatening precisely because of their greater potential to erupt into a firestorm of violation and offense. One respondent described the passive negativism that transforms innocuous statements of opinion into threatening statements of criticism, including the following: judgmental attitudes, standing or sitting in a defiant manner, looking around at whatever else is going on, calling out to others while one is still talking, and making little eye contact. The situation can be made even worse if there is a lot of active verbal abuse: critical statements, an unwillingness to listen by cutting the speaker off, changing the subject at whim, and dismissing one's needs to resolve protracted disagreements as unimportant. It is little wonder that individuals with strikingly different perspectives should try to avoid such conflicted confrontations.

Sometimes, however, there were hidden reasons for believing that it was meaningful to keep the lines of communication open. Unanticipated discoveries could suddenly come into plain view. These were often positive and significantly helpful, for they had the capacity to shed unexpected light on confused conditions that were shrouded in painful layers of misunderstanding and strident criticism. Typically, in sharp disagreements, the plethora of false assumptions—including labels, fuzzy conceptions, and rapid shifts into suddenly out-of-focus frames of reference—overwhelmed the ongoing effort to discover some basic point of common ground. When each one insisted on taking a totally opposite point of view, both would end up wanting to argue the point even further. Once the respective parties no longer cared about conflict resolution, they would say virtually anything that occurred to them. There may not seem to be any point in trying to arrive at a state of mutual accommodation where each party assumes that negative habits would overwhelm any interest in conducting their current affairs differently.

COMPATIBILITY OF VALUES

It is easier to foster a climate of interpersonal agreement when personal value systems are fully integrated and mutually accessible. Hence it can be quite difficult to sustain a congenial atmosphere when the value systems do not match up very well.

Agreement. R and W do not have to clarify what each one is trying to say because the other sees the topic from the same perspective. They are best friends who are majoring in psychology and share similar experiences with men. Each one hates Sigmund Freud. When sharing different views of others, they don't get into a disagreement. Each one states a point of view and concedes the other has a valid point, even though they may still end up holding differing positions. R and W have a similar approach to daily interactions with others—direct and honest yet with as much tact as possible. There is a great deal of silent, unspoken agreement. They often discover that the other person already agrees about something before a word is spoken. If one finds out about something that will affect the other one, she knows right away how the other will react to the news. R and W even had the same personality type on the Myers-type indicator. They can't remember ever disagreeing about anything.

Disagreement. K and H were raised in families with identical value systems yet their opinions and beliefs are still very different. Good-natured arguments are fairly characteristic. H often teases K about unshared ideals, and H does the same. They sometimes get into a debate over whose interests are "better" while knowing full well that neither one was about to change the opinions of the other. Even though K did not always understand H's point of view, their relationship was still amiable because they realized each one was quite different and both could accept the fact. K enjoys talking with H because it is so interesting to try to understand a perspective that is truly different from one's own. It seems as though H doesn't understand what makes K "tick" either. Sometimes the interactions are frustrating because K so much wants H to accept K's point of view. Such disagreements heighten K's sensitivity to the fact that others will not, and should not, always agree with K's own opinions and viewpoints.

Value orientations matter a great deal. Interpersonal agreements cluster around compatible value orientations. The following themes predominate. (a) *Respect:* D and E are engaged to be married; everything is based on mutual respect; they take the time to think things out and talk out personal differences; they don't dredge up old dirt, but it isn't fair to sweep things under the rug; neither believes such matters just go away; sticky issues will come up until they are finally resolved. (b) *Honesty:* W and D know a high level of honesty promotes a great deal of self-disclosure. (c) *Trust:* T and D consult one another as to what should be done next; it all comes down to trust and support; there is acceptance over little things, such as who should carry out a small task, that is, cleaning or washing dishes. There is also reference to (d) the *multiple virtues:* honesty, trust, self-worth, and independence.

Complementary value orientations facilitate the discovery of common ground. Shared beliefs and mutual respect for personal differences constitute the basis for solid human relations. When individual valuations match up quite well, interaction flows smoothly and helps form a stronger bond. There is no need for total agreement; agreement is only needed on the basic terms required to cover important issues. Consensus need not be all-inclusive for the respondents to talk freely about controversial concerns without worrying about being contradicted or further questioned.

Some respondents were exhilarated over the similarities and shared values that brought them close to one another. It is great to have someone with whom one can freely express any plan or option without fear of having to justify what one believes. Touchy issues can be raised in a calm and nonthreatening manner. No one has to struggle to clarify what is being expressed because the other sees the topic from a similar angle. Quite often, the depth of the bond was directly linked to the overall level of personal agreement present. In fact, there existed a deep bond between all who shared common value orientations, regardless of the nature of those values.

Confidence was important too. Respondents with well-matched value orientations showed a great deal of confidence in the belief that others *could* understand, accept, and value the effort to express or convey a sense of what matters in the long run. Such confidence lent predictability to present and future discussion by making individuals unafraid to be in one another's presence. Clearly, personal agreement made others feel more confident even when sharp differences were concerned. As a consequence, there was a lot of openness and mutual accessibility between those who shared similar values. Indeed, sharing went beyond factual information and included the sharing of each person's uniqueness and authenticity with the other. Physically, respondents leaned toward one another as they spoke, smiled, and made frequent eye contact while listening closely. Each one could grasp and comprehend, whether speaking or listening, while remaining sensitive to the meaning of tacit assumptions and innuendo. Others understand not only what you are saying, but what you mean, and take the time to tell you what they *think* you are trying to relate.

Severe disagreements may still lead to productive and supportive outcomes. Instead of reacting defensively, some would try and understand the other's views and in turn think about what each one might have done wrong. Indeed, it was this type of effective interchange that promoted a high level of acceptance, if not full agreement. There was added willingness to share different points of view and concede that the other had a valid point over a given point of opposition. In such a pragmatic climate, many persons were inclined to seek out one another for advice and counsel on personal problems and unresolved issues. When they did discuss sensitive or troubling matters, those who agreed over basic values took turns speaking and listening and were also quick to admit that they might be mistaken. No one wanted tension and strain to build up.

The potential for acute disagreement was minimized by listening to the other's point of view and taking it as seriously as one's own. Little things did not seem worth fighting over. Overall, when there was a core of shared values, beliefs, and attitudes, a spirit of mutuality prevailed. Renewed discovery of fresh and unexpected sources of common ground led to pleasure and delight for one another, for it also confirmed one's own values and beliefs. Validation of mutual viewpoints led to thoughtful reflection, and the broadening of one's understanding of the values, beliefs, and attitudes of each party. To live or work with someone who thought, felt, and believed as oneself made direct encounters a wonderful experience that deepened one's appreciation for self and other.

Unfortunately, however, a high level of pleasure did not hold when values, beliefs, and attitudes differed markedly. Without a central core of overlapping sensitivities, clashing perspectives became much harder to accept. There were, of course, various kinds of responses that people made when negotiating the validity of different points of view—for example, issues of policy or procedure. However, issues about what values were important in life often seemed much less negotiable. Respondents were taught to stick to their values and not to compromise on them. Partly for this reason, basic differences in attitudes, beliefs, and values created a wide spectrum of disputes of varying intensity and impact.

Disagreements have fantastic power to twist, invert, and displace value systems. As such, moral conflicts may escalate to a point where there is no technical solution in sight. It is a mistake to think that highly intelligent human beings can talk themselves into and out of virtually any sticky situation. The clash of incompatible value orientations resonates widely: J and K disagree at the deepest levels, such as religion and faith. J believes in God and K is an atheist. Person I is a pessimist, while Person T is an optimist; each one goes in circles to convince the other person, who in fact did not hear a word. The fact that they are always in debate is the reason the debate goes on and on; there is never an end and never a victor. D and W avoid talking about major issues because they are always at odds; they have reached the point where the subject in question is avoided at all costs. U and K provoke one another due to the constant clash of conflicting styles— the mix of (a) easygoing and (b) ultimately serious personalities leads to animus and hatred. A and S argue frequently; one is literal-minded while the other is the opposite, very dramatic and whimsical; each one translates back and forth in a joint exercise in futility. V and E take turns playing the devil's advocate; whenever one voices an opinion, the other will take the opposite stance; this just makes each party want to argue even more; they don't know why they bother to continue, on and on, stubborn, rigid, inflexible, and opin- ionated; even on trivial matters, what one views as the mere expression of opinion, the other will regard as highly personal criticism. O and S express clashing values; compromise cannot be reached by moving from extreme to middle ground; instead, one person just gives in, without consensus of any kind. Suppressed resentment makes the next issue even worse.

Receptivity toward personal differences was typical of those who agreed with one another most readily. Even under the best of circum- stances, however, there were desires that could, if not checked and monitored, lead to further discord. One of these was the subliminally tempting desire to change the way the other thought or felt so that his or her values, beliefs, and attitudes were closer to one's own. Each one strives to make the other see things in the same way. Greater levels of agreement were invariably desired but were not always realized, for several reasons. First, it took a lot of personal respect and appreciation to put severe disagreements into accurate and acceptable perspective. An equally important reason, however, was that it was not always easy to understand what the other was trying to say. Still another reason was that one party's desire to change the other was intense, and led to discomfort and frustration. As long as each party could control these mind-control urges, they were likely to avoid significant conflict—at least in the short term. It is not always easy to see how intense disagreement can heighten one's sensitivity to the fact that others will not, and should not, always agree with one's own opinions and viewpoints.

There were times, of course, when individuals pushed their points in an effort to get others to see things in the same way. This occurred with philosophical discussions over values and beliefs, because they rarely involved small talk and required a lot of thinking. As a rule, repeated pushing of one's point of view did little to assist in making the other agree; it also did very little to help the other understand. All that was left as a viable option was a chance to withdraw. The threat of withdrawal had become a primary way of dealing with the persistent lack of agreement. Personal philosophies might have been helpful when problem solving, but they were not a complete antidote for frustration, confusion, and strife. Some left valuable information unshared and feelings of frustration unspoken. The strategy of partial withdrawal to a superficial level was, at best, only a temporary fix.

Sometimes things just got worse. Deeply ingrained conflicts did not go away by themselves. After people held back deep-seated feelings of frustration and resentment long enough, they usually felt the need to "go verbal" with a pile of unresolved concerns. At first, the person would try to mention the issue in what seemed to be a positive way—usually by an indirect route. Sometimes, however, such attempts just did not "wash" with the person taken to be at fault. In some cases, the respective parties stopped trying to help one another understand, and they did not mind saying so. This was the time when verbal guerilla warfare turned into a savage verbal attack right out in the open. This was also the time when the wounds caused by the verbal onslaught became more severe, strengthening each person's resolve to continue the fight for as long as it took. Now everything was to be taken personally. Personal issues were obscured behind a jumble of point-making, accusation, and insult. A state of radical estrangement occurs when individuals disagree about anything and everything without end. No one makes an effort to accommodate or give in on any level. Such interactions are mostly adversarial and combative. The main concern is what one wins at someone else's expense.

SIMILARITY OF INTERESTS

Overlapping interests help to preserve all manner of friendships. The act of sharing joint interests enhances the pleasure of spending lots of time together.

Agreement. Q and Z agree on everything from life to relations. What transpires is almost scary—like interacting with oneself. They constantly hear the other say, "I know what you mean. I feel the same way." Each one knows the other isn't just saying such things to boost morale. Similar likes and dislikes make it so easy to talk and pour out one's heart. Direct contact is always rich, new, and exciting; Q and Z never cease to surprise and amaze one another. Although they haven't gotten to talk as much recently, when they do, conversation lasts for hours. Q and Z affirm and acknowledge and complement one another.

Disagreement. A and S argue frequently without reaching any solution. One big problem is due to differences in language use. S tends to be very literal and takes everything A says to be the case. A is very open, says what is on A's mind, and tries to speak as honestly as possible, but often not in "literal" terms. Differences in the explicit and implicit meanings placed on various words have led to even greater disagreement. A comes from a very open and loving family, while S never had close family ties. S's philosophy of life involves looking out for oneself and doing things for one's own gain first. A sees life quite differently. A places emphasis on how someone else will be affected by A's actions, while S feels one should not worry so much about everyone else. S thinks A thinks S gives people the benefit of the doubt too much and cares too much about what others think. Also, S's scientific way of viewing the world is very different from A's humanistic view.

It is, of course, easier to interact over similar interests than over widely divergent ones. What interests a person is not just a measure of relevance or salience per se. It is also the standard by which to determine what brings certain individuals together and drives others apart. Comparative analysis makes it possible to begin to see which types of personal interests brought people together—and, once together, which joint interests remained as sources of joy and fulfillment. Later, we will also examine which alternative interests tend to push people apart and how they count the cost.

The case studies on agreement show evidence of a strong *similarity* tendency at work. This term incorporates several domains of relevance. Respondents construe similarity across the following matters. (a) *Worldview:* P and Z view the world through similar eyes and rarely find themselves in a different place than the other. (b) *Viewpoints:* L and M have similar views about everything. (c) *Likes and dislikes:* Q and Z agree about everything; similar likes and dislikes make it very easy to talk with one another. (d) *Interests:* J and G interact with few conflicts; similar interests make conversations free and easy. (e) *Experience:* L and I find it easier to foster deep levels of agreement with someone who has shared a wide range of similar experiences. (f) *Beliefs:* N and K share the same beliefs about anything and everything. (g) *Personal philosophy:* T and E have identical conceptions of what is sacred or profane. (h) *Backgrounds:* E and R have known each other since kindergarten, with similar backgrounds, upbringing, values, goals, beliefs, and similar sets of influences. (i) *Families:* B and D have parents with similar values, family structures, gatherings, and socioeconomic class. (j) *Personal issues:* Each member has very similar opinions and views as to how issues should be solved.

The notion that opposites attract receives little support here. The idea barely shows up in the various descriptions of disagreement. The word *same* is hardly mentioned. What matters is some underlying sense of commonality. In the words of Richards (1925),

> An exceptional fund of common experience is needed, if people, in the absence of special communicative gifts, active and receptive, are to communicate, and with those gifts the success of the communication in difficult cases depends on the extent to which past similarities in experience can be made use of. (p. 179)

In effect, a sense of agreement arises from the tendency *to accentuate* a sense of similarity (resemblance) over the total magnitude of difference. In contrast, states of disagreement deflect attention away from what all individuals share in common—as members of the human race.

It is hard to say what it is that makes something similar to something else. The comparison of A to B may be ill-defined—an invitation to merely fill in the blank. When deciding what matches up well with what, there are multiple properties to consider. The objects of comparison must be brought into proper alignment to test the degree of correspondence or goodness of fit (Medin, Goldstone, & Gentner,

1993). Comprehension is a test. What matters is the degree of *respect* for which types of things fit together best. There may be some ingrained satisfaction in seeing things fit together in a coherent, pleasing, and well-grounded manner. It is not surprising, therefore, to find people who accentuate or exaggerate the magnitude of similarity (between self and other) to suit their own purposes—generally to enhance esteem, satisfaction, status, or sense of well-being (Acitelli, Douvan, & Veroff, 1993; Neimeyer & Mitchell, 1988).

In this study, references to *difference* show up in diverse types of associations. (a) *Realization:* A and B realize how unlike they are and hope disputes will not disrupt or erode relations. (b) *Viewpoints:* P and F see the world from different viewpoints. (c) *Orientations:* L and J have different secular orientations; neither one can compromise just for the sake of agreement; so they remain deadlocked when tension, friction, and strife prevail. (d) *Worldviews:* Each one tries to impose his or her own worldview on someone else, particularly when strong personalities clash. (e) *Expressive styles:* Y and B have so much in common but very different ways of expressing themselves; they talk briefly, but it is always one-sided and strictly on only one person's terms. (f) *Meanings:* Different things have different meanings to different people. (g) *Ideas:* C and D disagree because of opposed notions about how to deal with other people in situations where neither is going to change; each one knows how the other one feels, but it still makes no real difference. (h) *Excessiveness:* One is much too different from the other in outlook. (i) *Respectful:* This atmosphere is created when both assume that mutual understanding is strong enough to outweigh differences.

On the side of agreements, shared interests served as catalysts for communication. There may be no better reason for spending time together than similar interests and comparable ways of looking at the world. When good friends spend time talking to each other, they also go places and do specific things in which they both have a keen interest. Some, for example, liked staying home to watch movies. Others enjoyed doing any number of relaxing things together, including shopping, playing cards, or (inevitably) just talking for hours. Still others enjoyed karate, pool, tennis, basketball, lifting weights, and playing golf. Quite often people would inform close friends of their plans days and weeks ahead. This was true even among those who shared common interests but had not been together for some time.

Good friends get back together and re-create the magical sense that
"it's like we were never apart."

The chance to grow up together was viewed as a collective resource, a source of closeness, with similar values and interests as the
glue that kept each one happy and together. Of course, there were
times when forgetfulness or oversight caused problems within even
the closest of relationships. Friends and lovers who normally agreed
with one another suddenly and unpredictably let the information-
sharing process slide. These periods were offset, however, by the
magnitude of opportunity to share personal interests, including common artistic and professional goals, in complex and elaborated ways.
These vested interests formed the locus of conversation, while common artistic values invigorated individual skill. Inevitably, shared
projects and similar pursuits brought out the best in each member.

Agreement and cooperative work were generally held in high
esteem. Personal creativity was enriched by the depth of mutual
involvement. Ideas became richer. Anxiety was minimal. Beyond clearly
compatible sets of personal interests, respondents viewed common
values and goals as something beautiful and even spiritual in essence.
Feelings of oneness were a source of amazement and delight. During
routine interaction, or when reflecting on the uniqueness of what was
shared in common, many respondents found quiet joy within themselves. In those instances when one individual might disappoint the
other for some reason (e.g., miss a meeting), interaction took on an
aura of greater clarity, spiced with a sense of humor. A strong sense of
communication and togetherness did not suffer as a result.

The same thing was not true for individuals whose interests were
not similar or did not match up well, for very long. These individuals
almost invariably saw the other person as the reason that avoidance
or the path of least resistance was the least unfavorable course of
action. Usually periods of serious disagreement were followed by an
episode where the participants felt close once again. The prolonged
sense of growing distant after a sustained period of violated expectations lends itself to low-risk and insignificant levels of interchange later
on. Small talk, it turns out, is a strategic measure of how much
disagreement has already taken place. There is some protection in a
scene where neither party cares to know what the other takes to be
the case. Some seem to have a moody sense of powerlessness and
boredom. So what was of potential value and worth was reduced in

(psychological) size or weight through the application of the hidden agenda, an invisible mechanism of devaluation and discredit in the eyes of the beholder.

Not all respondents sounded so hardened against those with different interests, perspectives, and outlooks. Some realized they genuinely wanted closer relations, and tried hard to reduce levels of disagreement and to (re)discover areas of common ground. Despite the risks, heavily invested individuals persisted in actively looking for ways in which to discover areas of common interest. In some cases, however, the offended parties seemed unresponsive to even the most sustained efforts on behalf of someone else to minimize deprivation and loss.

DEPTH OF INVOLVEMENT

There is a depth dimension in human relations that fosters strong levels of interpersonal agreement. The subject becomes a central theme in the following instances.

Agreement. W and E enjoy their time together because they agree about so many things and can talk about matters of great personal concern. Conversations develop from superficial topics into very deep, sensitive issues. They find it easy to share personal issues because they have many of the same ideas, opinions, and attitudes. There is a great deal of mutual respect during conversations filled with good sound advice and solid reasons for any given course of action. W and E enjoy simply having fun and spending time with one another. They find the same things funny and can always make each other laugh. Time spent together is very rewarding. Although they agree on many things, not all goes smoothly. W seems to misunderstand E quite often, attributing selfish motives for courses of actions that actually do not have them. Agreement and understanding are not the same; the former does not imply the latter.

Disagreement. M and N disagree strongly. Usually N becomes impatient and feels the need to explain everything right down to the last detail. N tends to speak louder, faster than usual, and the pitch of N's voice goes up. N interrupts M frequently; eventually N becomes very defensive and tries to strike back. Sometimes N will ignore what M is saying and make a hasty generalization. N concentrates on the magnitude of difference rather than the potential for sensing similarity. Because M disagrees over one detail, N assumes that M will disagree on other aspects as well.

Shared experiences help people care more deeply about one another. Those who shared similarities over important issues often helped each other through the day. They found agreement on mundane issues, such as who would clean the apartment or wash the dishes. Related issues of when guests could visit, or who would use the bathroom at certain times, were discussed and resolved quite easily. Perhaps most rewarding for the respondents was the ease with which they made these day-to-day decisions. One is struck by the light atmosphere that prevailed during episodes of decision making where no one was ever nervous about bringing up personal issues to discuss.

I believe that it is this sense of ease and compatibility that, over time, encouraged individuals to share personal styles and life experiences in a more open manner. Indeed, those who discovered this dynamic sense of similarity allowed themselves to help one another on deeper levels. There was help through various difficulties where the respective parties tried to find solutions together and, in so doing, to acquire a better understanding of one another. Such realization led to the discovery that no one was actually alone. Each must deal with obstacles and learn to survive in spite of them.

It matters how various individuals resolved personal differences. Problem solving became critically important in those situations where disputes centered on a single theme. Each participant would assign priority to preferences and come up with the same pivotal issue over which a climate of opposition and divergence prevailed. Such critical matters tend to make or break close ties with other people. They show up strikingly in disagreement-making activity but not in agreement-making episodes. It takes time to share ingrained differences, work them through, and reach the highest level of consensus possible. This openness to alternative ways of seeing things may have led to mutual compromise. A process of give-and-take, along with mutual effort to increase personal understanding and shared decision making, often led to the most effective and acceptable course of action.

A sense of in-depth involvement was viewed as intrinsically valuable. As a further consequence of learning how to devise a working set of problem-solving skills, personal relations became more fully integrated and aligned than before. Mutual admiration and respect evolved into a highly refined sense of openness, receptivity, and spontaneity. Respondents who fit this profile sounded like fascinated observers as they watched the development of their affiliations with significant others. They made a distinction between a past in which very little was said to one another and a present characterized by much greater talking and sharing. Such high-quality interaction enriched self-esteem and self-worth for some time afterward because each party, in effect, confirmed the other's outlook and worldview. A sustaining sense of validity and validation coincided. In metaphorical terms, the reconstruction of what respondents shared was not unlike a sailor who scans the horizon and suddenly sees a point of land; just beyond the point is a lighthouse, and the promise of people to care about his safety and well-being.

There was also a strong sense of the importance of the time spent together. In caring, committed relations, proximity to significant others is of genuine importance. Particularly after long periods of absence, the interactants would spend time together and revel in each other's news, stories, insight, and decisions. Most important was the speaker's conviction of the authenticity of the listener's interest in, and understanding of, the one who spoke. When interactants achieved such authentic understanding, they became more deeply attached to one another. In this context, problem solving seemed to be a by-product of the primary concern—the quality and depth of what transpired.

For those who found widespread agreement together, life was considerably enriched. They shared themselves and their experiences more deeply with one another, and in the process learned much more about themselves and those with whom they were sharing their lives. Mutual support sometimes took the form of solving mundane, day-to-day issues; as a growing sense of communal identification evolved for each party, however, they were also able to empathize with one another at a much deeper and more significant level. These communicative processes led to the realization that each party had to struggle with the harshness of life. Indeed, the realization promoted the sense that there was a great deal of common ground to explore. Hence many made much more of an effort to be open, receptive, and attentive to the thoughts, feelings, and actions of each other. Inevitable difficulties posed no problems that could not be solved. As a result, individuals felt they were allowed to be themselves, and to move ahead in life with greater courage and confidence.

The adverse effects of sharp disagreement are most pronounced when there is also some degree of misunderstanding at work. One way in which this can occur is when one person does not feel able to share his or her point of view in any manner, shape, or form. The very assumption can be a stumbling block, which displaces formerly common ground and leaves a person believing that it has become very difficult to talk with the other. One's view may not be valued or deemed worthy of consideration. Without some clarification about the other's motives, the person in question would often assume that two-way communication would be implausible or virtually impossible to carry out. Even worse is where effort to establish sustaining conditions is met with a response that intimates the possibility of countermeasures in the form of verbal attack. The notion increased the risk of misinterpretation because behaviors such as these tended to encourage similar behaviors from the other person.

As anger and frustration increased, there was a growing tendency to focus exclusively on the magnitude of differences rather than keeping at least one eye firmly focused on the degree of similarity or common ground both still shared. This negative skew often resulted because individuals generalized disagreement in one area to the collective assumption that disagreement would be present in all areas. At the core of these problems is the reticence to talk with one another—a reality that increased the extent to which uninformed assumptions replaced more objective information. One can almost feel the weight of perpetual disagreement that continued to impose emotional pain on each member. Disillusionment seemed to be a tacitly stated outcome that promoted unrelenting finger-pointing and criticizing, during even minor disputes over inconsequential or trivial matters. It is not difficult to believe that, without some resolution of such chronic states of disagreement in sight, the individuals in question would continue to suffer or eventually decide to leave one another. A vague sense of troublesome forces lurks just below the surface.

Carelessness registered, as things got worse, in the tendency to displace blame and to dismiss any personal responsibility for the damage that was taking place. What often resulted was a blaming, attacking stance in which one denied all blame and accused the other of all that had gone wrong. When personal relations sink to this level of carelessness, it is nothing short of a state of verbal warfare taking place. Assumptions on both sides are distorted and lead to increased anxiety and higher levels of animosity. What was most discouraging was the probability that future involvements would continue to be divisive, negatively oriented, adverse, and ultimately alienating. The prospect of helping one another, resolving differences, strengthening close ties, and believing in the intrinsic value of what transpires is hardly a likely outcome for individuals who are entangled in this kind of interactive difficulty.

QUALITY OF INTERACTION

High levels of personal agreement were positively correlated with the total quality of the interaction. As the frequency and duration of disagreement increased, the quality of interaction decreased in turn. This finding has been replicated across a variety of marital and romantic settings (McGonagle, Kessier, & Gotlib, 1993; McGonagle, Kessier, & Shilling, 1992). Personal accounts make frequent reference to the depth and substance of personal encounters. The following are particularly striking.

Agreement. J and I share many things in common. This broadly based sense of common ground is very helpful. Communication is very deep and detailed on many subjects. Because they know one another so well, J and I have been able to analyze some topics in depth without a lot of explaining of trivial definitions and meanings. They also have a similar sense of humor, so that when kidding around, neither one has to say "just kidding" or "sorry, that was a little joke." It is always understood. When a problem occurs, either mutually or to one party, they either mutually agree or can offer relevant advice to each other. J and I agree on so many things primarily because of such extensive knowledge of each other's personalities, characters, lifestyles, and backgrounds; such honesty and openness make the relationship and tendency to agree very strong.

Disagreement. A and K are friends who don't agree on the state of their relationship. K demands a great deal of validation, which causes a knee-jerk reaction in A. Also, K displays a high level of confidence but feels inwardly that other people don't recognize his success; he makes comments like this one: "I can't wait until I can go where my friends understand me; I hate all my friends here." Of course, A is one of his "friends here" and that strikes a strong chord. A and K disagree with each other often, even on things they agree on; both have strong personalities and neither one wants to concede anything at all. A feels that if A gives an inch, K will use it to K's advantage instead of giving in a little on something else. Similarly, if K gives in on something, A will use it to A's advantage instead of reaching for a compromise. Much of the problem is that they like each other a lot and want the other person to be an image of the perfect person. K wants A to be more ambitious and A wants K to be more empathic toward other friends; A is content with his ambitions and K feels there is no need to be empathic toward those who don't extend the same courtesy. Even though K is one of A's closest friends, they have to limit the time spent together to avoid hurting one another. A thinks that K would not agree with any of this evaluation at all.

There was a lot of enthusiasm for a mutual sense of common ground. Respondents were enthusiastic because they saw themselves reflected in one another. Each party delighted in mutual understanding that could often be reached with only minimal use of words and gestures. They felt comfortable because they shared, like country club members, a sense of mutual membership in a way of life. The same neighborhoods, the same vocabulary, the same identities—the same everything—became the focus of their thinking and feeling, saying, and doing.

As one might expect, such interpersonal realities fostered a sense of identification and well-being. This was because the quality of interaction seemed directly related to quality of life, emotional health, clarity of thought, depth of understanding, and generosity of spirit. A broadly based sense of common ground was very helpful. Conversations just seemed to click. There was an in-depth sense of equivalence in matters of perspective and viewpoint. It is no small feat to be able to talk about trivial matters and find mutual connections. A sense of what is constant and consistent over time is a delightful reminder of unfulfilled potentialities.

Such revelations should come as no surprise, of course. Personal agreement, it seemed, had its foundation in an extensive awareness of each individual with a separate entity, personality, lifestyle, and background. A communal atmosphere develops slowly over time. Personal problems seem to become less massive when there is regular discussion of one another's feelings. Conversation examined these sensitive feelings and helped each party to make decisions about them. High-quality interaction generated a surplus of positive affect, particularly joy and happiness. Here contentment was used to indicate a high level of meaningfulness. Such relationships were flexible, intricate, and expansive. The sense of awe and wonder came in part not because life was always wonderful but because the respective parties encouraged one another under difficult circumstances as well as under easy ones. Take the bad with the good. What is right, by definition, is relative to what is wrong.

In contrast, severe disagreements caused much sorrow. Those with dissimilar backgrounds seemed to have the greatest difficulty relating well together. Unresolved friction, stress, and strife led to hurt feelings, fewer expressions of civility and cordiality, passive avoidance, and conversation that was no longer focused on substantive issues and core concerns. It is in just such circumstances of inarticulateness that people are prone to feel that they don't have much to say to one another. There was little to support the notion that people love to disagree and derive great pleasure from it (Kotthoff, 1993). Typically, the presence of explicit disagreement is sufficient to start up attempts to achieve agreement, at least in friendly conversations with an aim toward consensus (Bilmes, 1988; Pomerantz, 1984).

Protracted disagreement was often associated with a lack of flexibility in style of interaction. Different orientations may polarize people so that no single party can compromise merely for the sake of reaching an agreement. Such a possibility is ruled out in advance. It may be too high a price to pay. Even without anger and insult during conversation, each party may be locked into an adverse set of conditions that were unfulfilling because of all the tension, friction, and strife. Lack of flexibility created an uncomfortable climate that made withdrawal look like an appealing alternative. The decision to withhold one's most cherished thoughts and feelings might prevail over the risk of another painful confrontation with no resolution in sight. Usually it was the other person who was held to be mostly to blame for the tension and discomfort that still existed. Lack of flexibility meant that many would not see beyond this kind of perceptual error to the actual problems that each one brought to the table.

The urge to reach out may be neutralized or disregarded. When disagreement ruled, people tried out various ways to cope or compensate. Some tried to keep things going by constantly arguing about personal issues of one sort or another. Others, however, tried to accomplish the same thing by withholding vital information they believed would only promote ongoing conflict. When the resolution of differences seemed impossible, individuals often made valiant attempts to keep their opinions to themselves. Let other people have their say but keep one's own views to oneself at all costs. This repressive urge is understandable, because the expression of problematic points of view may not clarify or otherwise promote harmony but instead stress the magnitude of differences construed as firm obstacles.

At times, lack of flexibility can deteriorate into simple obstinacy. Often there was an unbending determination to keep up a constant state of competition and rivalry. It is curious that people who felt this way could often be close friends. They may have liked being with each other a lot, but had a hidden agenda resulting from the disparity in how each party wanted the behavior of the other to be manifest. The price such people paid for their obsessive demands was constant tension. Some needed to periodically separate themselves to avoid saying or hearing hurtful things. Sometimes, however, the unyielding tendency to change the other went beyond the humor that typically acted as a buffer. Verbal obstinacy can push reason out of the way with finger-pointing accusations and self-righteous indignation. Signs of frustration and alienation occurred more often because of the surplus negative slant that gave rise to adverse feelings, attitudes, and behaviors in repeated spirals and cycles.

EQUALITY OF INFLUENCE

Agreement. K and L share common assumptions, similar interests, and comparable ways of looking at the world. Lines of communication are always completely open—neither one holds anything back or feels uncomfortable discussing any topic. Knowing that they have the greatest respect for one another, constructive criticism is welcome. K and L share similar views on politics, religion, and most areas of public controversy. They confront areas of personal disagreement in the same fashion, and both parties adhere to quick and thorough methods of conflict resolution. Instead of stepping around areas of possible disagreement, they deal with them head on and enjoy the process of trying to understand the other person's perspective. K can tell L anything and (thinks) L can do the same. They never judge or condemn each other's actions or beliefs. L always looks forward to conversations with K and, the majority of the time, comes away feeling very satisfied. Success stems from (a) equality (lack of power struggles), (b) shared ideals of what constitutes respect, and (c) encouragement for feelings of self-worth and trust. L could never imagine having trust in K as a confidante violated. These attributes create an open system in which alternative points of view are encouraged, discussed, and evaluated.

Disagreement. S and Q are good friends. Nonetheless, S views Q as a control freak who manipulates people and tries to do the same with S. Both S and Q speak their minds and deal with most problems just fine, but when they go out together the trouble starts. Set plans will be changed before S arrives. Q makes other people wait for hours; S will speak to Q when this happens, but Q will get defensive and angry. Now that both are attending different universities, each is learning new things and meeting new people. When Q sees S, she crams all this stuff down S's throat; it is OK as long as S goes along with it, but there is a lot of disagreement because Q gets angry when S does not want to do what Q wants. If S tries to explain, Q can never see S's point; it gets irritating, but S begrudgingly admits that Q is still her friend.

It is no wonder, then, that high-quality performance should facilitate more equal access to available resources. An explicit stance helps to sustain a sense of shared construction and complex elaboration. Openness flourishes in close relations where there is little risk of betrayal and vulnerability to hurtful experiences such as criticism or domination. When we perceive such risks in our interactions with others, there is a tendency to close up, and the benefits of free and open deliberation cease to be available.

Those individuals who agreed with each other were likely to understand, respect, and trust one another as they moved ahead with their own lives. Individuals flourished where the mutual expression of diverse points of view was encouraged, discussed, and evaluated rather than suppressed or criticized. For those who made the effort to promote constructive agreements, openness and respect formed the basis of emotional health and personal well-being. For the fortunate, clear and articulate forms of self-expression often meant that it was safe to tell one another anything, and to abdicate any fearful desire to condemn the other's actions or beliefs.

Equality of influence was usually present when individuals genuinely confirmed one another's viewpoints. Equality of influence, at least as an ideal, distributes dividends and rewards as widely and fairly as possible. The process places checks on the urge to form power imbalances. Equality of influence encouraged feelings of safety, openness, and well-being and facilitated mutual comprehension of personal experience. Disputes fostered struggles for power and control over what transpired. Implicit in many power struggles are conflicting claims over what is better or worse, right or wrong, superior or inferior. A self-inflated sense of superiority is, in fact, a prime source of fuel for painful disagreement. Interactants seemed to be playing a game that puts one of them at the center of attention. When the other would question such calculating strategies, the offending person became self-righteous to the point of anger and indignation. The power game allowed the underdog to take on a superior attitude for the same purpose—getting an edge in the moral priority of the self in matters involving joint benefit.

Over time, of course, contentious attitudes become habitual ways of viewing and dealing with others. The superior view of the self becomes permanently established, and others are treated accordingly. Antagonizing moves cause injury to others, who feel that they deserve better treatment. People are left to hold negative feelings in check or to let them spill over into conversation, depending on the level of stress and friction at the time. Those who are prone to chronic disagreement complain loudly about the lack of respect. Disdain was designed to comfort the hurt feelings that disrespect brought with it. All too frequently, however, oppositional moves pushed interactants farther apart until they operated at opposite ends of the spectrum.

It was particularly sad to see close ties between family members or coworkers become so strained that, over time, the bond became weakened to the point where one became increasingly alienated from the other. What was so dismaying was that these individuals cared for one another, and wanted to live and work together. Usually, they had excellent reasons for wanting their relations to flourish; unfortunately, they defined everything they were or did together within extremely limiting and problematic definitions of right or wrong. Seen through such narrow and exclusive frameworks, interactants lost track of the larger and more complete picture that actually described them individually, and as caretakers of one kind or another.

Many lovers' quarrels can be attributed to shortsightedness. It is possible to get so caught up in the frenzy of the moment that one loses all sense of the larger perspective. What was terribly disturbing about such loving fights was that each interactant saw the unequal distribution of power and influence as being *reason enough* to think of the relationship as a war zone. Words such as *domineering* and *surrendering* give the mythic impression that battles had been going on for a long time, with both sides losing what they most valued in life. However, the issue of power and control, divorced from considerations of care and affection, was never far from the center of concern. The price paid in the loss of closeness and familiarity was a high one. Severely troubled relations did not retain a spirit of tender forgiveness after people experienced long periods of suffering.

FUTURE PLANS

Agreement. K and N are so alike that it is almost scary. They are attracted to the same types of people and work as a team when talking with others; they play off one another, love to joke around and be sarcastic. Both are always up for anything, but K draws the line at the exact place that N does. K and N don't have the type of relationship where one completely dominates the other; they strive to stay on common ground. K went to visit N in Alabama for spring break at Auburn University and realized how differences—political, social, and religious—can greatly affect the quality of interaction: N's roommates have very different political and religious views, and relations with them are very superficial. Neither one wanted to step on any toes, so N told K what to say and what not to say. K and N look forward to renewed conversation about serious matters without confronting personal differences.

There was little mention of the likelihood of future interaction in the disagreement section. This should come as no surprise. It is almost as if the prevalence of bickering and dispute cancels out the plausibility of planning similar courses of action in the distant future. Some reflect about how they might have altered the downward spiral of some current mode of questionable activity. Getting out of troubled situations was a frequently cited theme in respondents' reconstructed interactions. My conclusion is that the prospect of engagement in future interactions belongs to those who have taken good care of their past interactions.

CHAPTER 6

Understanding/ Misunderstanding

A t issue in misunderstanding is the possibility of minimizing misunderstanding and achieving a genuine understanding of other people. We must assume the risk of misunderstanding, and of being misunderstood, particularly in situations where it seems there is little or nothing that can be done. Perhaps a useful starting point is a tentative admission of our own powerlessness to create perfect understanding, free of errors, mistakes, and noise. It takes mutual struggle to dredge up the honesty to acknowledge that "I am not able to fully grasp the intent of the meanings you want me to grasp and comprehend." Such an acknowledgment provides a small but crucial opportunity for change that becomes available. Now there is renewed opportunity to experience a sense of healing and relief arising from the acceptance of the fallibility and limitations of our senses and thought habits—and of our conceptions generally. This opportunity can be used to look and listen rather than to be content to correct any misunderstanding of other people. In so doing, one may introduce an element of tenderness and forgiveness into turgid criticism and spiteful indictment of an interchange with adverse consequences. Possibilities open up as alternative conceptions can be shared. Suddenly there are new methods of inquiry to explore.

Consider a conundrum. Do basic disagreements lead to serious misunderstandings or is it actually the other way around? It's a tricky question for several reasons. The distinction between cause (antecedent) and effect (consequence) can be much too messy to figure out. Moreover, causal explanations cut two ways at once. What we assume to be the cause of something may be simply a delayed response to something that occurred previously (Pitt, 1988). Some respondents think they disagree *because* they misunderstand, whereas others invert the order of what comes first or last.

One thing seems clear. It is often easier to verify whether individuals agree or disagree than to figure out whether they actually do understand one another. As a rule, respondents have the greatest difficulty in reconstructing complex encounters where misunderstandings prevail. Public disagreements are self-evident—observable and demonstrative—whereas complex misunderstandings may operate below the surface and beyond anyone's current grasp. As a rule, serious misinterpretations extend beyond the scope of simple disagreements. It is not just a matter of whether differences and divergences outweigh similarities and convergences. Something far deeper is involved. Disagreements provide renewed opportunities to work through personal differences and move on. Misunderstandings, in contrast, require greater effort to reconcile incompatible or contradictory ways of making sense of things. Consequently, acts of miscommunication may reflect surface disagreements, deep-seated misunderstandings, or an uneven combination of both (Kenny, 1988; Semin & Gergen, 1990).

The concept of understanding is subject to the possibility of misunderstanding. There is no way around this humble admission. No other type of conception is worthy of consideration or defense in a dynamic social context. People get into trouble when they misunderstand what it means to grasp and comprehend the expressed activity of other creatures like themselves. The tendency toward mutual misinterpretation stems from misguided beliefs that lead all too easily to the conviction that the ideas we signify by our words and gestures are the same (coincidental) as others signify by the use of those same words and gestures (T. Taylor, 1992). Hence there is a widespread tendency, and great potential, for *perceived* agreement and understanding to be greater than is actually the case, particularly between close friends or long-term acquaintances (Monsour, Betty, & Kurzweil, 1993; Saidla, 1990).

Relational ties become collusive when the respective parties agree to act *as if* they agree or understand far more than they actually do (Laing et al., 1966). The illusion of complete consensus may safeguard and protect the most idealized versions of what is at stake. Moreover, it is tempting to assume that one's own personality is apparent to others, even during brief encounters with strangers. Also related is the tendency to trust generalized impressions of people to the point where moments of inattentiveness and lapses of concentration on current feedback reduce the accuracy of unique impressions even further (Malloy & Albright, 1990; Malloy & Janowski, 1992; Malloy & Kenny, 1986).

As a corrective, it is useful to think of human understanding as an incomplete and unfinished project. The process of interpretation is potentially infinite and inexhaustible rather than fixed or final, without further opportunity for revision or reinterpretation. It is also subject to endless reevaluation and cross-checking, bounded by tradition and context, and goes in circles rather than in a unilinear process or bold leap from ignorance to truth (Bauman, 1978). Hence even an interpretation that hits the mark is a matter of how much and what aspects of activity are brought under control and made available for further scrutiny (T. Taylor, 1992). In contrast, the search for universal, timeless principles, devoid of reference to particular contexts, leads only to a dead end. Toulmin (1972) locates relevant subject matter in the changing skills and abilities that individuals use to acquire and exercise a grasp of relevant concepts that facilitate ever more exacting methods of rational appraisal and criticism.

An act of understanding is precisely that—a construed action. It is, therefore, not a simple matter (yes/no or on/off) but an unfolding process, always on the move, never fully achieved, only partially shared, and construed from vague fragments of negotiation (H. Anderson & Gollishan, 1988; Shotter, 1993). So the critical question is whether the achievement is to be measured against obtainable and realistic standards or merely abstract, pure, or idealized notions, immune to falsification (Rommetveit, 1980, 1988; Wold, 1992). As a case in point, the puritanical search for a so-called politically correct way of speaking, now running amok on many college campuses, is based on a false set of linguistic premises. Because it is so oppressive and intolerant of free speech, the illusion of (political) purity and (ideological) correctness is liable to foster true believers, intellectual bigots, and self-righteous zealots who perpetrate the fiction that the meaning of an action can be reduced to a fixed idea (or vocabulary). Fanaticism, whether political, religious, or scientific, demands strict loyalty and blind obedience by the faithful to a particular way of speaking as sovereign or infallible.

The first step in freeing oneself from the correctness fallacy (in language use) is to step down from what amounts to a self-appointed throne. In this sense, it is better to be wise than smart. Wisdom is acquired through the realization that the whole of human reality is infinitely more than what can be said about it. As Madison (1982) states,

> Meaning is never perfect and univocal but always the product of our imperfect human understanding, which eagerly strives after meaning and, in its frustration at never finding it whole, posits identity—and definition—as a limiting case of its own vague, analogical, metaphorical way of grappling with things. (p. 127)

There is a reciprocal relation between the ability *to* understand and to *be* understood at the same time. It makes little sense, ordinarily, to express things in an idiom that others will not be able to grasp and comprehend. Therefore, conventional discursive practices are undertaken with a minimal presumption of some likelihood of success. Dascal and Berenstein (1987) refer to a duty or obligation to construe actions in light of their intended purposes. This makes the search for meaning a pragmatic as well as a semantic enterprise. The process unfolds directly, at the level of utterance, and indirectly, by working out, for oneself, implicit meanings, particularly when the latter differs from the former. The fallible or probabilistic aspects of such expectancies are often overlooked. The task of comprehension requires explicit interpretation, whereas grasping involves a more intuitive sense of how to work through the underlying implications. Failure to grasp the many purposes of expressive action will produce a kind of misunderstanding (indirect and elusive) that differs significantly from miscalculations associated with an inappropriate application of practical logic or reasoning.

The quality of human understanding is a reflection of the organization of conversation. There is a pattern of sound (talking) and silence (listening). Those who talk a great deal are likely to be quite confident of their ability to express things clearly. Talkative persons are prone to see themselves as dominant, self-accepting, powerful, self-assured, and relatively free of concerns about anxiety and self-esteem. Reticent persons, in contrast, not only talk less but feel more anxious, powerless, and isolated. Moreover, talkative subjects are inclined to think that they are better understood during brief interviews than those who view themselves as less verbally active. As a result, misunderstandings have a greater disruptive impact on the frequency, duration, and rate of verbal behavior than do mere disagreements. Finally, talkative persons take more credit for successfully transmitted utterances and attribute disproportionate blame to others for misinterpreting questionable lines of action (Arnston, Mortensen, & Lustig, 1980; Mortensen & Arnston, 1974; Mortensen, Arnston, & Lustig, 1977).

Subdivisions in this chapter revolve around central themes in respondents' reconstructed interactions. Preliminary analysis showed that basic distinctions could be identified along eight dimensions of consideration: (a) recognition of intent, (b) multiple perspective taking ability, (c) warrants and reasons, (d) tests of comprehension, (e) code switching, (f) synchrony and alignment of communicative styles, (g) working through problematic concerns, and (h) mutual struggle to minimize miscommunication.

RECOGNITION OF INTENT

In the first chapter, a state of effective communication was equated with the capacity and willingness to translate tacit, covert matters into overt, explicit form. We are struck by the variety of techniques and strategies that people employ to foster and maintain a strong sense of connection with others. Also impressive are the basic mechanisms associated with conditions that only make matters worse.

The problem begins with the recognition of underlying desires, purposes, intentions, and goals. We have already traced some basic pitfalls. There is no surefire way to read another's mind. What someone intends may not be obvious to anyone else. The meaning of behavior can be revealed or covered up. Sometimes we don't have direct access to our own intentions, much less those of others. Moreover, there is nothing to prevent the presumption that one knows why others act the way they do, even if the hunch is wrong or out of place. What we make of others' purposes may not be taken for granted as accurate or correct, with no or little effort at reality-checking along the way. Finally, it is as easy to misread as to construe in line with what others recognize as the main intention behind a given course of action.

We know that personal intent and mutual understanding go together, although not always in a neat and tidy way. Often there is just an intuitive sense of what self/other has in mind. At the center of much shared action is the ability to identify unstated urges, often without a word being spoken. This tendency shows up in a number of ways.

Understanding. R and B respond well to virtually any shift in mood or change from day to day. They share a similar range of moods quite often: joy, happiness, laughter, sadness, anger, and calm. Somehow they seem to know how to act when one feels one way while the other feels quite another. Both work hard to alleviate bad moods by leaving friendly notes, treats in the fridge, or cards on the desk. Usually R knows when to leave B alone, when B is in a mood to get picked on, or needs support. It is a result of making the effort plus natural rapport. Rarely do they get upset with one another. The common accent is on having fun: playing backgammon, studying, listening to music, or going out for a drink; it takes time and effort to achieve a spirit of genuine care and concern.

Misunderstanding. J and V fail to grasp the intentions, values, and ideas of one another as a matter of course. The severity of misunderstandings allows no room to step back and gain a better picture of what transpires. Preexisting frames of reference are automatically imposed on every little thing. One party will offer a response that fails to put oneself in the other's shoes or to account for why the other feels a certain way. Daily interactions are largely limited to matters of surface agreement but still ignore larger, underlying questions because of the pervasiveness of unresolved misunderstandings that do exist.

Now that we have examined personal accounts on both sides of the ledger, it is possible to focus on what is at stake. It does matter how well one can identify and recognize the purposes and intentions behind other people's actions. The quality of face-to-face interaction can be greatly enhanced by paying close attention and staying clearly focused. An intuitive grasp of what is implied is something to be achieved through hard work and concerted effort rather than something merely presumed or inherited as a special gift, trait, or attribute. Psychological expectations do matter. Some are predisposed to extend the benefit of doubt, take nothing for granted, and look only for the best of intentions. However, under less favorable conditions, there is a tendency to supply other people's intentions for them, usually with a negative or threatening overtone. The tenor of prior interaction sets the tone for what one is inclined to anticipate about the future.

The recognition of personal intent and mutual understanding go together somehow, although not always in a neat and tidy way. At the center of such dynamic action is the ability to identify unstated urges, often without a word being spoken. Often the observer is in a better position to recognize the intentions behind the action than the one who initiates it. There are any number of good reasons why people should be open to alternative readings of their behavior. Intentions may operate at the periphery of awareness. Although we cannot observe our own actions being performed, someone else can. I may not always be aware of my flushed cheeks, forehead wrinkles, pupil dilation, or rapid eye blinks when I speak, but you (as observer) can be. Hence it makes good sense to rely on one another to achieve a mutual understanding of any improvised course of action. This makes it possible to grasp another's intent even if the accompanying words and gestures do not convey the actual intent.

Overall, it takes considerably more effort to recognize personal intentions where protracted misunderstandings prevail. The sheer complexity of things often gets in the way. Individuals may come into close proximity with unique expectations about what is entailed and fail to express or convey unspoken urges with accuracy and precision. The longer they wait, the harder it becomes to bring such matters up. One party assumes the bills must be paid on time; another would just as soon wait—as long as possible. One person expects quiet during nighttime, while another insists on pulsating sound and light. To one a house is a home, while to another it is more like a hotel. So one party resorts to leaving passively aggressive notes of instruction and injunction while the other pretends not to notice from a stance of anxiety and fear. Because neither party knows how to deal with the mess they have made together, there is no genuine understanding of what to do or how to start anew. Under such circumstance, there is a global tendency to lose touch with other people's intentions over time. The failure to grasp the intentions of another can be all-embracing.

Mutual effort to fulfill individual intentions can lead to greater appreciation or respect for shared efforts to grasp the complexities of individual desire, intention, and purpose. It may also diminish any fear or apprehension to share what one had in mind, without cover-up, pretense, or deception. Finally, there is the virtue of validation, even when one can't grasp the expressed motives behind someone else's behavior. There may be a need for greater tolerance of misreading or inability to extract a sense of the reason behind what transpires.

Effective action can be best sustained among fluent and articulate individuals who know what to express and what to leave out. Unspoken convergences may be accomplished by staying in touch with hidden rules. There seems to be a connection between the skill to make implicit notions explicit and heavy reliance on nonverbal cues, without *having* to spell everything out in precise detail. Still, there is a great deal of expressive freedom coupled with an absence of compulsion or necessity to elaborate in either mode of self-expression.

The recognition of personal intent is closely associated with the identification of particular states of mind or prevailing mood changes. It is an advantage to be able to anticipate what broad courses of action will lead to particular types of mood change. Severe forms of reality-testing occur when moods change rapidly or unexpectedly shift toward the extreme.

Good observers rely heavily on body language, style, slant, and skew. They remain sensitive to the meaning of silence, the unspoken, what is left out, eye contact, facial expression, physical proximity, mood recognition, and *current* state or condition of another's well-being. Things click. Other things just happen. The fact that so many respondents can finish one another's sentences is an indication of strong empathy and a surplus of positive affect. In short, we see a profile of *mutual* effort to establish *individual* intent and a spirit of tolerance and patience with those segments of interchange that may not go smoothly or remain friction-free. Moreover, it is important to recognize that other people do things for complex reasons; some are unintended or totally garbled. There is much value in tolerating what goes wrong as a means to make it right. Staying in touch with the flow of intended meanings is coupled with an almost mystical faith in the ability to read interpretive actions constructively.

The cost of misreading others' intentions varies greatly. It is not always easy to separate the ability to make good sense of specific modes of action from the larger capacity to understand another person as a distinct entity. From this perspective, momentary lapses or minor miscalculations may not mean a thing. Sometimes misconstrued actions are subject to revision or subsequent alteration. At other times, certain frames of reference may be disputed or reclaimed. Of greatest concern is where interactants get stuck in faulty ways of making sense—of purpose and intent—and not be able to work their way out.

Respondents kept track of accumulated harms and injuries. There was a central tendency toward overreaction where interactants became too highly involved in what they are trying to express. In effect, they take themselves too seriously and hold others to overly demanding or unrealistic standards of account. The more complicated interaction becomes, the harder it is to deal with the entangled inferences and implications. If pressing issues are not resolved, the quality of interaction may deteriorate further. Those who lose touch with the underlying needs and desires of others may find subsequent interaction both bothersome and burdensome. Adverse effects include violated expectations, aimlessness, confusion, criticism, hurt feelings, a spirit of defensiveness, threat, and mistrust, and diminished optimism about the prospects of finding a better way. Over time, people may acquire a generalized apprehension about the prospect of having their intentions misconstrued, particularly when routinely translated into predetermined and unflattering characterizations. Miscommunication as a way of life seems pretty futile after all.

MULTIPLE PERSPECTIVE TAKING

Individual actions can be interpreted from alternative standpoints. It is important to be in a position to take as many of those operative frameworks into account within the shortest period of time.

We have already suggested a central mechanism consisting of the lingering, intuitive grasp of some unspoken urge. One may speak of an uncanny sense of another's position or place within the hierarchy of a given social situation. Under favorable conditions, one may become *almost* one with any other. What matters most decisively is the capacity and willingness to take into account the particular frame of reference of everyone else. Such moments help reduce conflict and promote a larger measure of comfort (in dialogue). In this domain, various personal problems can be addressed directly with no hesitation. It is a place where both parties know they will understand in any case.

A favorable linguistic atmosphere makes it easier to talk with one another. As a consequence, individual goals may be more readily achieved. Hence a state or condition of mutual understanding serves different purposes at different times—to entertain, solve problems, or simply fulfill the need to have someone to talk to about things. For these reasons, a tradition of successful interaction may become highly valued. We have selected case studies where acts of multiple perspective taking promote and foster a linguistic atmosphere of mutual understanding.

> *Understanding.* J and Q have been together for a long time and now know each other very well. Each one has a deep understanding of what is important to the other. J knows Q better than anyone else does and Q knows J better too. They share things never said or told to anyone else, and both show sides of themselves that others never see. J and Q know how to identify feelings and moods, and they appreciate and respect one another's beliefs and attitudes. Each one has acquired a deep appreciation for the unique contribution of the other.

> *Misunderstanding.* J and K don't have a chance to let the "meanings" sink in. Each one has become quite good at giving up when sick and tired of fighting and too stubborn to hear the other person's view. Usually fights end up in a fiasco of yelling and then there is no interaction for days on end. The main reason they don't let one another speak their piece is the matter of one-perspective goals. Often J will find herself regressing more and more into K's views of "my way or the highway." Often J is the only one who wishes for any change. Every

year it gets harder and harder to try to understand one another. Since J and K have drifted apart and now live separate lives, it is more difficult to know the other's real intentions. When they do fight, it is so easy to throw put-downs, which only produce more arguments. Finally, J and K never talk about the problem at hand. They are sure to move off the subject, even to the point where neither one realizes why they began fighting in the first place.

Once again, the contrasts in conditions are quite stark. Three types of interpretive sensibilities are at stake. The first is the capacity and willingness to take other people's perspectives into full account. This requires an intuitive grasp of someone's interpretive slant, usually based on appeal to shared history or the opportunity to construct one. It also presupposes the identification of expressed intent plus recognition of the other's point of view as an alternative to one's own. Notice how those who understand make repeated reference to what it takes to "put oneself in another's shoes" or to "see" things from the perspective of someone else. In contrast, protracted misunderstanding is equated with resistance, ever-present tension, and a generalized unwillingness to deal with multiple goals and objectives.

The second set of considerations goes beyond mere perspective-taking ability per se. Those who understand also demonstrate a willingness to explore as well as identify and acknowledge salient or relevant aspects of meaningful experience. Making sense of multiple perspectives can occur within narrow or broad limits. When people understand one another well, they are in a relatively better position to spell things out in greater depth and detail without always having to do so. Moreover, they are not as apt to be inhibited or uptight about what is still uncertain or unknown. There is not only a broad range of possibilities to explore but more ways to elaborate upon the complications and complexities that are revealed. Make no mistake: It is a decided advantage to be able to say more about less rather than less about more.

A third set of perspective-taking skills helps to validate and grant added psychological credit to relevant aspects of manifest action. We might call this the talent to establish salient parameters of validation. To see something as important or meaningful is to affirm its significance as intrinsically valuable. How we interpret the actions of others is not just a matter of accuracy and elaboration but of validation and confirmation as well. Accounts of mutual understanding are filled with references to the wide margin of credibility and support that clearheaded interpretations engender or confer upon the one who speaks. In contrast, those involving shared misunderstanding refer to devaluation of what people try to express or convey in the form of put-downs, criticism, harsh judgment, and lack of access to another's privileged or idealized meanings. Interaction is labored and talk is a chore where everything is taken wrong and meanings don't have a chance to sink in because of all the destructive cycles and snowball effects that stem from trying to prove someone else wrong.

WARRANTS AND REASONS

In this section, we compare the *personal logic* associated with various states of understanding and misunderstanding. A *warrant* is an explanatory mechanism that connects acts of observation to a given conclusion. What you see, hear, say, touch, and move leads—through personal logic—to a singular theme, assertion, or claim. The progression from premise through warrant to conclusion takes place in such a way as to unite observables with diverse inferences and implications in a coherent, goal-directed manner. Standards of reason help us make sense of things by arranging an array of particulars into a larger cluster, progression, or pattern of movement. Personal logic can be employed to support and nourish, or subvert and undermine, the vitality of the process.

We are interested in the reasoning principles used to explain what transpires in highly personal terms. The distinction between *participant* and *observer* is important. The behavior of A makes sense to B insofar as their own personal logic remains somehow accessible, compatible, or translatable. Highly interpretive actions are those that can be readily identified from multiple vantage points. In other words, the significance of personal conduct depends on the degree to which the process is viewed as self-explanatory to someone else.

Understanding. E and P enjoy one another, joke a good deal of the time, pick up on certain quirks, and use a lot of sarcasm. They like to laugh and try to say things that will cause more laughter to occur. It isn't picking on each other, they just say things that aren't true at all but would be funny if they were. It's hard to explain exactly what transpires, but they don't take it all apart and see what it means. They state their own position, make a comment, or ask a couple of questions, but usually without big discussion of any issue. The quality of interaction is high because both know how to respond to what the other needs.

What is so distinctive about the logic of understanding is how powerfully it supports the reproduction of the very conditions that give rise to constructive possibilities. Personal actions that exhibit sufficiently high levels of definitional, classificational, and explanatory force may be readily integrated into the interpretive frames of someone else. In the accounts of mutual understanding, ingrained personal logic was revealed in concrete actions that were broadly and deeply accessible to two individuals at once.

We see personal logic (at work) serving many useful functions. The first has to do with clarified reasons for actions, thoughts, and feelings. It is possible to see another's reasons right away or to state various perspectives without big issues arising. It isn't necessary to take it all apart and see what it means. Knowing why another takes a position makes it easier to address serious topics and still diffuse misunderstanding and conflict. The second has to do with the incremental gain and pleasure of being in touch with the way that someone else makes sense of things. Respondents speak of the pleasure of reasoning out things together. There is a heightened sense of responsiveness in knowing how to react or anticipate the replies of others who are close by. As pleasure shifts into playfulness, there is expanded margin of opportunity for joking, laughing, teasing, and making fun. When interactants feel safe and secure, the process of making sense of things can become quite heavy and tense, hence the need to take refuge in what makes no sense—the ludicrous features of being human.

The third function is compensatory. There is irony in the discovery that we may not know why or how we express the things we do. Other people may help us find out what our own reasons actually are. Notice reference to conditions where one knows more about the other than the other knows about him- or herself. It is not just a matter of providing much-needed signs of social support. More significant is the measure of reassurance in understanding why people feel the way they do, particularly during moments of uncertainty or self-doubt.

Fourth, the application of sound personal logic is a useful steering mechanism. It helps regulate interchange between the participants and outside interventions with second and third parties. Notice where respondents seem to know what the other means although others don't have a clue. One may explain things for someone on behalf of someone else. Being able to explain one another's conduct to a wider circle of associates produces a deeper sense of personal connectedness. One fringe benefit is greater tolerance for what is difficult or implausible to discuss in the immediate situation.

The logic of misunderstanding is quite compelling as well. Here a central theme is shallow and superficial forms of involvement without being able to fathom how or why others may pursue a given course of action.

> *Misunderstanding.* P and O would be more understanding if only they had not disagreed so much over so many little things along the way. O knows for a fact that P misconstrues O's intentions at many times. O will pay P a compliment and P will think that O is being sarcastic just to annoy P. At times, they do it to each other. When O tries to apologize for acting a certain way, P interprets O's action as antagonizing P even more. O feels some of the ideas going through P's head are simply wrong, but maybe if O could understood why P believes the way P does, O would see or even agree with P's viewpoint. O sees misunderstanding as a huge and overwhelming obstacle to overcome.

It is a mistake to think that personal logic somehow disappears or disintegrates during acts or episodes of collusion or mystification. It is rather that one person's logic may interfere with the application of alternative ways of making sense of things from multiple vantage points. The personal logic of one may negate or contradict the application of any other source. Some respondents give accounts of contradiction based upon unpredictability or massive doses of change. The central tendency is for people to impose their own valuative standards on the problematic behavior of others rather than to encourage their own unique methods of assessment. There is also the presence of power struggles over which standards will apply in any given case. When there is a lack of explicit interaction over implicit motives, people are least likely to know why others act the way they do. The clash of competing logic is described in terms of barriers, walls, and obstacles and the invisible consequences of not being able to follow along.

TESTS OF COMPREHENSION

Some explanations are better than others. Those that carry the most weight enable us to figure out—to measure or estimate—what another does against some standard of personal relevance. What we observe is a function of a search for plausible explanations. So what it means to grasp and comprehend the actions of another is a matter of viewing the activity in question from all possible angles. First consider central themes gathered under conditions of mutual understanding.

Understanding. L and R know better than one another's close friends. The odd thing is that L has never met R face-to-face because they talk by computer on Telnet every night. L has an amazing mental connection with R even though R lives in Colorado. L and R know each other only through written words, yet they can still interact quite effectively. L and R have an uncanny intuitive sense of one another; each one can tell just by the words how the other is feeling. Also, when they talk, L feels at ease, safe, and connected. L has discussed things with R that L has never mentioned to other buddies, that is, his friend's death from cancer and father's death from a heart attack. It is amazing that L can, in a way, feel R's understanding of L's problems through R's words on a computer screen. Even when talking of nonemotional (low-risk) information, L and R can follow clearly. Despite some conflict, L and R have established a level of understanding that will overcome any differences that may come between them.

Misunderstanding. Y and U have had a lot of misunderstandings lately. Y was brought up in a family that didn't promote a lot of direct exchange and Y doesn't know the rules of everyday conversation. Y says things that make U mad and this makes Y even more mad. The other morning after U was curling her hair, U asked Y if Y wanted the curling iron left on. Y said, "No," as if U had asked if U could burn Y with it. Deep down, U knows Y didn't mean it, but it still makes U furious. Eventually U stopped talking to Y because U didn't like to be treated this way. This went on for a while before they finally broke the barrier, and now everything is back to normal. If Y and U could learn to understand how the other feels, things would improve and unnecessary misunderstanding would be a thing of the past.

We have equated comprehension with the power to distinguish and discriminate between one thing and another. Personal actions acquire definitional clarity by being subject to reality-testing against the standards of the observer(s). Somehow matters of definition, questions of classification, and modes of explanation work together, either under conditions favorable or adverse to the achievement of mutually acknowledged forms of identification and recognition. On the side of understanding, there is a frequent mention of a strong need to make sense, a mutual refusal to give up, and genuine willingness to do everything possible to make things happen. There is a spirit of perseverance, hard work, sustained effort, goodwill, and support over criticism.

In matters of misunderstanding, we document a tendency to cover up evidence of personal difficulty in figuring out what's going on or what something means. A certain amount of slippage is to be expected or tolerated. Some respondents are passive, avoidant, or resigned. Others search through noise and confusion to no avail. Still others acquire a measure of relief from all the fuss where keeping things in perspective becomes a constant chore. There is considerable frustration associated with the effort to act *as if* nothing is wrong. Futility registers in the fear of saying the wrong thing where people have no idea why their respective methods of logic remain so inaccessible, even when they do everything possible to break through, only to find it is still not enough.

CODE SWITCHING

It is a strategic advantage to be able to translate (back and forth) from one idiom to another. We notice that people who achieve high levels of mutual understanding are better able to stay in touch with a wider range of viewpoints.

Understanding. L and T interact well together. They do not let problems stand in the way for very long. It is not necessary to spell everything out in verbal terms; there is more of an unspoken knowledge of the other. When T walks into the room, L knows right away whether T is stressed, upset, happy, tired, and so on, and vice versa. Both know when it is a good time to talk and when it is better to leave one another alone. L and T know how hard to push for information and when to back off; they know what secrets can be told to others and which ones must be kept strictly confidential. The list goes on. They can tell each other things neither one could ever tell to anyone else. They can laugh at things no one else would find even remotely funny. There is shared determination to maintain a high level of mutual understanding.

Misunderstanding. J and T drive one another crazy. Simple body language provides a strong indication of the level of mutual intolerance. Due to extremely different styles and outlooks on virtually everything, routine interaction is plagued by constant disputes and endless misunderstandings. The comments directed at J, or others, that T considers to be harmless, J views as incredibly inconsiderate and hurtful. Sarcastic comments that J throws out to lighten the tension only end up irritating T even more. Also, T misreads J's actions while staying mainly on the defensive. Most of the direct exchanges are guarded, adversarial, and combative. J and T refuse to open up to one another and take down the walls that have been erected to protect themselves. There is nothing more frustrating than to try to interact in a friendly and effective manner and then end up at an impasse. Recently, J and T have not bothered to try. Constructive criticism is blown out of proportion and taken as a personal attack by one or both parties. Small talk is analyzed again and again to find some hidden insult or discredit. Incompatible styles of self-presentation and discordant viewpoints produce disastrous failures. After such unfulfilling, frustrating encounters, J and T decide to give up and settle instead for a state of perpetual confusion and misunderstanding.

M and N had engaged in a great deal of personal contact in the past. Recently, however, due to persistent misunderstandings, they have begun to avoid each other. M thinks the problem lies in different approaches to language use. N goes on and on, talking about basic information in a highly elaborated stream of opinion and speculation. Lots of other topics are constantly sprinkled in. M cannot follow the abstract thought processes that N is putting straight into words without any editing or refinement. Sometimes when N is talking about something, M finds himself nodding in agreement, only to find out 5 minutes later that he initially had an entirely wrong idea about what N was trying to express. They must have incompatible styles because M doesn't think that N would be where N is today if everyone felt as confused as M does. M feels uneasy talking with N, who seems to misinterpret M's remarks and get the wrong idea entirely. Sometimes N acts as though M has offended N with some other intended meaning by hint or implication. M is more careful than usual not to use unclear language that could lead to confusion over the flow of intended meanings.

Respondent accounts document what it takes to speak someone else's language. It is not just a matter of saying the right thing at the right time and place. There is an atmosphere of expressive freedom and interpretive responsiveness. Where agreements and understandings flourish, a more democratic and egalitarian climate will find support. Notice the creative use of special vocabularies, slant, mannerisms, and the efficacious use of in-group codes. There is a striking absence of *logophobia,* the fear of expressing oneself freely before others. Progressive movement makes difficult issues somehow easier to deal with in constructive ways. Methods of reasoning dovetail, even where complex issues are at stake.

In sharp contrast are daily contacts where matters of vocabulary, idiom, and code do not fit well together well. The respective parties too often hear themselves say, "I don't get it." Participants inhabit different spheres where it becomes almost impossible to explain complex matters to one another. Lack of vocabulary and the inability to explain things effectively virtually rule out the possibility of grasping complex matters. Methods of reasoning do not translate into equivalent terms. What hurts one helps another. It becomes easier to reach an impasse. One may be tempted to settle for perpetual confusion where nothing seems important anymore. It is possible to fall into a habit of misreading other people and not be able to find a quick way out. Sometimes it is not worth the effort to pay attention and follow along.

SYNCHRONY AND ALIGNMENT
OF COMMUNICATIVE STYLES

One good measure of compatibility is the degree of synchrony and alignment in the various styles of personal conduct. Those who stay in synch and remain closely aligned are in a more favorable position to integrate and unify the particulars of what is said and done into a larger coherent narrative.

Understanding. J and V are very comfortable sharing personal feelings with one another. Neither one is afraid to say whatever comes to mind because each one knows the other *will* understand. Sometimes J or V will sense what the other is feeling before the other does. This leads to comfortable interactions where conversations flow smoothly, except where each one starts talking at the same time because each one knows exactly what the other is trying to express. Because each one senses the other's frame of reference, it is easy to talk about personal problems. Such skills promote and foster a strong level of personal bond.

Misunderstanding. U and P are roommates who don't get along very well. There is considerable misunderstanding, but they never discuss what matters most. U doesn't understand what P wants in response to P's millions of comments. U has to listen to P talk to other friends to make sense of what P is saying. U tries to joke with P as with other friends, but P still doesn't respond well.

They have drifted into a passive relationship. They rarely sit down and talk. Conversations revolve around trivial comments. U thinks about the bothersome implications of not being able to get along and not knowing how or what to say or do.

There is some measure of consistency in how fine-tuned relations evolve over time. Respondents are flexible and tolerant of risk and change. A spirit of accommodation and compromise enables each one to make the best of the situation and not let petty mistakes or miscalculations stand in the way. Respondents speak of working hard to talk things through and of concentrated effort to make sure everyone understands what transpires at each step along the way. There is ample opportunity to go back over what remains unclear as well as skill in knowing how much to explain and when to leave well enough alone. Notice references both to not having to spell everything out in detail and the willingness to go back over troubling issues as much as necessary. Some give credit to the unique modes of language that are employed. Others stress matters of affection—empathy, positive regard, social support, or reciprocated matters of trust and respect. Still others appeal to the sheer strength or salience of the bond, as with soul mates or a spirit of love. Also relevant are frequent references to an underlying sense of safety and security. It is not simply a matter of being unafraid to speak out but also a willingness to reveal almost anything. Equally important is the tendency for the various styles of interchange to become more alike over time. It takes a lot of time, patience, and determination to overcome the many obstacles.

Something quite different happens where interactants find themselves working at cross-purposes. It is difficult to say what is more troubling—not being able to get along or not knowing how or what to say about it. We notice a strong tendency for those in highly strained relations to take refuge in silence and verbal cover-up of what goes wrong. Small talk is a central mechanism of compensation for lack of breadth or depth of relevant subject matter. Mistakes are repeated over and over in the manner of a game without end. Some feel trapped in a perpetual state of miscommunication. After periods of prolonged separation, attributional biases take the form of blaming the other disproportionately for what goes wrong together with loose rationalizations for why a better means of communication has yet to be devised.

WORKING THROUGH
PROBLEMATIC CONCERNS

Our respondents used a wide range of strategies and tactics to work through various communicative difficulties and address problematic concerns.

Understanding. O and R lived together for several years. Through considerable effort, O knows what types of situations make R happy, sad, agitated, or irritated, and how to deal with difficult times. R has also learned to identify and deal with similar feelings and reactions on O's part. They are very open with one another and work hard at looking at complex situations from the other's point of view. O is always willing to place R's personal problems and crises ahead of O's own. Both avoid judgment and condemnation and instead rely on honesty and trust. Although O listens to Rush Limbaugh and R is a strong Bill Clinton supporter, they can discuss their political differences in a pleasurable and nonthreatening manner. When R acts in a hostile, irrational, or irritating manner, the chances are pretty good that O will be able to understand why, provide comfort, and diffuse tense situations by talking through touchy feelings and concerns.

Misunderstanding. D and V disagree a lot. D is serious, quiet, and reserved, while V can also be quiet but is mostly loud, rowdy, and sarcastic. Conversations are skewed because neither one knows how to interpret the most sensitive feelings of the other. D interprets much of what V says as sarcasm. As a result, D has become irritated, defensive, and no longer opens up out of a fear of a sarcastic reaction. In a sense, D has become gun-shy. The biggest problems arise when V is trying to be sincere and doesn't intend to create difficulties. D and V remain good friends but are still quite anxious. Now when D speaks of a problem, V responds with V's own feelings. Because D. expects the worst, D is overly sensitive to V's comments and remains on the defensive because of an inability to tell the difference between V's sincerity and sarcasm.

Several major themes stand out. Where firm understandings prevail, personal weaknesses, deficiencies, and vulnerabilities are treated with sensitivity and care. People do not take advantage of weakness or disadvantage but take such considerations into special account. Instead of giving in to the urge to push someone else's buttons, it is thought better to leave well enough alone. As a rule, respondents find it useful to know each other's limitations—soft spots—and devise specialized tactics or subroutines to circumvent or work around what cannot be addressed in conventional terms. In such settings, there is less reason to get defensive as a means to ward off potential threat. Irrational or irritating actions can be deflected, neutralized, or diffused as a means to bring comfort or relief. Respondents speak of soothing troubled feelings. Support is discovered in the transition from crisis to routine. It can take a great deal of person-specific knowledge of unfulfilled needs, wants, and desires to keep everything intact and alleviate worry, anxiety, and doubt.

An effective interactant might be defined as one who can move in and out of whatever communicative difficulties come to the fore. Where misunderstandings rule, it is the other way around. We notice that most interpersonal entanglements can be taken as an excuse or rationalization for almost any form of abuse or neglect. Because we do not see eye to eye about X, Y, or Z, there is nothing more we can do (about all the other stuff). If no one else takes the initiative, why should I? Indifference takes the form of not having any idea of what goes wrong or sense of why others do the things they do. Utter resignation enables everything to be left up in the air and nothing gets resolved. Diminished expectations are equated with undaunted rivalry, fear of speaking up, a sense of loss, negativity, pessimism, paranoia, and hope the situation will change soon.

MUTUAL STRUGGLE TO
MINIMIZE MISCOMMUNICATION

It takes hard work to maintain close ties with others. At issue is what it takes to get into and out of various types of communicative difficulties. We were impressed with two basic considerations. First, some people are more skilled and better able to deal with problematic circumstances than others. Second, the transition between crisis and routine is not always successfully accomplished. There are images of interpersonal entanglements where sense-making practices hinge on poor performances sustained as a matter of course. Others are in a better position to help us find our way. At one end of the spectrum are acts of giving up or giving in, and at the other the possibility of shared resolve to stick it out and see things through. We focus now on protracted struggles to avoid, diminish, minimize, neutralize, or transcend episodes of difficult circumstances where the load shifts back and forth in highly improvised trajectories of relational amplification and compression. One thing is sure. Some people get into and out of trouble better than others. We want to know what sorts of things make things better or worse along the way. At issue are the intrinsic features of situations where individuals find a way to work things through as opposed to those where they don't. Often there is a circuitous journey governed by a partially refined game of trial and error.

Understanding. T and Y are best friends who know one another's moods, views, and emotions very well. Whenever either person has a problem or wants to discuss some outstanding issue, he turns to the other. Each one knows how to listen actively and to give unbiased advice, despite the potential of opposing views. When personal flaws are revealed, neither counters with "I told you so." There is a strong tendency to accept and support new efforts to do better. When addressing the other's "stupid" mistakes or problems, both reveal a strong sense of morality and common sense. Various problems or mistakes are not allowed to become obstacles or harm someone's future. Despite great strain and confusion, both know what it is like to truly care about one's partner when conflicts arise. T and Y base personal advice on personal experience and on putting themselves in the other's position. Any major falling out ends up with each one crying, apologizing, and explaining. A strong spirit makes relations stronger and makes understanding of one another so much clearer.

Misunderstanding. L and X live together but rarely see each other anymore. This makes even the most simple task appear to be the most imposing. When they do talk, one will get the wrong meaning from what was said. L avoids X, who becomes defensive and takes things the wrong way. L can also tell how X feels about things because X doesn't voice deep feeling or show much emotion. The solution to so many misunderstandings has been just to let them pass. This hasn't been effective, however, as it produces very negative feelings. L thinks X bottles things up inside more than X used to. Because X is not around much, X doesn't understand L or what L means to say. The same holds for L's situation because L hardly knows X anymore. Sometimes when L and X are around one another long enough, they begin to listen to each other better. This effort reduces some misunderstandings and shows that, if only they would make the effort, the relationship would work out better than before.

Personal accounts provide vivid testimony about what goes right or wrong in the course of human encounters. It seems clear that communicative competence is broadly associated with the capacity and willingness to produce a broad spectrum of agreements and understandings. Likewise, the inability or unwillingness to make well-reasoned sense together constitutes a severe liability. The process of communication can make things better or worse, depending largely on the goodness of fit between two or more distinctive ways of dealing with matters of complexity and complication. Obviously, *more* communication does not always make things better. Sometimes, less is more.

The risk of miscommunication is part of the price of admission. It cannot be eliminated, but it can be subject to a greater degree of volitional control. The greatest danger is mindless repetition or entrapment in low-quality performances from which there is dim prospect of alleviation or escape. Closely related is the willingness to use evidence of miscommunication as a rationalization or excuse for not giving one's best. Avoiding the trap is crucial to the pursuit of social harmony and individual well-being. The central question is whether outmoded or ineffectual methods of relating can be recast and then transformed into productive and efficacious ways of taking care of unfinished business.

CHAPTER 7

Personal Transformation

The capacity and willingness to encounter others as directly as possible is risky business. It takes conscious effort to put individual egos on hold and withdraw the presumption that someone else is largely responsible for whatever has gone wrong. In so doing, we run the risk of assigning proportionate responsibility to ourselves for gradations of success and failure. Other types of possibilities arise insofar as we strive to become as sensitive to the effects of our own behavior on others as we are to the effects of others' behavior on ourselves. What is required is the willingness to go beyond ordinary reframing exercises into a whole new conception—a different model or paradigm—of who we are in the eyes of one another. Part of the larger process entails the ability and willingness to transform first person perspectives into a broader and more inclusive framework of inquiry. The central objective is to arrive at a radical acceptance of the distinct reality of other living beings. The willingness to accept others for what they are (as living subjects) can nurture the same spirit toward ourselves. Such a massive shift in personal priorities makes it possible to work together for genuine and authentic forms of sense-making practice. The pursuit of optimum conditions fosters the design of the most favorable systems of interactive methodology so that one's personal and social relationships can become as fully articulated and effective as possible. At issue is the possibility of a metamorphosis from one way of doing business into a whole new way. A spirit of renewal and restoration occurs when what was feared and relived is replaced with a vision of shared hope for the acquisition of a more humane way of dealing with unfinished business.

Our final task is to explore the possibility of devising new methods of communication to replace those that work poorly or not at all. As a standard of measurement, an *effective interactant* is defined as someone who can move into and out of a wide range of communicative difficulties with other people. At issue is the larger capacity and willingness to deal with a broad spectrum of problematic concerns, unresolved issues, and complex forms of risk and change. The main goal is to be in a favorable position to make clear and cogent sense of what takes place from as many vantage points as possible. The quest is full of risks: Not everything works out well for all of the people all of the time; one person's success may be construed as another person's failure.

So the enterprise, however laudable, is subject to reservation. Not every way or means of conducting daily business may be worth saving. For instance, it is not possible to envision starting over where the weight of the past is considered far too great or faith in unfinished human possibilities much too small. Also, the search for shared solutions can be easily subverted or undermined, particularly where one strives for constructive change while no one else around seems to care. Moreover, where the mix of personal resources is too unevenly distributed, the prospects for modest, short-term gain remain quite slim. In effect, there may be no reason to cling to false hope. A wide spectrum of things *could* or *might* go wrong, hold us back, or stand in our way. Admittedly, it is not always possible to see the intrinsic worth of trying to make the world a better place. However, the goal is worth pursuing, even when encountering those who seem to presume otherwise.

The main objective is to work to improve the quality of face-to-face interaction around us. To this end, it is important to understand what facilitates or interferes with the (re)production of a long succession of clear, transparent, sense-making practices. After all, it does little good to know what goes wrong if one lacks the resources or inclination to make things right. Three types of conceptual-analytical skills are involved. First is the basic diagnostic ability to discover what it takes to foster, promote, and maintain a climate of life-affirming interchange with other living creatures like ourselves. Second is the magnitude of mutual determination to avoid (internal) distraction or (outside) interference and deal with the pressing business at hand. Third is the ability to cope with powerful, large-scale events over which one may exert only a small measure of control.

RECEPTIVITY TO CHANGE

A first step is to see fatalism as the enemy of constructive change. Static or faulty conditions may be repeated in the manner of a bad habit or poorly executed routine. There is a tendency to repeat the same mistakes over and over. In matters of acquired deficiency, the focal points of subject matter may change rapidly while the underlying misconstructive processes remain much the same. Fatalism implies bargaining in bad faith: Things have always been this way and they will never change. People get stuck in a litany of poor performance with no way out and no better way to alter the failing system.

As a corrective, a minimal requirement is some small measure of faith in the possibilities of changing the very processes of miscommunication that interfere most severely with the acquisition of one's highest aspirations. The measure of change may involve an incremental or stepwise gain, or assume a more sweeping and inclusive form that affects the character, condition, and context of interaction. In either case, a steady succession of faulty performances may only be arrested at the deepest levels of collective resource and personal skill. Appeal to matters of belief or faith affirms that what has gone wrong is still capable of being made right. At stake is an imprecise but complex matter of trial and error with renewed opportunity for reconsideration along the way. Nothing is set in stone. A measure of (individual) risk blends with a margin of (collective) opportunity.

The personal accounts reveal different levels of preparation for significant change. The distinction between first- and second-order activity is basic to the age-old question of persistence and change in human affairs. What qualifies as questionable or problematic is not to be treated as absolute or inherent in the great scheme of things but as quite dependent on the particular mix of circumstance and behav-

ior (Watzlawick, Weakland, & Fisch, 1974). In a context of miscommunication, two issues surface: (a) How does an unwelcome or undesirable situation persist? (b) What is required to change it? *Persistence*
refers to small-scale change (one state to another) within the same
basic level or type of activity (type 1). *Transformation,* in contrast, refers
to a dramatic or sudden shift in a wider domain of one's behavior (type
2). The urge to minimize acts of miscommunication is revealed in (a)
the same way of conducting business (more or less) or else in (b) a
sudden shift, a jump, out of a faulty system (all or nothing).

Instances of first-order condition: Games without end contain no
provision for their termination. What is quite obvious is the most
difficult thing to grasp (Watzlawick et al., 1974, p. 77). The following
are examples of second-order instances:

> something uncontrollable, even incomprehensible, a quantum jump,
> a sudden illumination which unpredictably comes at the end of a long,
> often frustrating mental and emotional labor, sometimes in a dream,
> sometimes almost as an act of grace in the theological sense. (p. 23)

Expressions of nonsense and confusion are pervasive where long
sequences of questionable behaviors are taken at the wrong level or
where multiple levels of operation shift suddenly without notice. The
idea that the fault lies with the working premises can be unbearable
(Watzlawick et al., 1974, p. 55). Someone who is disposed to see no
problem where there is one may well encounter someone who is
inclined to see a solution where there is none. Still, a host of faulty
performances can be subverted, neutralized, or undermined by paying strict and close attention to what kinds of wrong or misguided
solutions are helping to maintain them (p. 160).

Tolerance for change acquires definition from the point of greatest resistance. The baseline is a state or condition of sheer intolerance
toward any type of change in any form. One may decide to cling to a
set of *static* conditions. A central theme found in respondents' reconstructed interactions was the desire to keep things just the way they
are right now and to not change a thing. The sweep of the desire is
unquestioned (by implication). A minimum point of departure occurs
in the willingness to tolerate a small measure of *incremental* or momentary change but only for a specified period of time. One might be
capable or willing to alter someone or something in one way or

another for a short-term gain. There was willingness to settle for a slow succession of slight improvements that would leave the larger picture intact. Slight signs of change might be begrudgingly accepted. *Episodic* change registers in minor adjustments and accommodations to the larger forces of risk and change at work within a given place, time, and circumstance. *Generalized* change registers as a major shift in (a) the definition and direction of human relations during some critical or decisive period or else in (b) one's prevailing ways of dealing with people in general. More visible is *extensive* change because it can be dramatic, elaborated, and a complete break from the collective weight of the past. Beyond the province of ordinary events is the possibility to envision *radical* change in the larger scheme of things. A vision of *transformational* change enables someone to behave in a whole new way, as in a quest for a new way of life.

THE 5% SOLUTION

Consider a modest proposal. A group of undergraduates (from UWM) were given a small amount of "psychological credit" (chits) to be applied toward a 5% increase in the quality of their daily interactions with other people. The specific task was to allocate the credit to ensure a modest increase in the quality of a specified aspect or domain of face-to-face interaction. The effort could be defined at the level of (a) a specific person, (b) a type of person or situation, or (c) persons in general. The credit could apply anywhere, anytime, for a 3-month period.

Conceptions of modest improvement dovetail nicely with the central concerns of this study. The envisioned remedies are quite striking. One accent is with sustained effort to assume a more open, receptive, and constructive spirit in dealing with other people in general. Here are located mostly modest visions for improvement. Each one is enacted bit by bit, act by act, episode by episode, one person, subject, or situation at a time. The larger process involves a little bit of a whole lot of things. One may seek to make each daily contact better in some small way. The initial aspiration may be directed toward greater attentiveness and sensitivity to shared activities in general. People treat you better if you pay close attention and remember exactly what they say to you. If you are not fully alert, the words will go in one ear and out the other.

It is wise to avoid those methods of exchange that diminish your own faith in yourself and your total sense of well-being. You might begin by addressing personal feelings of weakness and inadequacy. Everyone has room for improvement. No one individual is flawless. Some benefit by learning how to confront other people, instead of just letting everything stay bottled up inside. Others have to acquire the courage to stand up and say what they have to say once and for all. It is important to speak out, say what one thinks, and not be so afraid of how others will react. The biggest change would be less of a fear of telling others what one is actually thinking or feeling at the time. Still others must come to know that their opinions are as important and valuable as those of anyone else. Any gain would help avoid conflicts over saying the sorts of things that one will only later regret.

Do not bother to be content simply to strike a calm and tranquil pose. Make intentions clear and explicit. Keep an open mind toward the unstated intentions of others. Personal differences of opinion need not indicate the presence of a threat. Address personal problems when they occur rather than waiting until they boil over. It is not necessary, after all, to rush to any premature judgment. Straight talk is better than a host of hidden meanings and veiled suggestions.

Some people learn to be more empathic and less critical. It is a mistake to keep thinking that one is always right and others are always wrong. One needs to think more carefully about the expressions of sharp opinion and decide if it is actually worth arguing over. It may be also necessary to swallow one's pride—put a little more thought into what is said instead of just flying off the handle. Constructive change can be measured by whether people actually converse or just shout and yell and tell others what to do. Concerted effort to create more open and fluid lines of communication will permit other things to fall into place. Constructive change would enhance the ability to establish a wider range of personal contacts in the future: Generate relevant questions. Meet one new person a day. Interact on a broader basis. One standard of measurement is the wisdom that is acquired along the way. The best achievement would be to overcome one's own worst fears of being wrong, misinterpreted, or misunderstood.

It may be possible, under certain circumstances, to transform the actual course of face-to-face interaction into a far more favorable state or condition. Respondent accounts document a broad tendency for considerable improvement to be acquired through the patient cultivation of (slightly more) favorable conditions for human interaction to accrue over time. From a communicative standpoint, favorable conditions facilitate the ability to integrate one's sense of what is taking place in the wider context of the collective strivings for a greater measure of constructive change. The act of living fully in the absolute present tense may be taken as a model. Present-centered activity encourages the acquisition of varied sensibilities as to what nonverbal cues, spoken acts, and personal idioms could and should embody or aspire. The main intent is to conceive of, and then attribute, realistically based forms of value to whatever bits of actions serve to meet the deepest personal longings and desires. This is what keeps hope alive.

The ultimate state is to be receptive to the full spectrum of unfinished possibilities. One plausible standard is realized by taking into account the very best that every other person has to offer. This is an implicit presumption that applies to everyone who is concerned. At stake is an open communication network that links a shifting aggregate of first, second, and third parties into a much more deeply and richly integrated sense of each one's own position and place within the larger scheme of things. What is advanced is an idealized vision that can be realized in the form of an appeal to each member to perform at the outer limits of determination and resolve. What is at stake is a pragmatic and operative ideal that has a lot going for it. It is plausible, widely applicable, and does not discriminate against any one person, or class of people, because no one is cut out of the equation. After all, every person, and every creature, lives through its own unique possibilities.

To be "all that one can be" is to attain a privileged stance as the living embodiment of an individual and collective ideal. Maximum performance unfolds where each one uses everything there is to use to make the most of yet another uniquely constituted opportunity. Productive encounters open the way for a greater range of alternatives, while faulty encounters are prone to close them down. The best standard turns out to be an obtainable standard that remains just out of reach. Such a condition is sufficient, rather than utopian or rationalistic, because it envisions a state or conditions where fully functioning individuals are fully functioning with one another—no more, no less.

SUPPORTIVE COMMUNICATION

It is important not to look at the question of psychological support in a social vacuum. How much recognition one receives is relative to what is lacking or missing somewhere else. Access to a sufficient level of social support acquires definition by the proximity to its absence. So instead of asking simply *whether* an observer recognizes or acknowledges the expressed activity of another person as intrinsically valuable, it is more useful to locate questionable matters across a wide range of contested possibilities. The spectrum is anchored at one end by a state of unconditional or unqualified support or regard and at the other by a condition of utter discredit or disregard. The opposite of support (credit) is subversion (discredit) by any means.

To support personal conduct is to affirm the conditions required to repeat such highly valued sources of shared action over and over again. To subvert the action of another, in contrast, is to deny the conditions required to repeat the basic sequence indefinitely. Hence the magnitude of supportive communication is a powerful force, when fully present, to sustain and preserve, or, when inadequate, defective, or insufficient, to undermine and subvert the perpetuation of the existing state of affairs (Valentiner et al., 1994). Conversely, even the threat of negation or denial, inaction, or withdrawal may be sufficient to alter the course of events. A clear display of support, affirmation, or recognition is whatever one can make of it—a scarce resource at a time of greatest need.

The magnitude of available support is an important human resource. It is useful to think about supportive interaction as an ecological asset, much like food and water for sustenance. Vaux (1988, 1990) views support along three main dimensions: network resource, supportive behavior, and personal appraisals. Here is presumed (a) individual access (direct/mediated) to others for assistance in dealing with stressful environmental demands and difficult behaviors, (b) basic interchange predicated on the assumption of helpfulness to sustain someone in a goal or cause, and (c) personal appraisals of the use (or misuse) of collective resources. Support is on the side of a greater or wider measure of human contact that is repeated on a regular basis. The central test is how well (or badly) one uses existing networks of association and/or finds suitable replacements. A central goal is to preserve and protect the material, economic, and symbolic resources that people already value (Hobfoll, Freedy, Lane, & Geller, 1990).

Supportive conditions are a source of stability and persistence in changing times. Supportive circumstances include benefits derived from secure connections; satisfaction that is moderately stable, owing to the temporal and spatial consistency of individual characteristics and social milieus; ability to maintain cross-situational consistency in the average level of success during daily interchange; and mutual tolerance of difficulties when close connections are lacking, ambiguous, or insecure (Newcomb, 1990). The full measure of support comes and goes—from family, peers, communal ties, and general attachments to people, places, and things. It is positively associated with the willingness to provide aid to peers who are themselves faced with major stressful conditions (Dunkel-Schetter & Skokan, 1990).

Personal support provides warmth and comfort to compensate for feelings of hurt, disappointment, and distress. What matters is how explicitly the adverse feelings of the distressed are acknowledged and elaborated (Burleson, 1994). Sophisticated comforting strategies are associated with (a) a greater degree of involvement with distressed others and their difficulties, (b) neutral forms of personal evaluation, (c) awareness and sensitivity to stressful feelings, (d) acceptance and validation of the other's distress, and (e) clear explanations for the urgency of another's condition (Burleson, 1994). The supportive person provides valuable but intangible resources—warmth, reassurance, help, assistance, and aid for troubled times. The degree of success increases the willingness to deal with signs of distress in far greater complexity and detail (Notarius & Herrick, 1988; Samter, Burleson, & Basden-Murphy, 1989).

There is an important connection between levels of support and matters of good health and well-being (Sarason, Pierce, & Sarason, 1990; Schwarzer & Leppin, 1991). Global conceptions of support help shape one's sense of being worthy of help and assistance (Sarason, Pierce, Bannerman, & Sarason, 1993). Support availability includes a general sense of nourishment and support plus specific orientations toward significant persons seen as caregivers (Milardo, 1992; Pierce, Sarason, & Sarason, 1992). There is growing recognition that supportive actions are powerful forces in solving problems (Tardy, 1994), forming amicable and productive work relations (Albrecht & Hall,

1991; Zimmermann & Applegate, 1994), friendships, romantic ties, and other types of enduring relations (Adelman, Parks, & Albrecht, 1987; Rawlins, 1992), healthy family life (Julien & Markman, 1991), and global measures of interpersonal competence and compatibility (Barnes & Duck, 1994; Burleson, Albrecht, & Sarason, 1994).

The achievement of multiple goals is associated with a sense of well-being. Lack of opportunity, control, and support, in contrast, impairs well-being and poses a threat to the achievement of highly valued aspirations (Brunstein, 1993; Omodie & Wearing, 1990; Ruehlman & Wolchik, 1988). The focus on others, rather than the self, provides a greater sense of social support (Gore, Aseltine, & Colten, 1993), but it can also lead to a greater measure of distress if one is sensitive to the stresses and tensions of others (McGrath, Keita, Strickland, & Russo, 1990). Learned resourcefulness may be viewed as a self-regulated means of coping with aversive situations (Hart, Hittner, & Paras, 1991; Weisenberg, Wolf, Mittwoch, & Mikulincer, 1990). Closely related is the general finding that people who are well adjusted are most likely to seek social support when it is needed (Conn & Peterson, 1989). Conversely, a relative lack of social support is associated with the poor adjustment and poor health of people in dire need (Holahan & Moos, 1981, 1982). Deficiencies in support often accompany pronounced feelings of loneliness and estrangement (Berg & McQuinn, 1989; Samter, 1994).

Social support can be given or taken away. Much depends on the prevailing climate or milieu. There is a higher level of support for the production of those rituals, projects, and routines where a broad spectrum of agreements and understandings prevails than where a stockpile of disagreements and misunderstandings rules the day. Respondents reveal considerable attentiveness and sensitivity to questionable matters of who supports (or subverts) whom, what or why, and at what cost. Hence dual movement (into or out) of either supportive or subversive lines of action can be traced in outline form.

In this study, agreements are more highly valued than disagreements. A number of factors come into play. Those who readily agree are the most likely to have similar value systems, stay open to worthwhile ideas, validate opinion and share preferences, priorities, and beliefs over basic issues, analyze everything or anything in detail, make mutual decisions, and see the world for what it is. If something is important to one, it will seem important to the other as well. The uncanny ability of some to concur on almost any topic never ceases to be amazing.

Personal agreement is viewed as an important sign of social support. It is often equated with socially desirable frames of action. There is encouragement, recognition, and appreciation for matters of personal definition and identity. A free atmosphere promotes greatly enhanced feelings of self-esteem, self-worth, and a renewed sense of self. There is no offense taken to all the little things that would otherwise bother or annoy. Help is available whenever necessary to get out of a rough spot or during hard times. One may look to others for guidance when confused or upset, offer sound advice and good reasons for personal belief, give validity to choice and decision, or find out what the other would have said or done in the same situation. It is like talking to your own conscience. The responses of others help to justify your own ideals. Moral consensus abounds. There is shared acceptance of personal fault and failure, a reluctance to criticize or condemn, and mutual awareness of what to avoid without running out of things to say. A spirit of mutual affirmation helps close relations feel safe and secure.

Strong agreement is equated with highly valued outcomes. It is taken as a source of helpfulness through trying situations, makes personal criticism more tolerable, and enhances the ability to deal with serious disagreements head on. If something is wrong, there is a shared impulse to take care of it right away. Intense interactions do not have to be strained or forced. It is possible to talk often and long about nearly every aspect of life. Respondents share personal plans, which strengthens the desire to continue, provides incentive to get along, maintains close ties that cannot be broken, and helps them look forward to future plans.

Serious disagreement is less highly valued than strong agreement. There is very good reason for this to be the case. What is exciting and interesting to one may be a matter of total indifference to another. Respondents speak of the detriment of failing to take one another seriously. There is added difficulty in trying to establish the intrinsic worth of any questionable lines of activity where one does not fully realize what is taking place (at the time) or care about getting more deeply involved. Opposing tendencies often cancel out the distinction between winners and losers and short-circuit efforts to find compromise and middle ground. When multiple methods of personal calculation clash repeatedly, what one presumes to be right or correct is taken by someone else to be wrong or incorrect.

Serious disagreement discounts, discredits, downgrades, or disconfirms the validity of one's own beliefs or ideals. The imposition of conflicting values is dismissed as belittled effort. Hasty generalization, sweeping judgments, constant badmouthing, and self-serving bias only compound the magnitude of miscalculation and error. Respondents appeal to militant metaphors to explain what it is like to have one's ideas attacked, twisted, and torn apart. In the conflict of vested interests, the fight for power and control produces lack of respect or appreciation for mostly futile or useless efforts at adaptation and accommodation. Where no one is willing to look carefully at any other point of view, too many aspects of the larger picture will be ruled out. Those who love to argue, prove others wrong, and challenge little things are likely to make others feel uptight, anxious, and uncomfortable. Potential threats to existing values are ruled out as taboo, forbidden topics. Hence unstated problems may get worse before they have a chance to get any better. Disputes often end where one party walks away or shuts the other out.

Severe disagreements are taken as mixed signals. Mainstream disagreements occur often in causal or short-lived relations where there is very little acknowledgment and recognition from the outset. Such relations are particularly fragile during initial stages, where the initial pull of positivity and idealized expectations hold sway. With less of a safety net, the occasion for adverse or critical remarks may be assigned highly inflated negative values, particularly where there are power imbalances, a climate of defensiveness, or a lingering sense of threat. Hence sometimes a measure of social support starts to erode or slip away. It may simply be a case where anything one says is met with the opposite response. Trying to alter someone else's lack of flexibility seems futile in the end. Highly adversarial and combative styles may become so deeply ingrained that basic differences cannot be overcome. Some disputes go in circles without end. Prospects for accommodation, much less resolution, may appear quite slim.

Severe disagreement is usually equated with disruptive tactics and adverse outcomes. Total disagreement over everything leaves room for virtually nothing—just trivia and small talk. The only exceptions are where the respective parties (a) know how to argue about political or religious issues in a good-natured way, (b) use disputes as a stimulating corrective to boredom, (c) find it interesting or exciting to understand a personal perspective so foreign to one's own, or (d) withstand unwelcome modes of conflict, due to the sheer strength of the bond, the length of friendship, or the magnitude of love and affection. Touchy subjects can bring about the downfall of affection, particularly where the methods of confrontation are not sufficient to break a deadlock or impasse. Nothing does much good when such harm is caused. Social support is prone to vanish during protracted disagreements. This (a) heightens anxiety and uncertainty over the prospects for future interaction, (b) causes some to stop talking to one another, (c) drives people apart, or (d) dissolves well-established networks of exchange.

Personal understandings are the most highly valued of affiliative signs. They are equated with the ability to sustain a sense of mutual agreement and so much more. In powerful and passionate metaphors, often invoking images of knowledge as power, respondents struggle to account for the highest ranking of social achievements, often without an adequate vocabulary. There is a pervasive sense of being in a favorable position to understand persistent and changing aspects of source and subject matter, often without being able to explain the how, what, or why. In effect, the power of human understanding transcends what can be said about it. Such an idealized but obtainable state is, in a word, joyful, but inexplicable at the same time.

Prevailing metaphors are expansive and inclusive rather than strictly linear and unidirectional. The rite of passage from a state of initial uncertainty to one of more established knowledge is not to be reduced to a simple transition from point A to point B. Rather, A and B are taken as codetermined and codetermining sources of sense-making practice. Specifically, each one earns the presumption that someone else will understand in any case and no matter what. It is not an easy journey, to be sure. Preparation must deal with basic considerations of openness, receptivity, trust, honesty, and respect. Empathy for another's feelings creates a supportive bond. Over time, it gets easier to talk about pressing personal problems. Solid knowledge, patiently acquired, allows each one to see things in a totally new light.

As a statement of faith, unveil any problems. Do what it takes. Come to a mutual understanding. Discover how to deal with questionable situations across the board. Avoid harsh judgment. Confront tense situations and diffuse tensions by talking at the level of one's deepest strivings and concerns. To understand what another explains is, in fact, to be overcome with a sort of calm where there is, for a time, no further need to question or defend. Mutual realization contributes to matters of health and well-being. It is possible to learn to make opposing viewpoints fuse or dissolve. Talk through things to make sure everyone does understand. Fine-tune ideas. Show concern for the welfare of one another. Make each contact seem distinctive and worthwhile. However, it is only when close relations are worth the work in total that it actually pays to hammer out differences until they can be reconciled or resolved one way or another.

There is often a deeply ingrained and inherent sense of what each one wants to say or leave alone. Usually there is more than enough access to help for personal problems. The point of salvation is the knowledge of why others reach the conclusions they do without having to agree with the particular conclusions themselves. There need be no pretense or inhibition. Both parties may strive to deal with misunderstandings by explaining things in as many ways as necessary. There is a fine line between the topics to be handled with extra sensitivity or else confronted in a more straightforward manner. It is amazing how much one can learn from the sheer pleasure of talking to someone who understands one's own unique circumstance. This makes it possible to share things that have never been said or done with anyone else.

By adapting fluid and shifting perspectives, one may be persuaded to see things in a whole new light. Concerted effort is required to understand how a given person will act, to agree with the position taken, and to understand precisely why. A keen level of mutual understanding reduces discord and increases the sense of pleasure and reward. Personal differences do not have to tear people apart. It helps to spend considerable time on metacommunication as well, discussing where communication might have gone wrong and possible ways to minimize unwelcome change.

It is hard to see much value in misunderstanding other people. Virtually all the linguistic credit goes to the other side of the ledger. The crude formula—that human misunderstandings are worthless— is not far from the mark. Very few, if any, respondents consider the prize worth the cost. Instead, looking backward, there is mostly allowance for lament and resignation. Protracted misunderstandings are the most difficult to justify. Intractable forms have the power to drive people apart and sever long-standing accords. Some look back to an entire lifetime filled with lots of misunderstandings that were fabricated almost as a matter of course. So what one discovers may be the opposite of what is needed to feel important as a person. The stronger the desire for relevance and meaning (for someone), the greater the potential threat of irrelevance and indifference (for someone else). Every fresh construction may be subject to further reinterpretation. Things cancel out. Possibilities dissolve. Foundations crumble while protective covenants are ripped asunder.

Severe misunderstandings undermine social support in diverse ways. They make it more difficult to empathize with someone else's unfulfilled needs. Say something and someone else will take it the wrong way. There may be offense taken no matter what was said or done. Low-quality interaction is often forced or strained, even when no one can say how or why. Everyone may stay on edge for some time. One may come to know that another person didn't actually "mean it," but that does little good in the end. Common is the tendency to read too much into other people's minds. If the respective parties can't agree on anything, they can't possibly understand one another either.

Strong feelings of mutual intolerance abound. Some people seem impossible to read. Incompatible styles and outlooks on virtually everything cause daily interaction to be plagued by constant personal misunderstanding. What one considers harmless and innocent another will construe to be inconsiderate and spiteful. Sarcasm lightens tension. Stay on guard. Refuse to open up. Things get blown out of proportion. Look constantly for hidden signs of insult or attack. Routine matters become nothing short of a chore. Mindless disputes over trivia produce circular arguments where each one may accept part of the blame but nothing is resolved. It may be impossible to reach conclusions. If the other person isn't going to understand anyway, there is no need to get into muddled or sticky business. One small slip is all it takes to cross the line. Some things will never be figured out.

Misery follows misunderstanding. Some misguided actions are driven underground, never to be acknowledged or recognized explicitly again. Having to deal with mass confusion on a daily basis may not change a thing. Nine times out of ten it is the other person who is presumed to misunderstand the most—rather than the other way around. Understand what *I* am saying; the *burden* is on you. Such distorted emphasis makes it seem, in the manner of a convincing illusion, that the entire source of misunderstanding can be reduced to a specific source or location, most notably locked up tightly in someone else's misguided mind. At times of greatest frustration, virtually anyone may start to blurt out the wrong thing. At the point of greatest upset, the hottest issue will get dropped. The spiral of silence sets in. Some refuse to express any further opinion, out of a generalized expectation that it would all be garbled in translation and not mean a thing.

A general rule is that as the severity of misunderstanding increases, the frequency of interaction will decrease in turn. The movement away from a condition of integration and interdependence is how social support is, in small slices, diluted, neutralized, or undermined. Future possibilities are minimized after a lot of ambiguity and confusion has set in on all sides. No matter hard one may try, others will never get the point. There is no intrinsic reason to put a lot of effort into trying to grasp what others try to say. Because it takes so much to search for a suitable topic of conversation, there is a common tendency to feel the process is now less important.

In a downward spiral, an impending sense of unimportance leads to inattentive listening and focused effort to sustain the existing framework of communication in any manner. One may find it easier to fall into a habit of misunderstanding than to find a quick way out. Everything stays the same if no one is motivated to take the initiative and ask others why the possibility of direct communication is so often denied or avoided.

There is a redeeming value to what is subject to mutual resolution. The magnitude of misunderstanding, once resolved and upon reflection, may put people back in touch with so much of what they have taken for granted, namely, the capacity and willingness to make well-directed sense of things in the past, present, and future tense. There is more than solace in the resolution of prior misunderstandings. Most important is renewed faith in the shared ability to work through complexities and complications to know and understand one another better. Here is mutual resolve to clear up the confusion, find out where things went wrong, so as not to make the same mistakes over and over again. It is possible, due to the sheer weight of misunderstanding, to gain a deeper measure of insight and to resolve to transform what went wrong. Even trivial concerns over little things may be taken into consideration, calculated down to the smallest detail.

WHAT HAS COMMUNICATIVE
VALUE TO SOMEONE ELSE

A considerable amount of miscommunication is due to the sheer clamor of clashing viewpoints and the stressful outcomes of opposition and resistance. These are the very social conditions that prove so difficult to reconcile at a personal level. Either there is a problem in interpretation or some course of action proves resistant to the fulfillment of an alternative source of goal-directed action. A counterproductive cycle is set in motion when faulty or distorted perspective taking interferes with behavioral objectives, which in turn makes it even more difficult to see things clearly (Mortensen, 1976). Harsh criticism may foster the appearance of incompetence where underestimated or ignored abilities are discounted or negated out of a false sense of not being able to do something when faced with someone else's expectation of being able to do it (Philips & Zimmerman, 1990). The danger of labeling someone "incompetent" encourages the illusion of a person with a fixed state of personality or character (Langer & Park, 1990).

Underdeveloped or negative conceptions of self-worth may persist, despite the possession of some requisite ability. Hence it is possible to experience much difficulty performing effectively, even if one has the necessary skills, due to an inaccurate or misguided conception of accessible personal resources or capacities (Markus, Cross, & Wurf, 1990). Just as persons define themselves in terms of characteristics they have not acquired, so also may they fail to assign any value to untapped potentials. That is, I define myself as a good person who has not acquired the tendency to "fly off the handle." Hence a part of my self picture includes items that I have consciously excluded from consideration, as in "I am not a mean person." So I fail to assign any value to my untapped potential to be unreasonable or excessively aggressive. Thus, the evaluation of social skill cannot be realistically assessed apart from the full range of present opportunities. As Markus et al. (1990) conclude, "Unless somebody believes a person can develop certain skills, such hidden potential may never be realized. The creation of a possible self-structure may foster the development of the desired attribute or ability, the surest route out of incompetence" (p. 223).

Running through the current of much misguided difficulty is a striking tendency to apply double standards. One set of appraisals is seen to apply to the party who initiates something, and another set of evaluative measures to those who observe or respond. At the level of a hidden agenda, a superior-inferior distinction is set in motion. In attributive slant, the standards that apply to one party are presumed to apply to everyone else, but the respective measures of everyone else are treated as somehow irrelevant, unknown, or inaccessible. In such circumstances, a rule of interpretive equity is violated—that of assigning no more or no less significance to the actions of others than to the actions of oneself. Violations are measured in terms of the total magnitude of disproportion that is introduced. At such times, it is easy to forget that other people are in exactly the same position as oneself—in a broad communal sense. After all, everyone is at the mercy of his or her own hunches and devices to make sense of things.

Fluent and articulate interactants are able to keep more things in better perspective. They are less likely to engage in heavily edited versions of concrete events. Most assume appropriate balance between issues of involvement and detachment. Prior interchange is not construed as burdensome, nor is the future construed as bleak. What matters to one is strictly relative to the concerns of everyone else. Closely related is a strong sense of communal orientation. Free-spirited participation matters more (in the long run) than who is above, below, ahead, or behind the others (in the short run).

Under favorable conditions, it is easier, perhaps, to stay in touch with what has distinct communicative value to other people. It is not just a matter of sizing up an audience, analyzing motives, and telling them what they are supposed to want to hear in the manner of (mere) rhetoric. The struggle for efficacy leads to a greater measure of resourcefulness in the expenditure of scarce resources. Change becomes systemic; that is, alter the system and not just the participants one by one. Now every member is in a realistic position to assign, and be assigned, commensurate levels of importance and weight. At last, the transactional process is the way that it could, should, or might have been at a great number of points along the way. Considerations of power, affection, and involvement now come more fully into play. Things merge and coalesce into the more sustaining, nurturing, and enduring of human forms.

Conditions are now in place for a greater proliferation of life-affirming acts. When we focus all of our performance skills and resources on those issues that still stand before us, rather than a litany of friction, strife, and strain, we put ourselves in a more favorable position to be faithful to the search for mutual truth rather than to narrow demands and sudden impulses. With mutual acceptance, change for the better is not just an empty possibility but a sheer necessity.

ULTIMATE CONSIDERATIONS

The quality of life registers in the tone and texture of human communication. As a consequence, a substratum of miscommunication may erode or undermine a spirit of mutuality through a process of reduction, simplification, misapplication, and elimination. Sometimes slippery mechanisms work out well as a matter of convenience: miss out on something over here; omit something else over there; fail to anticipate or follow through; short-circuit; pull up short; give up too soon; stop short of the mark; miss crucial opportunities; confuse time, place, or date; get lost and wander about; ask the wrong questions or search for the right answers in all the wrong places. Ergo, the simple failure to fulfill existing opportunities is a common malady. Optimism insists that whatever shortcomings cannot be eliminated may still be subject to a greater measure of regulation and control (Carnelley & Janoff-Bulman, 1992; Fletcher & Kininmonth, 1992; Rusbult, Onizuka, & Lipkus, 1993).

Ultimate considerations depend on whether face-to-face interaction facilitates or interferes with matters of personal health and well-being. The main way to find out is to live through the consequences of one's own choices and decisions. In the activities that people pursue and forgo, they cultivate the capacity and performance records that give them a sense of self-worth (Bandura, 1990; Zimmerman, 1990). The credit to be assigned to self and other (as interactants) is global, whereas appraisals of individual competence are more context- and task-specific. Esteem is derived from fulfilling standards of meaning and acclaim. Devaluation prompts corrective measures. Not a surprise, the more people feel that significant others have regard for them, the higher their self-worth and the greater regard they have for themselves (Harter, 1990). In effect, the goal to maximize interactive opportunities makes for a prudent personal policy (J. Griffin, 1990).

The best models for emulation are those that invoke deliberate practice in the acquisition of expert performance. Questions of communicative competence eventually must be reality-tested in the arena of concrete practice. Recent studies of expertise show that high-quality performance cannot be separated from (a) environmental circumstance and (b) opportunity for extraordinary skills to be acquired through protracted experience and the effect of practice on performance (Chi, Glaser, & Farr, 1988; Ericsson & Smith, 1991; Sternberg & Kolligian, 1990). In other words, when conditions are stable and personal actions well founded, there is the greatest margin of opportunity to work through expressed difficulties and problematic concerns.

Progress is often slow during initial stages of skill acquisition. Performance is increased in direct relation to the total amount of time that is devoted to deliberate practice. The larger effort may not be intrinsically enjoyable, particularly during the transition to greater involvement and increased levels of personal commitment. The ability to recognize abstract patterns is related to the capacity to view complex activities as a whole (Proctor & Dutta, 1995). Extended experience is associated with global conceptions of increased refinement, generalization, and discrimination (Ackerman, 1992). Expertise involves the ability to integrate embedded chunks of information in large units, the skillful coordination of specific units of complex tasks, and greater sensitivity to matters of evaluated progress (Proctor & Dutta, 1995; Schneider, 1985).

One qualification is in order. There is no guarantee that sheer persistence will do the trick. In a review of relevant findings, Ericsson et al. (1993) conclude,

> The maximal level of performance for individuals in a given domain is not attained automatically as a function of extended experience, but the level of performance can be increased even by highly experienced individuals as a result of deliberate efforts to improve. (p. 366)

As the complexity of tasks increases, so also must the number of functional methods increase as well. New methods must be devised to replace those that no longer work out well. There is no point in clinging to modes of existence that have outlived their usefulness. It is better to focus on activities that maximize improvement slowly. Finally, deliberate practice is an effortful activity that can only be sustained at peak levels for so long. Hence it is necessary to leave time to recover on a regular basis. At stake is the willingness to understand the full range of possible adaptations and methods for circumventing limits (Ericsson & Smith, 1991). In effect, the ability to maintain close and caring ties cannot be separated from the difficulties to be faced when those ties are themselves under the greatest degree of review, scrutiny, or doubt.

References

Abrahams, M. F. (1994). Perceiving flirtatious communication: An exploration of the perceptual dimensions underlying judgments of flirtatiousness. *Journal of Sex Research, 31,* 1-10.

Acitelli, L. K., Douvan, E., & Veroff, J. (1993). Perceptions of conflict in the first year of marriage: How important are similarity and understanding? *Journal of Social and Personal Relationships, 10,* 5-19.

Acker, M., & Davis, M. H. (1992). Intimacy, passion, and commitment in adult romantic relationships: A test of the triangular theory of love. *Journal of Social and Personal Relationships, 9,* 21-50.

Ackerman, P. L. (1992). Predicting individual differences in complex skill acquisition: Dynamics of ability determinants. *Journal of Applied Psychology, 77,* 598-614.

Adelman, M. B., Parks, M. R., & Albrecht, T. L. (1987). Supporting friends in need. In T. L. Albrecht & M. B. Adelman (Eds.), *Communicating social support* (pp. 105-125). Newbury Park, CA: Sage.

Airenti, G., Bara, B. G., & Colombetti, M. (1993). Failures, exploitations and deceits in communication. *Journal of Pragmatics, 20,* 303-326.

Albrecht, T. L., & Hall, B. J. (1991). The role of personal relationships in organizational innovation. *Communication Education, 29,* 158-170.

Aldous, J., & Ganey, R. (1989). Families' definition behavior of problematic situations. *Social Forces, 67,* 870-896.

Altman, L., & Taylor, D. A. (1973). *Social penetration: The development of interpersonal relationships.* New York: Holt, Rinehart & Winston.

Ambady, N., & Rosenthal, R. (1992). Thin slices of expressive behavior as predictors of interpersonal consequences: A meta-analysis. *Psychological Bulletin, 111,* 256-274.

American Psychiatric Association. (1987). *Diagnostic and statistical manual of mental disorders* (3rd ed.). Washington, DC: Author.

Amy, D. (1983). Environmental mediation: An alternative approach to policy stalemates. *Policy Sciences, 15,* 345-365.

Anderson, C. A. (1989). Causal reasoning and belief perseverance. In D. W. Schumann (Ed.), *Proceedings of the Society for Consumer Psychology* (pp. 115-120). Knoxville: University of Tennessee.

224

Anderson, H., & Gollishan, H. (1988). Human systems as linguistic systems: Evolving ideas about the implications for theory and practice. *Family Process, 27,* 371-393.

Anderson, J. R. (1991). The adaptive nature of human categorization. *Psychological Review, 98,* 409-429.

Anderson, R. L., & Mortensen, C. D. (1967). The logic of marketplace argumentation. *Quarterly Journal of Speech, 53,* 143-151.

Anderson, S. M., & Cole, S. W. (1990). "Do I know you?" The role of significant others in general social perception. *Journal of Personality and Social Psychology, 59,* 384-399.

Antaki, C. (1994). *Explaining and arguing: The social organization of accounts.* London: Sage.

Argyle, M., & Furnham, A. (1983). Sources of satisfaction and conflict in long-term relationships. *Journal of Marriage and the Family, 45,* 481-493.

Arnston, P. H., Mortensen, C. D., & Lustig, R. (1980). Predispositions toward verbal behavior in task-oriented interaction. *Human Communication Research, 6,* 239-252.

Aron, A., Aron, E. N., & Smollan, D. (1992). Inclusion of other in the self-scale and the structure of interpersonal closeness. *Journal of Personality and Social Psychology, 63,* 596-612.

Aronoff, J., Stollak, G. E., & Woike, B. A. (1994). Affect regulation and the breadth of interpersonal engagement. *Journal of Personality and Social Psychology, 67,* 105-114.

Axelrod, R. (1984). *The evolution of cooperation.* New York: Basic Books.

Axelrod, R., & Hamilton, W. D. (1981). The evolution of cooperation. *Science, 211,* 1390-1396.

Backman, C. W. (1988). The self: A dialectical approach. *Advances in Experimental Social Psychology, 21,* 229-260.

Bandura, A. (1990). Conclusion: Reflections on nonability determinants of competence. In J. Kolligian, Jr., & R. J. Sternberg (Eds.), *Competence considered* (pp. 315-362). New Haven, CT: Yale University Press.

Bargh, J. A. (1989). Conditional automaticity: Varieties of automatic influence in social perception and cognition. In J. S. Uleman & J. A. Bargh (Eds.), *Unintended thought* (pp. 3-51). New York: Guilford.

Bargh, J. A. (1994). The four horsemen of automaticity: Awareness, intention, efficiency, and control in social cognition. In R. S. Wyer, Jr., & T. K. Srull (Eds.), *Handbook of social cognition: Vol. 1. Basic processes* (2nd ed., pp. 1-40). Hillsdale, NJ: Lawrence Erlbaum.

Barnes, M. K., & Duck, S. (1994). Everyday communicative contexts for social support. In B. R. Burleson, T. L. Albrecht, & I. G. Sarason (Eds.), *Communication of social support: Messages, interactions, relationships, and community* (pp. 175-194). Thousand Oaks, CA: Sage.

Baron, R. A. (1988). Negative effects of destructive criticism: Impact on conflict, self-efficacy, and task performance. *Journal of Applied Psychology, 73,* 199-207.

Bartholomew, K. (1990). Avoidance of intimacy: An attachment perspective. *Journal of Social and Personal Relationships, 7,* 147-178.

Bartsch, R. (1987). *Norms of language.* London: Longman.

Bateson, G. (1972). *Steps to an ecology of mind.* New York: Ballantine.

Baum, A., & Paulus, P. B. (1987). Crowding. In D. Stokols & I. Altman (Eds.), *Handbook of environmental psychology* (pp. 533-570). New York: John Wiley.

Bauman, Z. (1978). *Hermeneutics and social science.* New York: Columbia University Press.

Baumhart, R. (1968). *An honest profit.* New York: Prentice Hall.

Bavelas, J. B. (1983). Situations that lead to disqualification. *Human Communication Research, 9,* 130-145.

Bavelas, J. B., Black, A., Chovil, N., & Mullett, J. (1990). *Equivocal communication.* Newbury Park, CA: Sage.

Bavelas, J. B., & Smith, B. J. (1982). A method for scaling verbal disqualification. *Human Communication Research, 8,* 214-227.

Baxter, L. A. (1984). Trajectories of relationship disengagement. *Journal of Social and Personal Relationships, 1,* 29-48.

Baxter, L. A. (1985). Accomplishing relationship disengagement. In S. Duck & D. Perlman (Eds.), *Understanding personal relationships: An interdisciplinary approach* (pp. 243-265). Beverly Hills, CA: Sage.

Baxter, L. A. (1986). Gender differences in the heterosexual relationship rules embedded in break-up accounts. *Journal of Social and Personal Relationships, 3,* 289-306.

Baxter, L. A. (1990). Dialectical contradictions in relationship development. *Journal of Social and Personal Relationships, 7,* 69-88.

Baxter, L. A., & Dindia, K. (1990). Marital partners' perceptions of marital maintenance strategies. *Journal of Social and Personal Relationships, 7,* 187-208.

Baxter, L. A., & Simon, E. P. (1993). Relationship maintenance strategies and dialectical contradictions in personal relationships. *Journal of Social and Personal Relationships, 10,* 225-242.

Baxter, L. A., & Wilmot, B. (1984). Secret tests: Social strategies for acquiring information about the state of the relationship. *Human Communication Research, 11,* 171-201.

Baxter, L. A., Wilmot, W. W., Simmons, C. A., & Swartz, A. (1993). Ways of doing conflict: A folk taxonomy of conflict events in personal relationships. In P. J. Kalbfleisch (Ed.), *Interpersonal communication: Evolving interpersonal relationships* (pp. 89-107). Hillsdale, NJ: Lawrence Erlbaum.

Belk, S. S., & Snell, W. E. (1988). Avoidance strategy use in intimate relationships. *Journal of Social and Clinical Psychology, 7,* 80-96.

Bell, R. A., & Daly, J. (1984). The affinity-seeking function of communication. *Communication Monographs, 51,* 91-115.

Bell, R. A., Daly, J. A., & Gonzalez, C. (1987). Affinity-maintenance in marriage and its relationship to women's marital satisfaction. *Journal of Marriage and the Family, 49,* 445-454.

Bendor, J. (1993). Uncertainty and the evolution of cooperation. *Journal of Conflict Resolution, 37,* 709-734.

Bennett, L. (1992). Legal fictions: Telling stories and doing justice. In M. L. McLaughlin, M. J. Cody, & S. J. Read (Eds.), *Explaining one's self to others: Reason-giving in a social context* (pp. 149-165). Hillsdale, NJ: Lawrence Erlbaum.

Bentley, A. F. (1926). *Relativity in man and society.* New York: G. P. Putnam.

Berg, J. H., & McQuinn, R. D. (1989). Loneliness and aspects of social support networks. *Journal of Social and Personal Relationships, 6,* 359-372.

Berger, C. R., & Calabrese, R. J. (1975). Some explorations in initial interaction and beyond: Toward a developmental theory of interpersonal communication. *Human Communication Research, 1,* 99-112.

Berger, C. R., & Kellermann, K. A. (1989). Personal opacity and social information gathering: Explorations in strategic communication. *Communication Research, 16,* 314-351.

Berger, C. R., & Kellermann, K. A. (1994). Acquiring social information. In J. A. Daly & J. M. Wiemann (Eds.), *Strategic interpersonal communication* (pp. 1-31). Hillsdale, NJ: Lawrence Erlbaum.

Berry, D. S. (1990). The perceiver as naive scientist or the scientist as naive perceiver? An ecological view of social knowledge acquisition. *Contemporary Social Psychology, 14,* 145-153.

Berry, D. S. (1991). Accuracy in social perception: Contributions of facial and vocal information. *Journal of Personality and Social Psychology, 61,* 298-307.

Berscheid, E., Snyder, M., & Omoto, A. M. (1989). The Relationship Closeness Inventory: Assessing the closeness of interpersonal relationships. *Journal of Personality and Social Psychology, 57,* 792-807.

Betz, B. (1991). Response to strategy and communication in an arms race-disarmament dilemma. *Journal of Conflict Resolution, 35,* 678-690.

Bienenfeld, F. (1985). The power of child custody mediation. *Mediation Quarterly, 9,* 35-47.

Bilmes, J. (1988). The concept of preference in conversational analysis. *Language in Society, 17,* 161-181.

Blalock, H. M. (1989). *Power and conflict: Toward a general theory.* Newbury Park, CA: Sage.

Bluhm, C., Widiger, T. A., & Miele, G. M. (1990). Interpersonal complementarity and individual differences. *Journal of Personality and Social Psychology, 58,* 464-471.

Bochner, A. (1984). The functions of human communication in interpersonal bonding. In C. Arnold & J. Bowers (Eds.), *Handbook of rhetorical and communication theory* (pp. 544-621). Boston: Allyn & Bacon.

Bok, S. (1978). *Lying: Moral choice in public and private life.* New York: Vintage.

Bond, C. F., Jr., Kahler, K. N., & Paolicelli, L. M. (1985). The miscommunication of deception: An adaptive perspective. *Journal of Experimental Social Psychology, 21,* 331-345.

Bond, C. F., Jr., Omar, A., Pitre, U., & Lashley, B. R. (1992). Fishy looking liars: Deception judgment from expectancy violation. *Journal of Personality and Social Psychology, 63,* 969-977.

Bond, C. F., Jr., & Robinson, M. (1988). The evolution of deception. *Journal of Nonverbal Behavior, 12,* 295-307.

Booth-Butterfield, S., & Booth-Butterfield, M. (1987, April). *Untangling the tangled web: Theory and empirical tests of interpersonal deception.* Paper presented at the annual convention of the International Communication Association, Montreal, Canada.

Borgida, E., & Howard-Pitney, B. (1983). Personal involvement and the robustness of perceptual salience effects. *Journal of Personality and Social Psychology, 45,* 560-570.

Borkenau, P. (1986). Toward an understanding of trait interrelations: Acts as instances for several traits. *Journal of Personality and Social Psychology, 51,* 371-381.

Bornstein, G., Erev, I., & Goren, H. (1994). The effect of repeated play in the IPG and IPD team games. *Journal of Conflict Resolution, 38,* 690-707.

Boulding, K. E. (1990). *Three faces of power.* Newbury Park, CA: Sage.

Bowman, M. L. (1990). Coping efforts and marital satisfaction: Measuring marital coping and its correlates. *Journal of Marriage and the Family, 52,* 463-474.

Bradac, J. J. (1990). Language attitudes and impression formation. In H. Giles & W. P. Robinson (Eds.), *Handbook of language and social psychology* (pp. 387-412). Chichester: Wiley.

Bradac, J. J., Wiemann, J. M., & Schaefer, K. (1994). The language of control in interpersonal communication. In J. A. Daly & J. M. Wiemann (Eds.), *Strategic interpersonal communication* (pp. 91-108). Hillsdale, NJ: Lawrence Erlbaum.

Bradac, J. J., & Wisegarver, R. (1984). Ascribed status, lexical diversity, and accent: Determinants of perceived status, solidarity, and control of speech style. *Journal of Language and Social Psychology, 3,* 239-255.

Bradbury, T. N., & Fincham, F. D. (1992). Attributions and behavior in marital interaction. *Journal of Personality and Social Psychology, 63,* 613-628.

Brams, S. J., & Doherty, A. E. (1993). Intransigence in negotiations: The dynamics of disagreement. *Journal of Conflict Resolution, 37,* 692-708.

Broderick, J. E., & O'Leary, K. D. (1986). Contributions of affect, attitudes, and behavior to marital satisfaction. *Journal of Consulting and Clinical Psychology, 54,* 514-517.

Brown, D. E. (1991). *Human universals.* Philadelphia: Temple University Press.

Brunstein, J. C. (1993). Personal goals and subjective well-being: A longitudinal study. *Journal of Personality and Social Psychology, 65,* 1061-1070.

Buck, R. (1988). *Human motivation and emotion* (2nd ed.). New York: John Wiley.

Buller, D. B., Strzyzewski, K. D., & Comstock, J. (1991). Interpersonal deception: I. Deceivers' reactions to receivers's suspicions and probing. *Communication Monographs, 58,* 1-24.

Bullis, C., Clark, C., & Sline, R. (1993). From passion to commitment: Turning points in romantic relationships. In P. J. Kalbfleisch (Ed.), *Interpersonal communication: Evolving interpersonal relationships* (pp. 213-236). Hillsdale, NJ: Lawrence Erlbaum.

Burger, J. M. (1990). Desire for control and interpersonal interaction style. *Journal of Research on Personality, 24,* 32-44.

Burger, J. M., & Palmer, M. L. (1992). Changes in and generalization of unrealistic optimism following experiences with stressful events: Reaction to the 1989 California earthquake. *Personality and Social Psychology Bulletin, 18,* 39-43.

Burgoon, J. K., & Buller, D. B. (1994). Interpersonal deception: III. Effects of deceit on perceived communication and nonverbal behavior dynamics. *Journal of Nonverbal Behavior, 18,* 155-184.

Burgoon, J. K., Buller, D. B., Ebesu, A. S., & Rockwell, P. (1994). Interpersonal deception: V. Accuracy in deception detection. *Communication Monographs, 61,* 303-325.

Burgoon, J. K., Buller, D. B., Guerrero, L. K., Afifi, W. A., & Feldman, C. M. (1996). Interpersonal deception: XII. Information management dimensions underlying deceptive and truthful messages. *Communication Monographs, 63,* 50-69.

Burgoon, J. K., & LePoire, B. (1993). Effects of communication expectancies, actual communication, and expectancy disconfirmation on evaluations of communicators and their communication behavior. *Human Communication Research, 20,* 67-96.

Burgoon, J. K., & Walther, J. B. (1990). Nonverbal expectancies and the evaluative consequences of violations. *Human Communication Research, 17,* 232-265.

Burleson, B. R. (1994). Comforting messages: Features, functions, and outcomes. In J. A. Daly & J. M. Wiemann (Eds.), *Strategic interpersonal communication* (pp. 135-161). Hillsdale, NJ: Lawrence Erlbaum.

Burleson, B. R., Albrecht, T. J., & Sarason, L. G. (Eds.). (1994). *Communication of social support: Messages, interactions, relationships, and community.* Thousand Oaks, CA: Sage.

Burling, R. (1986). The selective advantage of complex language. *Ethology and Sociobiology, 7,* 1-16.

Burnstein, E., Crandall, C., & Kitayama, S. (1994). Some neo-Darwinian decision rules for altruism: Weighing cues for inclusive fitness as a function of the biological importance of the decision. *Journal of Personality and Social Psychology, 67,* 773-789.

Buunk, B. P., Doosje, B. J., Jans, L. G. J., & Hopstaken, L. E. M. (1993). Perceived reciprocity, social support, and stress at work: The role of exchange and communal orientation. *Journal of Personality and Social Psychology, 65,* 801-811.

Buunk, B. P., & VanYperen, N. W. (1991). Referential comparisons, relational comparisons, and exchange orientation: Their relation to marital satisfaction. *Personality and Social Psychology Bulletin, 17,* 709-716.

Byrd, M. (1988). Adult age differences in the ability to comprehend ambiguous sentences. *Language and Communication, 8,* 135-146.

Canary, D. J., Cunningham, E. M., & Cody, M. J. (1988). Goal types, gender, and locus of control in managing interpersonal conflict. *Communication Research, 15,* 426-446.

Canary, D. J., & Stafford, L. (1993). Preservation of relational characteristics: Maintenance strategies, equity, and locus of control. In P. J. Kalbfleisch (Ed.), *Interpersonal communication: Evolving interpersonal relationships* (pp. 237-259). Hillsdale, NJ: Lawrence Erlbaum.

Carlson, J. G., & Hatfield, E. (1992). *Psychology of emotion.* Fort Worth, TX: Harcourt Brace Jovanovich.

Carnelley, K. B., & Janoff-Bulman, R. (1992). Optimism about love relationships: General vs specific lessons from one's personal experience. *Journal of Social and Personal Relationships, 9,* 5-20.

Carpenter, B. N., Hansson, R. O., Rountree, R., & Jones, W. H. (1983). Relational competence and adjustment in diabetic patients. *Journal of Social and Clinical Psychology, 1,* 359-369.

Cegala, D. J., Savage, G. T., Brunner, C. C., & Conrad, A. B. (1982). An elaboration of the meaning of interaction involvement: Toward the development of a theoretical concept. *Communication Monographs, 49,* 229-248.

Chelune, G. J. (1979). *Self-disclosure: Origins, patterns, and implications of openness in interpersonal relationships.* San Francisco: Jossey-Bass.

Chi, M. T. H., Glaser, R., & Farr, M. J. (Eds.). (1988). *The nature of expertise.* Hillsdale, NJ: Lawrence Erlbaum.

Chisholm, R. M., & Freehan, T. D. (1977). The intent to deceive. *Journal of Philosophy, 74,* 143-159.

Chovil, N. (1994). Equivocation as an interactional event. In W. R. Cupach & B. H. Spitzberg (Eds.), *The dark side of interpersonal communication* (pp. 105-123). Hillsdale, NJ: Lawrence Erlbaum.

Christensen, A., & Heavey, C. I. (1990). Gender and social structure in the demand/withdrawal pattern of marital conflict. *Journal of Personality and Social Psychology, 59,* 73-81.

Clark, A. J. (1984). Evolutionary epistemology and ontological realism. *Philosophical Quarterly, 34,* 482-490.

Clark, H. H., & Schunk, D. H. (1980). Polite responses to polite requests. *Cognition, 8,* 111-143.

Clark, M. S. (1984). Record keeping in two types of relationships. *Journal of Personality and Social Psychology, 47,* 549-557.

Clark, M. S., Mills, J., & Powell, M. C. (1986). Keeping track of needs in communal and exchange relationships. *Journal of Personality and Social Psychology, 51,* 333-338.

Clark, M. S., Ouellette, R., Powell, M. C., & Milberg, S. (1987). Recipient's mood, relationship type, and helping. *Journal of Personality and Social Psychology, 53,* 94-103.

Clark, M. S., & Waddell, B. (1985). Perception of exploitation in communal and exchange relationships. *Journal of Social and Personal Relationships, 2,* 403-413.

Cody, M. J. (1982). A typology of disengagement strategies and an examination of the roles intimacy, reactions to inequity, and relational problems play in strategy selection. *Communication Monographs, 49,* 148-170.

Coker, D. A., & Burgoon, J. K. (1987). The nature of conversational involvement and nonverbal encoding patterns. *Human Communication Research, 13,* 463-494.

Collins, N. L., & Miller, L. C. (1994). Self-disclosure and liking: A meta-analytic review. *Psychological Bulletin, 116,* 457-475.

Collins, R. (1975). *Conflict sociology: Toward an explanatory science.* New York: Academic Press.

Collins, R. (1985). *Three sociological traditions.* New York: Oxford University Press.

Colvin, C. R., & Block, J. (1994a). Do positive illusions foster mental health? An examination of the Taylor and Brown formulation. *Psychological Bulletin, 116,* 3-20.

Colvin, C. R., & Block, J. (1994b). Positive illusions and well-being revisited: Separating fiction from fact. *Psychological Bulletin, 116,* 1-28.

Conlon, D., & Fasolo, P. (1990). The influence of speed of third-party intervention and outcome on negotiator and constituent fairness judgments. *Academy of Management Journal, 33,* 833-846.

Conn, M. K., & Peterson, C. (1989). Social support: Seek and ye shall find. *Journal of Social and Personal Relationships, 6,* 345-358.

Coombs, C. H. (1987). The structure of conflict. *American Psychologist, 42,* 355-363.

Coombs, C. H., & Avrunin, G. S. (1988). *The structure of conflict.* Hillsdale, NJ: Lawrence Erlbaum.

Corson, D. J. (1993). Discursive bias and ideology in the administration of minority group interests. *Language and Society, 22,* 165-191.

Coupland, N., Giles, H., & Wiemann, J. M. (Eds.). (1991). *"Miscommunication" and problematic talk.* Newbury Park, CA: Sage.

Cowley, S. J. (1994). Conversational functions of rhythmical patterning: A behavioural perspective. *Language and Communication, 14,* 353-376.

Cross, R. (1977). Not can but will college teaching be improved. *New Directions for Higher Education, 17,* 1-15.

Cupach, W. R. (1994). Social predicaments. In W. R. Cupach & B. H. Spitzberg (Eds.), *The dark side of interpersonal communication* (pp. 159-180). Hillsdale, NJ: Lawrence Erlbaum.

Cupach, W., & Metts, S. (1986). Accounts of relational dissolution: A comparison of marital and non-marital relationships. *Communication Monographs, 53,* 311-334.

D'Agostino, P. R., & Fincher-Kiefer, R. (1992). Need for cognition and the correspondence bias. *Social Cognition, 10,* 151-163.

D'Andrade, R. G., & Wish, M. (1985). Speech act theory in quantitative research on interpersonal behavior. *Discourse Processes, 8,* 229-259.

Daly, J. A., Diesel, C. A., & Weber, D. (1994). Conversational dilemmas. In W. R. Cupach & B. H. Spitzberg (Eds.), *The dark side of interpersonal communication* (pp. 127-158). Hillsdale, NJ: Lawrence Erlbaum.

Dascal, M., & Berenstein, I. (1987). Two modes of understanding: Comprehending and grasping. *Language and Communication, 7,* 139-151.

Daves, W. F., & Holland, C. L. (1989). The structure of conflict behavior of managers assessed with self- and subordinate ratings. *Human Relations, 42,* 741-756.

Davis, K. E., Kirkpatrick, L. A., Levy, M. B., & O'Hearn, R. E. (1994). Stalking the elusive love style: Attachment styles, love styles, and relationship development. In R. Erber & R. Gilmour (Eds.), *Theoretical frameworks for personal relationships* (pp. 179-210). Hillsdale, NJ: Lawrence Erlbaum.

Deaux, K. (1992). Focusing on the self: Challenges to self-definition and their consequences for mental health. In D. N. Ruble, P. R. Costanzo, & M. E. Oliveri (Eds.), *The social psychology of mental health: Basic mechanisms and applications* (pp. 301-327). New York: Guilford.

Deluga, R. J. (1991). The relationship of upward-influencing behavior with subordinate-impression management characteristics. *Journal of Applied Social Psychology, 21,* 1145-1160.

DePaulo, B. M., Blank, A. L., Swaim, G. W., & Hairfield, J. G. (1992). Expressiveness and expressive control. *Personality and Social Psychology Bulletin, 18,* 276-285.

DePaulo, B. M., Kirkendol, S. E., Tang, J., & O'Brien, T. P. (1988). The motivational impairment effect in the communication of deception: Replications and extensions. *Journal of Nonverbal Behavior, 12,* 177-201.

DePaulo, B. M., LeMay, C. S., & Epstein, J. A. (1991). Effects of importance of success and expectations for success on effectiveness at deceiving. *Personality and Social Psychology Bulletin, 17,* 14-24.

deTurck, M. A., Harszlak, J. J., Bodhorn, D. J., & Texter, L. A. (1990). The effects of training social perceivers to detect deception from behavioral cues. *Communication Quarterly, 38,* 1-11.

deTurck, M. A., & Miller, G. R. (1985). Deception and arousal: Isolating the behavioral correlates of deception. *Human Communication Research, 12,* 181-201.

deTurck, M. A., & Miller, G. R. (1990). Training observers to detect deception: Effects of self-monitoring and rehearsal. *Human Communication Research, 16,* 603-620.

Devine, P. G. (1989). Automatic and controlled processes in prejudice: The roles of stereotypes and personal beliefs. In A. R. Pratkanis, S. J. Breckler, & A. G. Greenwald (Eds.), *Attitude structure and function* (pp. 181-212). Hillsdale, NJ: Lawrence Erlbaum.

Dillard, J. P., Kinney, T. A., & Cruz, M. G. (1996). Influence, appraisals, and emotions in close relationships. *Communication Monographs, 63,* 105-130.

Dillon, J. T. (1990). *The practice of questioning.* London: Routledge.

Dindia, K., & Allen, M. (1992). Sex differences in self-disclosure: A meta-analysis. *Psychological Bulletin, 112,* 106-124.

Dindia, K., & Baxter, L. (1987). Strategies for maintaining and repairing marital relationships. *Journal of Social and Personal Relationships, 4,* 143-158.

Dindia, K., & Canary, D. J. (1993). Definitions and theoretical perspectives on maintaining relationships. *Journal of Social and Personal Relationships, 10,* 163-173.

Douglas, W. (1991). Expectations about initial interaction: An examination of the effects of global uncertainty. *Human Communication Research, 17,* 355-384.

Driscoll, D. M., Hamilton, D. L., & Sorrentino, R. M. (1991). Uncertainty orientation and recall of person-descriptive information. *Personality and Social Psychology Bulletin, 17,* 494-500.

Druckman, D. (1993). The situational levers of negotiating flexibility. *Journal of Conflict Resolution, 37,* 236-276.

Druckman, D. (1994). Determinants of compromising behavior in negotiation. *Journal of Conflict Resolution, 38,* 507-556.

Duck, S. (1981). Toward a research map for the study of relationship breakdown. In S. Duck & R. Gilmour (Eds.), *Personal relationships: Vol. 3. Personal relationships in disorder* (pp. 1-29). New York: Academic Press.

Duck, S. (1982). A topography of relationship disengagement and dissolution. In S. Duck (Ed.), *Personal relationships: Vol. 4. Dissolving personal relationships* (pp. 1-30). New York: Academic Press.

Duck, S. (1991). *Understanding relationships.* New York: Guilford.

Duck, S. (1994). Stratagems, spoils, and a serpent's tooth: On the delights and dilemmas of personal relationships. In W. R. Cupach & B. H. Spitzberg (Eds.), *The dark side of interpersonal communication* (pp. 3-24). Hillsdale, NJ: Lawrence Erlbaum.

Duck, S., & Gilmour, R. (Eds.). (1981). *Personal relationships: Vol. 3. Personal relationships in disorder.* New York: Academic Press.

Dudley, C. J., & Brown, E. (1981). Social relativity: The motion of groups and actors. *Sociological Quarterly, 22,* 313-326.

Dummett, M. (1993). *The seas of language.* New York: Oxford University Press.

Dunbar, R. I. M. (1987). Sociobiological explanations and the evolution of ethnocentrism. In V. Reynolds, V. Falger, & I. Vine (Eds.), *The sociobiology of ethnocentrism: Evolutionary dimensions of xenophobia, discrimination, racism and nationalism* (pp. 48-59). London: Croom Helm.

Dunkel-Schetter, C., & Skokan, L. A. (1990). Determinants of social support provision in personal relationships. *Journal of Social and Personal Relationships, 7,* 437-450.

Dunning, D., Meyerowitz, J. A., & Holzberg, A. D. (1989). Ambiguity and self-evaluation: The role of idiosyncratic trait definitions in self-serving assessments of ability. *Journal of Personality and Social Psychology, 57,* 1082-1090.

Dunning, D., & Stern, L. B. (1994). Distinguishing accurate from inaccurate eyewitness identification via inquiries about decision processes. *Journal of Personality and Social Psychology, 67,* 818-835.

Edwards, D., & Potter, J. (1993). Language and causation: A discursive action model of description and attribution. *Psychological Review, 100,* 23-41.

Eisenberg, E. M. (1984). Ambiguity as strategy in organizational communication. *Communication Monographs, 51,* 227-242.

Ekman, P. (1980). *The face of man: Expressions of universal emotions in a New Guinea village.* New York: Garland STPM.

Ekman, P. (1988). Lying and nonverbal behavior: Theoretical issues and new findings. *Journal of Nonverbal Behavior, 12,* 163-175.

Ekman, P. (1994). Strong evidence for universals in facial expressions: A reply to Russell's mistaken critique. *Psychological Bulletin, 115,* 268-287.

Ekman, P., & O'Sullivan, M. (1991). Who can catch a lie? *American Psychologist, 46,* 913-920.

Emmons, R. A. (1987). Narcissism: Theory and measurement. *Journal of Personality and Social Psychology, 52,* 11-17.

Epstein, S. (1990). Cognitive-experiential self-theory. In L. Pervin (Ed.), *Handbook of personality theory and research* (pp. 165-191). New York: Guilford.

Epstein, S., & Meier, P. (1989). Constructive thinking: A broad coping variable with specific components. *Journal of Personality and Social Psychology, 57,* 332-350.

Erber, R., & Tesser, A. (1994). Self-evaluation maintenance: A social psychological approach to interpersonal relationships. In R. Erber & R. Gilmour (Eds.), *Theoretical frameworks for personal relationships* (pp. 211-233). Hillsdale, NJ: Lawrence Erlbaum.

Ericsson, K. A., Krampe, R. T., & Tesch-Romer, C. (1993). The role of deliberate practice in the acquisition of expert performance. *Psychological Review, 100,* 363-406.

Ericsson, K. A., & Smith, J. (Eds.). (1991). *Toward a general theory of expertise: Prospects and limits.* Cambridge: Cambridge University Press.

Falbo, T., & Peplau, L. A. (1980). Power strategies in intimate relationships. *Journal of Personality and Social Psychology, 38,* 618-628.

Fenigstein, A., & Abrams, D. (1993). Self-attention and the egocentric assumption of shared perspective. *Journal of Experimental Social Psychology, 29,* 287-303.

Fincham, F. D. (1992). The account episode in close relationships. In M. L. McLaughlin, M. J. Cody, & S. J. Read (Eds.), *Explaining one's self to others: Reasoning-giving in a social context* (pp. 167-182). Hillsdale, NJ: Lawrence Erlbaum.

Fincham, F. D., & Bradbury, T. N. (1987). The impact of attributions in marriage: A longitudinal analysis. *Journal of Personality and Social Psychology, 53,* 510-517.

Fincham, F. D., & Bradbury, T. N. (1989). The impact of attributions in marriage: An individual differences analysis. *Journal of Social and Personal Relationships, 6,* 69-85.

Firestone, R. W. (1987). *The fantasy bond: Effects of psychological defenses on interpersonal relations.* New York: Human Sciences Press.

Fischer, K. (1989). The functional architecture of adaptive cognitive systems—with limited capacity. *Semiotica, 68*(3/4), 191-248.

Fish, S. (1989). *Doing what comes naturally.* Durham, NC: Duke University Press.

Fiske, A. P. (1992). The four elementary forms of sociality: Framework for a unified theory of social relations. *Psychological Review, 99,* 689-723.

Fiske, S. T. (1980). Attention and weight in person perception: The impact of negative and extreme forms of behavior. *Journal of Personality and Social Psychology, 38,* 889-906.

Fiske, S. T., & Taylor, S. E. (1991). *Social cognition* (2nd ed.). New York: McGraw-Hill.

Fleming, J. H., & Darley, J. M. (1991). Mixed messages: The multiple audience problem and strategic communication. *Social Cognition, 9,* 25-46.

Fletcher, G. J. O., & Kininmonth, L. A. (1992). Measuring relationship beliefs: An individual differences scale. *Journal of Research in Personality, 26,* 371-397.

Fletcher, G. J. O., Reeder, G. D., & Bull, V. (1990). Bias and accuracy in attitude attribution: The role of attributional complexity. *Journal of Experimental Social Psychology, 26,* 275-288.

Fletcher, G. J. O., Rosanowski, J., & Fitness, J. (1994). Automatic processing in intimate contexts: The role of close-relationship beliefs. *Journal of Personality and Social Psychology, 67,* 888-897.

Fletcher, G. J. O., Rosanowski, J., Rhodes, G., & Lange, C. (1992). Accuracy and speed of causal processing: Experts versus novices in social judgment. *Journal of Experimental Social Psychology, 28,* 320-338.

Flett, G. L., Blankstein, K. R., Pliner, P., & Bator, C. (1988). Impression management and self-deception components of appraised emotional experience. *British Journal of Social Psychology, 27,* 67-77.

Funder, D. C. (1987). Errors and mistakes: Evaluating the accuracy of social judgment. *Psychological Bulletin, 101,* 75-90.

Funder, D. C., & Colvin, C. R. (1988). Friends and strangers: Acquaintanceship, agreement, and the accuracy of personality judgment. *Journal of Personality and Social Psychology, 55,* 149-158.

Furedy, J. J., & Ben-Shakhar, G. (1991). The roles of deception, intention to deceive, and motivation to avoid detection in the psychophysiological detection of guilty knowledge. *Psychophysiology, 28,* 163-171.

Furnham, A. (1992). Lay explanations. In M. L. McLaughlin, M. J. Cody, & S. J. Read (Eds.), *Explaining one's self to others: Reason-giving in a social context* (pp. 83-104). Hillsdale, NJ: Lawrence Erlbaum.

Galin, K. E., & Thorn, B. E. (1993). Unmasking pain: Detection of deception in facial expressions. *Journal of Social and Clinical Psychology, 12,* 182-197.

Geertz, C. (1975). On the nature of anthropological understanding. *American Scientist, 63,* 47-53.

Gelman, R. (1991). Epigenetic foundations of knowledge structures: Initial and transcendent constructions. In C. Carey & R. Gelman (Eds.), *The epigenesis of mind: Essays on biology and cognition* (pp. 293-322). Hillsdale, NJ: Lawrence Erlbaum.

Gibbons, P., Bradac, J. J., & Busch, J. (1992). The role of language in negotiations: Threats and promises. In L. Putnam & M. Roloff (Eds.), *Communication and negotiation* (pp. 156-175). Newbury Park, CA: Sage.

Gibbons, P., Busch, J., & Bradac, J. J. (1991). Powerful versus powerless language: Consequences for persuasion, impression formation, and cognitive response. *Journal of Language and Social Psychology, 10,* 115-133.

Giddens, A. (1994). *Modernity and self-identity.* Stanford, CA: Stanford University Press.

Gilbert, D. T. (1991). How mental systems believe. *American Psychologist, 46,* 107-119.

Gilbert, D. T. (1993). The assent of man: Mental representation and the control of belief. In D. M. Wegner & J. W. Pennebaker (Eds.), *The handbook of mental control* (pp. 57-87). Englewood Cliffs, NJ: Prentice Hall.

Gilbert, D. T., Pelham, B. W., & Krull, D. S. (1988). On cognitive busyness: When person perceivers meet persons perceived. *Journal of Personality and Social Psychology, 54,* 733-741.

Goetz, E. T. (1979). Inferring from text: Some factors influencing which inferences will be made. *Discourse Processes, 2,* 179-195.

Goetze, D. (1994). Comparing prisoner's dilemma, commons dilemma, and public goods provision designs in laboratory experiments. *Journal of Conflict Resolution, 38,* 56-86.

Goffman, E. (1959). *The presentation of self in everyday life.* Garden City, NY: Doubleday Anchor.

Goleman, D. J. (1989). What is negative about positive illusions? When benefits for the individual harm the collective. *Journal of Social and Clinical Psychology, 8,* 190-197.

Goodwin, C. (1987). Forgetfulness as an interactive resource. *Social Psychological Quarterly, 2,* 115-130.

Goodwin, C., & Goodwin, M. H. (1990). Interstitial argument. In E. Grimshaw (Ed.), *Conflict talk: Sociolinguistic investigations of arguments in conversations* (pp. 85-117). Cambridge: Cambridge University Press.

Goodwin, M. H., & Goodwin, C. (1987). Children's arguing. In S. U. Philips, S. Steele, & C. Tanz (Eds.), *Language, gender and sex in comparative perspective* (pp. 200-248). Cambridge: Cambridge University Press.

Gore, S., Aseltine, R. H., Jr., & Colten, M. E. (1993). Gender, social-relational involvement, and depression. *Journal of Research on Adolescence, 3,* 101-125.

Gottman, J. M. (1994). *Why marriages succeed or fail.* New York: Simon & Schuster.

Gottman, J. M., & Krokoff, L. J. (1989). Marital interaction and satisfaction: A longitudinal view. *Journal of Consulting and Clinical Psychology, 57,* 47-52.

Gottman, J. M., & Levenson, R. W. (1992). Marital processes predictive of later dissolution: Behavior, physiology, and health. *Journal of Personality and Social Psychology, 63,* 221-233.

Grace, G. W. (1987). *The linguistic construction of reality.* London: Croom Helm.

Graesser, A. C., Singer, M., & Trabasso, T. (1994). Constructing inferences during narrative text comprehension. *Psychological Review, 101,* 371-395.

Graziano, W. G., & Musser, L. M. (1982). The joining and the parting of the ways. In S. Duck (Ed.), *Personal relationships: Vol. 4. Dissolving personal relationships* (pp. 75-106). New York: Academic Press.

Greene, J. O. (1995). An action-assembly perspective on verbal and nonverbal message production: A dancer's message unveiled. In D. E. Hewes (Ed.), *The cognitive bases of interpersonal communication* (pp. 51-85). Hillsdale, NJ: Lawrence Erlbaum.

Greenwald, A. G., & Pratkanis, A. R. (1984). The self. In R. S. Wyer & T. K. Srull (Eds.), *Handbook of social cognition* (Vol. 3, pp. 129-178). Hillsdale, NJ: Lawrence Erlbaum.

Grice, H. P. (1989). *Studies in the way of words.* Cambridge, MA: Harvard University Press.

Griffin, D., & Bartholomew, K. (1994). Models of the self and other: Fundamental dimensions underlying measures of adult attachment. *Journal of Personality and Social Psychology, 67,* 430-445.

Griffin, J. (1990). *Well-being.* Oxford: Clarendon.

Grimshaw, A. D. (1990). Research on conflict talk: Antecedents, resources, findings, directions. In A. D. Grimshaw (Ed.), *Conflict talk: Sociolinguistic investigations of arguments in conversations* (pp. 280-324). Cambridge: Cambridge University Press.

Grover, S. L. (1993). Lying, deceit, and subterfuge: A model of dishonesty in the workplace. *Organizational Science, 4,* 478-495.

Grundy, K. W., & Weinstein, M. A. (1974). *The ideologies of violence.* Columbus, OH: Merrill.

Gryl, F. E., Stith, S. M., & Byrd, G. W. (1991). Close dating relationships among college students: Differences by use of violence and by gender. *Journal of Social and Personal Relationships, 8,* 243-264.

Gudjonsson, G. H. (1990). Self-deception and other-deception in forensic assessment. *Personality and Individual Differences, 11,* 219-225.

Haley, J. (1959). An interactional description of schizophrenia. *Psychiatry, 22,* 321-332.

Handworker, W. P. (1989). The origins and evolution of culture. *American Anthropologist, 91,* 313-326.

Harris, M. J., & Rosenthal, R. (1985). Mediation of interpersonal expectancy effects: 31 meta-analyses. *Psychological Bulletin, 97,* 363-386.

Hart, K. E., Hittner, J. B., & Paras, K. C. (1991). Sense of coherence, trait anxiety, and the perceived availability of social support. *Journal of Research on Personality, 25,* 137-145.

Harter, S. (1990). Causes, correlates, and the functional role of global self-worth: A life-span perspective. In J. Kolligian, Jr., & R. J. Sternberg (Eds.), *Competence considered* (pp. 67-97). New Haven, CT: Yale University Press.

Hartladge, S., Alloy, L. B., Vazques, C., & Dykman, D. (1993). Automatic and effortful processing in depression. *Psychological Bulletin, 113,* 247-278.

Haslam, N. (1994). Mental representation of social relationships: Dimensions, laws, or categories? *Journal of Personality and Social Psychology, 67,* 575-584.

Haslam, N., & Fiske, A. P. (1992). Implicit relationship prototypes: Investigating five theories of the cognitive organization of social relationships. *Journal of Experimental Social Psychology, 28,* 441-474.

Heidegger, M. (1962). *Being and time* (J. Macquarrie & E. Robinson, Trans.). New York: Harper & Row.

Hewes, D. E. (1995). Cognitive processing of problematic messages: Reinterpreting to "unbias" texts. In D. E. Hewes (Ed.), *The cognitive bases of interpersonal communication* (pp. 113-138). Hillsdale, NJ: Lawrence Erlbaum.

Hewes, D., & Planalp, S. (1987). The individual's place in communication science. In C. R. Berger & S. H. Chaffee (Eds.), *Handbook of communication science* (pp. 146-183). Newbury Park, CA: Sage.

Higgins, E. T. (1987). Self-discrepancy: A theory relating self and affect. *Psychological Review, 94,* 319-340.

Higgins, E. T. (1989). Knowledge accessibility and activation: Subjectivity and suffering from unconscious sources. In J. S. Uleman & J. A. Bargh (Eds.), *Unintended thought* (pp. 75-123). New York: Guilford.

Higgins, E. T., & Bargh, J. A. (1987). Social cognition and social perception. *Annual Review of Psychology, 38,* 369-425.

Higgins, E. T., & Bargh, J. A. (1992). Unconscious sources of subjectivity and suffering: Is consciousness the solution? In L. L. Martin & A. Tesser (Eds.), *The construction of social judgments* (pp. 67-103). Hillsdale, NJ: Lawrence Erlbaum.

Hill, C. T., Rubin, Z., & Peplau, L. A. (1976). Breakups before marriage: The end of 103 affairs. *Journal of Social Issues, 32,* 147-168.

Hill, T., Lewicki, P., Czyzewski, M., & Boss, A. (1989). Self-perpetuating development of encoding biases in person perception. *Journal of Personality and Social Psychology, 57,* 373-387.

Hiltrop, J. (1989). Factors associated with successful labor mediation. In K. Kressel & D. G. Pruitt (Eds.), *Mediation research* (pp. 241-262). San Francisco: Jossey-Bass.

Hobfoll, S., Freedy, J., Lane, C., & Geller, P. (1990). Conservation of social resources: Social support resource theory. *Journal of Social and Personal Relationships, 7,* 465-478.

Holahan, C. J., & Moos, R. H. (1981). Social support and psychological distress: A longitudinal analysis. *Journal of Abnormal Psychology, 90,* 365-370.

Holahan, C. J., & Moos, R. H. (1982). Social support and adjustment: Predictive benefits of social climate indices. *American Journal of Community Psychology, 10,* 403-415.

Hopper, R., & Bell, R. A. (1984). Broadening the deception construct. *Quarterly Journal of Speech, 70,* 288-300.

Hornstein, G. A. (1985). Intimacy in conversational style as a function of the degree of closeness between members of a dyad. *Journal of Personality and Social Psychology, 49,* 671-681.

Howells, K. (1981). Social relationships in violent offenders. In S. Duck & R. Gilmour (Eds.), *Personal relationships: Vol. 3. Personal relationships in disorder* (pp. 215-234). New York: Academic Press.

Huston, T. L., & Vangelisti, A. L. (1991). Socioemotional behavior and satisfaction in marital relationships: A longitudinal study. *Journal of Personality and Social Psychology, 61,* 721-733.

Hyman, R. (1989). The psychology of deception. *Annual Review of Psychology, 40,* 133-154.

Ickes, W. (Ed.). (1985). *Compatible and incompatible relationships.* New York: Springer-Verlag.

Infante, D. A., Chandler, T. A., & Rudd, J. E. (1989). Test of an argumentative skill deficiency model of interpersonal violence. *Communication Monographs, 56,* 163-177.

Infante, D. A., Sabourin, T. C., Rudd, J. E., & Shannon, E. A. (1990). Verbal aggression in violent and nonviolent marital disputes. *Communication Quarterly, 38,* 361-371.

Izard, C. E. (1980). Cross-cultural perspectives on emotion and emotion communication. In H. Triandis & W. Lonner (Eds.), *Handbook of cross-cultural psychology: Basis processes* (Vol. 3, pp. 185-222). Boston: Allyn & Bacon.

Izard, C. E. (1990). Facial expressions and the regulation of emotions. *Journal of Personality and Social Psychology, 58,* 487-498.

Izard, C. E. (1994). Innate and universal facial expressions: Evidence from developmental and cross-cultural research. *Psychological Bulletin, 115,* 288-299.

Jacobs, B. A. (1992). Undercover deception: Reconsidering presentations of self. *Journal of Contemporary Ethnography, 21,* 200-225.

Jacoby, L. L., Lindsay, S. D., & Toth, J. P. (1992). Unconscious influences revealed: Attention, awareness, and control. *American Psychologist, 47,* 802-809.

Janoff-Bulman, R. (1979). Characterological versus behavioral self-blame: Inquiries into depression and rape. *Journal of Personality and Social Psychology, 37,* 1798-1809.

Janoff-Bulman, R. (1992). *Shattered assumptions: Toward a new psychology of trauma.* New York: Free Press.

Jaworski, A. (1993). *The power of silence.* Newbury Park, CA: Sage.

John, O. P., & Robins, R. W. (1994). Accuracy and bias in self-perception: Individual differences in self-enhancement and the role of narcissism. *Journal of Personality and Social Psychology, 66,* 206-219.

Jones, D. H. (1989). Pervasive self-deception. *Southern Journal of Philosophy, 27,* 217-237.

Jones, E. E., & Gerald, H. B. (1967). *Foundations of social psychology.* New York: John Wiley.

Jones, W. H. (1985). The psychology of loneliness: Some personality issues in the study of social support. In I. G. Sarason & B. R. Sarason (Eds.), *Social support: Theory, research, and application* (pp. 225-241). The Hague, the Netherlands: Martinus Nijhof.

Jourard, S. (1964). *The transparent self.* New York: Van Nostrand.

Judd, C. M., & Park, B. (1988). Out-group homogeneity: Judgments of variability at the individual and group levels. *Journal of Personality and Social Psychology, 54,* 778-788.

Judd, C. M., Ryan, C. S., & Park, B. (1991). Accuracy in the judgment of in-group and out-group variability. *Journal of Personality and Social Psychology, 61,* 366-379.

Julien, D., & Markman, H. J. (1991). Social support and social networks as determinants of individual and marital outcomes. *Journal of Social and Personal Relationships, 8,* 549-568.

Jussim, L. (1991). Social perception and social reality: A reflection-construction model. *Psychological Review, 98,* 54-73.

Kalbfleisch, P. J. (1992). Deceit, distrust and the social milieu: Application of deception research in a troubled world. *Journal of Applied Communication Research, 20,* 308-334.

Kasof, J., & Lee, J. Y. (1993). Implicit causality and implicit salience. *Journal of Personality and Social Psychology, 65,* 877-891.

Katz, L., & Epstein, S. (1991). Constructive thinking and coping with laboratory-induced stress. *Journal of Personality and Social Psychology, 61,* 789-800.

Kellermann, K. (1992). Communication: Inherently strategic and primarily automatic. *Communication Monographs, 59,* 288-300.

Kellermann, K., Reynolds, R., & Chen, J. B. (1991). Strategies of conversational retreat: When parting is not sweet sorrow. *Communication Monographs, 58,* 362-383.

Kelley, D. L., & Burgoon, J. K. (1991). Understanding marital satisfaction and couple type as functions of relational expectations. *Human Communication Research, 18,* 40-69.

Kemper, S., Estil, R., Otalvaro, N., & Schadler, M. (1985). Questions of facts and questions of inference. In A. C. Graesser & J. B. Black (Eds.), *The psychology of questions* (pp. 227-246). Hillsdale, NJ: Lawrence Erlbaum.

Kemper, S., & Thissen, D. (1981). Memory for the dimensions of requests. *Journal of Verbal Learning and Verbal Behavior, 20,* 552-563.

Kenny, D. A. (1988). Interpersonal perception: A social relations analysis. *Journal of Social and Personal Relationships, 5,* 247-261.

Kenny, D. A. (1991). A general model of consensus and accuracy in interpersonal perception. *Psychological Review, 98,* 155-163.

Kenny, D. A. (1994). *Interpersonal perception: A social relations analysis.* New York: Guilford.

Kenny, D. A., & DePaulo, B. M. (1993). Do people know how others view them? An empirical and theoretical account. *Psychological Bulletin, 114,* 145-161.

Kernis, M. H., Brockner, J., & Frankel, B. (1989). Self-esteem and reactions to failure: The mediating role of overgeneralization. *Journal of Personality and Social Psychology, 57,* 707-714.

Kernis, M. H., Cornell, D. P., Sun, C. R., Berry, A., & Harlow, T. (1993). There's more to self-esteem than whether it is high or low: The importance of stability of self-esteem. *Journal of Personality and Social Psychology, 65,* 1190-1204.

Kernis, M. H., Grannemann, B. D., & Barclay, L. C. (1992). Stability of self-esteem: Assessment, correlates, and excuse-making. *Journal of Personality, 60,* 621-644.

Kihistrom, J. F. (1987). The cognitive unconscious. *Science, 237,* 1445-1452.

Kihistrom, J. F., & Klein, S. B. (1994). The self as a knowledge structure. In R. S. Wyer, Jr., & T. K. Srull (Eds.), *Handbook of social cognition: Vol. 1. Basic processes* (2nd ed., pp. 153-208). Hillsdale, NJ: Lawrence Erlbaum.

Kim, M., & Wilson, S. R. (1994). A cross-cultural comparison of implicit theories of requesting. *Communication Monographs, 61,* 210-235.

Kimble, C. E., & Musgrove, J. I. (1988). Dominance in arguing mixed-sex dyads: Visual dominance patterns, talking time, and speech loudness. *Journal of Research on Personality, 22,* 1-16.

King, L. A., & Emmons, R. A. (1990). Conflict over emotional expression: Psychological and physical correlates. *Journal of Personality and Social Psychology, 58,* 864-877.

Kitayama, S. (1990). Interaction between affect and cognition in word perception. *Journal of Personality and Social Psychology, 58,* 209-217.

Knowles, P. L., & Smith, D. L. (1984). The ecological perspective applied to social perception: Revision of a working paper. *Journal of the Theory of Social Behavior, 12,* 53-78.

Komorita, S. S., Hilty, J. A., & Parks, C. D. (1991). Reciprocity and cooperation in social dilemmas. *Journal of Conflict Resolution, 35,* 494-518.

Kotthoff, H. (1993). Disagreement and concession in disputes: On the context sensitivity of preference structures. *Language in Society, 22,* 193-216.

Kramer, R. M., Pommerenke, P., & Newton, E. (1993). The social context of negotiation: Effects of social identity and interpersonal accountability on negotiator decision making. *Journal of Conflict Resolution, 37,* 633-654.

Kressel, K., & Pruitt, D. (1989). Conclusion: A research perspective on the mediation of social conflict. In K. Kressel & D. G. Pruitt (Eds.), *Mediation research* (pp. 394-436). San Francisco: Jossey-Bass.

Kring, A. M., Smith, D. A., & Neale, J. M. (1994). Individual differences in dispositional expressiveness: Development and validation of the emotional expressivity scale. *Journal of Personality and Social Psychology, 66,* 934-949.

Krokoff, L. J. (1987). The correlates of negative affect in marriage. *Journal of Family Issues, 8,* 111-135.

Kruglanski, A. W. (1990). Motivations for judging and knowing: Implications for causal attribution. In E. T. Higgins & R. M. Sorrentino (Eds.), *The handbook of motivation and cognition: Foundations of social behavior* (Vol. 2, pp. 333-368). New York: Guilford.

Kruglanski, A. W., & Mayseless, O. (1988). Contextual effects in hypothesis testing: The role of competing alternatives and epistemic motivations. *Social Cognition, 6,* 1-21.

Kurdek, L. A. (1987). Sex role of self schema and psychological adjustment in coupled homosexual and heterosexual man and women. *Sex Roles, 17,* 549-562.

Kurdek, L. A. (1991a). Correlates of relationship satisfaction in cohabiting gay and lesbian couples: Integration of contextual, investment, and problem-solving models. *Journal of Personality and Social Psychology, 61,* 910-922.

Kurdek, L. A. (1991b). Predictors of increases in marital distress in newlywed couples: A 3-year prospective longitudinal study. *Developmental Psychology, 27,* 627-636.

Laing, R. D., Phillipson, J., & Lee, A. R. (1966). *Interpersonal perception: A theory and a method of research.* New York: Springer.

Lamb, R., & Lalljee, M. (1992). The use of prototypical explanations in first- and third-person accounts. In M. L. McLaughlin, M. J. Cody, & S. J. Read (Eds.), *Explaining one's self to others: Reason-giving in a social context* (pp. 21-39). Hillsdale, NJ: Lawrence Erlbaum.

Lambert, A. J., & Wedell, D. H. (1991). The self and social judgment: Effects of affective reaction and "own position" on judgments of unambiguous and ambiguous information about others. *Journal of Personality and Social Psychology, 61,* 884-897.

Langer, E. J., & Park, K. (1990). Incompetence: A conceptual reconsideration. In J. Kolligian, Jr., & R. J. Sternberg (Eds.), *Competence considered* (pp. 146-166). New Haven, CT: Yale University Press.

Langston, C. A. (1994). Capitalizing on and coping with daily-life events: Expressive responses to positive events. *Journal of Personality and Social Psychology, 67,* 1112-1125.

Larwood, L., & Whittaker, W. (1977). Managerial myopia: Self-serving biases in organizational planning. *Journal of Applied Psychology, 62,* 194-198.

Lee, D. A., & Peck, J. J. (1995). Troubled waters: Argument as sociability revisited. *Language in Society, 24,* 29-52.

Lehman, D. R., Wortman, C. B., & Williams, A. F. (1987). Long-term effects of losing a spouse or child in a motor vehicle crash. *Journal of Personality and Social Psychology, 52,* 218-231.

Leippe, M. R., Manion, A. P., & Romanczyk, A. (1992). Eyewitness persuasion: How and how well do fact finders judge the accuracy of adults' and children's memory reports? *Journal of Personality and Social Psychology, 63,* 181-197.

LePoire, B. A., & Burgoon, J. K. (1994). Two contrasting explanations of involvement violations: Expectancy violations theory versus discrepancy arousal theory. *Human Communication Research, 20,* 560-591.

Lepore, S. J., Evans, G. W., & Schneider, M. L. (1991). Dynamic role of social support in the link between chronic stress and psychological distress. *Journal of Personality and Social Psychology, 61,* 899-909.

Levenson, E. (1972). *The fallacy of understanding: An inquiry into the changing structure of psychoanalysis.* New York: Basic Books.

Levine, T. R., & McCornack, S. A. (1992). Linking love and lies: A formal test of the McCornack and Parks model of deception detection. *Journal of Personal and Social Relationships, 9,* 143-154.

Levinson, D. (1994). Ethnocentrism. In *Ethnic relations: A cross-cultural encyclopedia.* Santa Barbara, CA: ABC-CLIO.

Linkey, H. E., & Firestone, I. J. (1990). Dyad dominance composition effects, nonverbal behaviors, and influence. *Journal of Research on Personality, 24,* 206-215.

Lippard, P. V. (1988). "Ask me no questions, I'll tell you no lies": Situational exigencies for interpersonal deception. *Western Journal of Speech Communication, 52,* 91-103.

Loftus, E. (1992). When a lie becomes a memory's truth: Memory distortion after exposure to misinformation. *Current Directions in Psychological Science, 1,* 121-123.

Logan, G. D. (1989). Automaticity and cognitive control. In J. S. Uleman & J. A. Bargh (Eds.), *Unintended thought* (pp. 52-74). New York: Guilford.

Long, E. C. J., & Andrews, D. W. (1990). Perspective taking as a predictor of marital adjustment. *Journal of Personality and Social Psychology, 59,* 126-131.

Lykken, D. T. (1984). Polographic interrogation. *Nature, 307,* 681-684.

MacDonald, M. C. (1993). The interaction of lexical and syntactic ambiguity. *Journal of Memory and Language, 32,* 692-715.

MacDonald, M. C. (1994). Probabilistic constraints and syntactic ambiguity resolution. *Language and Cognitive Processes, 9,* 157-201.

MacDonald, M. C., Pearlmutter, N. J., & Seidenberg, M. S. (1994). Lexical nature of syntactic ambiguity resolution. *Psychological Review, 101,* 676-703.

Madison, G. B. (1982). *Understanding: A phenomenological-pragmatic analysis.* Westport, CT: Greenwood.

Magnusson, D., & Endler, N. S. (1977). Interactional psychology: Present status and future prospects. In D. Magnusson & N. S. Endler (Eds.), *Personality at the crossroads: Current issues in interactional psychology* (pp. 3-36). Hillsdale, NJ: Lawrence Erlbaum.

Makau, J. M. (1990). *Reasoning and communication.* Belmont, CA: Wadsworth.

Malloy, T. E., & Albright, L. (1990). Interpersonal perception in a social context. *Journal of Personality and Social Psychology, 58,* 419-428.

Malloy, T. E., & Janowski, C. L. (1992). Perceptions and metaperceptions of leadership: Components, accuracy, and dispositional correlates. *Personality and Social Psychology Bulletin, 18,* 700-708.

Malloy, T. E., & Kenny, D. A. (1986). The social relations model: An integrative methodology for personality research. *Journal of Personality, 54,* 199-225.

Marks, G., & Duval, S. (1991). Availability of alternative positions and estimates of consensus. *British Journal of Social Psychology, 30,* 179-183.

Marks, G., & Miller, N. (1987). Ten years of research on the false consensus effect: An empirical and theoretical review. *Psychological Bulletin, 102,* 72-90.

Markus, H., Cross, S., & Wurf, E. (1990). The role of the self-system in competence. In *Competence considered* (pp. 205-225). New Haven, CT: Yale University Press.

Markus, H. R., & Kitayama, S. (1991). Culture and the self: Implications for cognition, motivation, and emotion. *Psychological Review, 98,* 224-253.

Mayer, B. (1985). Conflict resolution in child protection and adoption. *Mediation Quarterly, 7,* 69-81.

Maynard, D. W., & Clayman, S. E. (1991). The diversity of ethnomethodology. *Annual Review of Sociology, 17,* 385-418.

McAdams, D. P. (1985). *Power, intimacy and the life story.* Homewood, IL: Dorsey.

McAdams, D. P. (1993). *The stories we live by: Personal myths and the making of the self.* New York: William Morrow.

McCall, G. (1982). Becoming unrelated: The management of bond dissolution. In S. Duck (Ed.), *Becoming unrelated: The management of bond dissolution* (pp. 211-231). New York: Academic Press.

McClure, J. (1992). An economy of explanations. In M. L. McLaughlin, M. J. Cody, & S. J. Read (Eds.), *Explaining one's self to others: Reason-giving in a social context* (pp. 61-82). Hillsdale, NJ: Lawrence Erlbaum.

McCornack, S. A. (1992). Information manipulation theory. *Communication Monographs, 59,* 1-16.

McCornack, S. A., & Levine, T. R. (1990). When lovers become leery: The relationship between suspicion and accuracy in detecting deception. *Communication Monographs, 57,* 219-230.

McCornack, S. A., Levine, T. R., Morrison, K., & Lapinski, M. (1996). Speaking of information manipulation: A critical rejoinder. *Communication Monographs, 63,* 83-92.

McCornack, S. A., & Parks, M. R. (1990). What women know that men don't: Sex differences in determining the truth behind deceptive messages. *Journal of Social and Personal Relationships, 7,* 107-118.

McGonagle, K. A., Kessier, R. C., & Gotlib, I. H. (1993). The effects of marital disagreement style, frequency, and outcome on marital disruption. *Journal of Social and Personal Relationships, 10,* 385-404.

McGonagle, K. A., Kessier, R. C., & Schilling, E. A. (1992). The frequency and determinants of marital disagreements in a community sample. *Journal of Social and Personal Relationships, 9,* 507-524.

McGrath, E., Keita, G. P., Strickland, B. R., & Russo, N. F. (Eds.). (1990). *Women and depression: Risk factors and treatment issues.* Washington, DC: American Psychological Association.

McKoon, G., & Ratcliff, R. (1992). Inference during reading. *Psychological Review, 99,* 440-466.

McLaughlin, M. L., Cody, M. J., & Read, S. J. (Eds.). (1992). *Explaining one's self to others: Reason-giving in a social context.* Hillsdale, NJ: Lawrence Erlbaum.

Medin, D. L., Goldstone, R. L., & Gentner, D. (1993). Respects for similarity. *Psychological Review, 100,* 254-278.

Merydith, S. P., & Wallbrown, F. H. (1991). Reconsidering response sets, test-taking attitudes, dissimulation, self-deception, and social desirability. *Psychological Reports, 69,* 891-905.

Metts, S. (1989). An exploratory investigation of deception in close relationships. *Journal of Social and Personal Relationships, 6,* 159-179.

Metts, S. (1994). Relational transgressions. In W. R. Cupach & B. H. Spitzberg (Eds.), *The dark side of interpersonal communication* (pp. 217-239). Hillsdale, NJ: Lawrence Erlbaum.

Metts, S., & Chronis, H. (1986, April). *An exploratory investigation of deception in close relationships.* Paper presented at the annual meeting of the International Communication Association, Montreal.

Metts, S., & Cupach, W. R. (1986, April). *Disengagement themes in same-sex and opposite-sex friendships.* Paper presented to the Interpersonal Communication Interest Group, Western Speech Communication Association, Tucson, AZ.

Metts, S., & Cupach, W. R. (1990). The influence of relationship beliefs and problem-solving responses on satisfaction in romantic relationships. *Human Communication Research, 17,* 170-185.

Mikulincer, M., & Nachshon, O. (1991). Attachment styles and patterns of self-disclosure. *Journal of Personality and Social Psychology, 61,* 321-331.

Milardo, R. M. (1992). Comparative methods for delineating social networks. *Journal of Social and Personal Relationships, 9,* 447-461.

Millar, A. (1991). *Reasons and experience.* Oxford: Clarendon.

Millar, K. U., & Tesser, A. (1988). Deceptive behavior in social relationships: A consequence of violated expectations. *Journal of Psychology, 122,* 263-273.

Millar, S. (1993). In pursuit of clarity: An analysis of speech education manuals. *Language & Communication, 13,* 287-303.

Miller, D. T., & Turnbull, W. (1986). Expectancies and interpersonal processes. In M. R. Rosenzweig & L. W. Porter (Eds.), *Annual review of psychology* (Vol. 37, pp. 233-256). Palo Alto, CA: Annual Reviews.

Miller, G. R., Mongeau, P. A., & Sleight, C. (1986). Fudging with friends and lying to lovers: Deceptive communication in personal relationships. *Journal of Social and Personal Relationships, 3,* 495-512.

Miller, G. R., & Parks, M. R. (1982). Communication in dissolving relationships. In S. Duck (Ed.), *Personal relationships: Vol. 4. Dissolving personal relationships* (pp. 127-154). New York: Academic Press.

Miller, G. R., & Stiff, J. B. (1993). *Deceptive communication.* Newbury Park, CA: Sage.

Miller, L. C. (1990). Disclosure liking effects at the individual and dyadic level: A social relations analysis. *Journal of Personality and Social Psychology, 59,* 50-60.

Mills, J., & Clark, M. S. (1994). Communal and exchange relationships: Controversies and research. In R. Erber & R. Gilmour (Eds.), *Theoretical frameworks for personal relationships* (pp. 29-42). Hillsdale, NJ: Lawrence Erlbaum.

Monsour, M. (1992). Meanings of intimacy in cross- and same-sex friendships. *Journal of Social and Personal Relationships, 9,* 277-295.

Monsour, M., Betty, S., & Kurzweil, N. (1993). Levels of perspectives and the perception of intimacy in cross-sex friendships: A balance theory explanation of shared perceptual reality. *Journal of Social and Personal Relationships, 10,* 529-550.

Montgomery, B. M. (1993). Relationship maintenance versus relationship change: A dialectical dilemma. *Journal of Social and Personal Relationships, 10,* 205-223.

Moore, A. W. (1987). Points of view. *Philosophical Quarterly, 37,* 1-20.

Mortensen, C. D. (1976). A transactional paradigm of verbalized social conflict. In G. R. Miller & H. W. Simons (Eds.), *Perspectives on communication in social conflict* (pp. 90-124). Englewood Cliffs, NJ: Prentice Hall.

Mortensen, C. D. (1987). *Violence and communication: Public reactions to an attempted presidential assassination.* Lanham, MD: University Press of America.

Mortensen, C. D. (1991). Communication, conflict, and culture. *Communication Theory, 1,* 273-293.

Mortensen, C. D. (1994). *Problematic communication: The construction of invisible walls.* Westport, CT: Praeger.

Mortensen, C. D., & Arnston, P. H. (1974). The effect of predispositions toward verbal behavior on interaction patterns in dyads. *Quarterly Journal of Speech, 60,* 421-430.

Mortensen, C. D., Arntson, P. H., & Lustig, R. (1977). The measurement of verbal predispositions: Scale development and application. *Human Communication Research, 3,* 146-158.

Murray, S. L., & Holmes, J. G. (1993). Seeing virtues in faults: Negativity and the transformation of interpersonal narratives in close relationships. *Journal of Personality and Social Psychology, 65,* 707-722.

Neimeyer, R. A., & Mitchell, K. A. (1988). Similarity and attraction: A longitudinal study. *Journal of Social and Personal Relationships, 5,* 131-148.

Neuberg, S. L., & Fiske, S. T. (1987). Motivational influences in impression formation: Outcome dependency, accuracy-driven attention, and individuating processes. *Journal of Personality and Social Psychology, 53,* 431-444.

Neuliep, J. W., & Mattson, M. (1990). The use of deception as a compliance-gaining strategy. *Human Communication Research, 16,* 409-421.

Newcomb, M. D. (1990). Social support by many other names: Towards a unified conceptualization. *Journal of Social and Personal Relationships, 7,* 479-494.

Newcomb, M. D., & Bentler, P. M. (1981). Marital breakdown. In S. Duck & R. Gilmour (Eds.), *Personal relationships: Vol. 3. Personal relationships in disorder* (pp. 57-94). New York: Academic Press.

Newell, S. E., & Stutman, R. K. (1988). The social confrontation episode. *Communication Monographs, 55,* 266-285.

Nezlek, J. B. (1993). The stability of social interaction. *Journal of Personality and Social Psychology, 65,* 930-941.

Nicotera, A. M. (1994). The use of multiple approaches to conflict: A study of sequences. *Human Communication Research, 20,* 592-621.

Niedenthal, P. M. (1989). Implicit perception of affective information. *Journal of Experimental Social Psychology, 26,* 505-527.

Nöelle-Neumann, E. (1984). *The spiral of silence.* Chicago: University of Chicago Press.

Nöelle-Neumann, E. (1991). The theory of public opinion: The concept of the spiral of silence. In J. A. Anderson (Ed.), *Communication yearbook 14.* Newbury Park, CA: Sage.

Noller, P. (1985a). Negative communications in marriage. *Journal of Personal and Social Relationships, 2,* 289-301.

Noller, P. (1985b). Video primacy: A further look. *Journal of Nonverbal Behavior, 9,* 28-47.

Norem, J. K., & Cantor, N. (1986). Defensive pessimism: "Harnessing" anxiety as motivation. *Journal of Personality and Social Psychology, 51,* 1208-1217.

Notarius, C. L., Benson, P. R., Sloane, D., Vanzetti, N., & Hornyak, L. M. (1989). Exploring the interface between perception and behavior: An analysis of marital interaction in distressed and nondistressed couples. *Behavioral Assessment, 11,* 39-64.

Notarius, C. L., & Herrick, L. R. (1988). Listener response strategies to a distressed other. *Journal of Social and Personal Relationship, 5,* 97-108.

Nowicki, S., Jr., & Manheim, S. (1991). Interpersonal complementarity and time of interaction in female friendships. *Journal of Research in Personality, 25,* 322-333.

O'Hair, D., & Cody, M. J. (1994). Deception. In W. R. Cupach & B. H. Spitzberg (Eds.), *The dark side of interpersonal communication* (pp. 181-213). Hillsdale, NJ: Lawrence Erlbaum.

Omodie, M. M., & Wearing, A. J. (1990). Need satisfaction and involvement in personal projects: Toward an integrative model of subjective well-being. *Journal of Personality and Social Psychology, 59,* 762-769.

Orive, R. (1988). Social projection and social comparison of opinions. *Journal of Personality and Social Psychology, 54,* 953-964.

Osborne, R. E., & Gilbert, D. T. (1992). The preoccupational hazards of social life. *Journal of Personality and Social Psychology, 62,* 219-228.

Owen, W. F. (1993). Metaphors in accounts of romantic relationship terminations. In P. J. Kalbfleisch (Ed.), *Interpersonal communication: Evolving interpersonal relationships* (pp. 261-278). Hillsdale, NJ: Lawrence Erlbaum.

Paniagua, F. A. (1989). Lying by children: Why children say one thing, do another? *Psychological Reports, 64,* 971-984.

Parks, C. D., & Vu, A. D. (1994). Social dilemma behavior of individuals from highly individualistic and collectivistic cultures. *Journal of Conflict Resolution, 38,* 708-718.

Paulhus, D. L., & Reid, D. B. (1991). Enhancement and denial in socially desirable responding. *Journal of Personality and Social Psychology, 60,* 307-317.

Paunonen, S. V. (1991). On the accuracy of ratings of personality by strangers. *Journal of Personality and Social Psychology, 61,* 471-477.

Pearce, W. B. (1989). *Communication and the human condition.* Carbondale: Southern Illinois University Press.

Pearson, J. N., Thoennes, N., & Vanderkooi, L. (1982). The decision to mediate: Profiles of individuals who accept and reject the opportunity to mediate contested child custody and visitation issues. *Journal of Divorce, 6,* 17-35.

Peirce, C. S. (1955). *Philosophical writings of Peirce* (J. Buchler, Ed.). New York: Dover.

Pennebaker, J. W., & Beall, S. K. (1986). Confronting a traumatic event: Toward an understanding of inhibition and disease. *Journal of Abnormal Psychology, 95,* 274-281.

Peterson, B. E., Winter, D. G., & Doty, R. M. (1994). Laboratory tests of a motivational-perceptual model of conflict escalation. *Journal of Conflict Resolution, 38,* 719-748.

Petronio, S. (1991). Communication boundary management: A theoretical model of managing disclosure of private information between marital couples. *Communication Theory, 1,* 311-335.

Petty, R. E., & Cacioppo, J. T. (1986). The elaboration likelihood model of persuasion. In L. Berkowitz (Ed.), *Advances in experimental social psychology* (Vol. 19, pp. 123-205). San Diego, CA: Academic Press.

Philips, D. A., & Zimmerman, M. (1990). The developmental course of perceived competence and incompetence among competent children. In J. Kolligian, Jr., & R. J. Sternberg (Eds.), *Competence considered* (pp. 41-66). New Haven, CT: Yale University Press.

Pierce, G. R., Sarason, B. R., & Sarason, I. G. (1992). General and specific support expectations and stress as predictors of perceived supportiveness: An experimental study. *Journal of Personality and Social Psychology, 63,* 297-307.

Pitt, J. C. (Ed.). (1988). *Theories of explanation.* New York: Oxford University Press.

Pittman, T. S., & D'Agostino, P. R. (1989). Motivation and cognition: Control deprivation and the nature of subsequent information processing. *Journal of Experimental Social Psychology, 25,* 465-480.

Planalp, S., & Honeycutt, J. M. (1985). Events that increase uncertainty in personal relationships. *Human Communication Research, 11,* 593-604.

Polanyi, M. (1967). *The tacit dimension.* Garden City, NY: Anchor.

Pomerantz, A. (1984). Agreeing and disagreeing with assessments: Some features of preferred/dispreferred turn shapes. In M. Atkinson & H. Heritage (Eds.), *Structures of social action* (pp. 57-102). New York: Cambridge University Press.

Poole, G. D., & Craig, K. D. (1992). Judgments of genuine, suppressed, and faked facial expressions of pain. *Journal of Personality and Social Psychology, 63,* 797-805.

Posner, M. L., & Rothbart, M. K. (1989). Intentional chapters on unintended thoughts. In J. S. Uleman & J. A. Bargh (Eds.), *Unintended thought* (pp. 450-469). New York: Guilford.

Proctor, R. W., & Dutta, A. (1995). *Skill acquisition and human performance.* Thousand Oaks, CA: Sage.

Raskin, R., Novacek, J., & Hogan, R. (1991a). Narcissism, self-esteem, and defensive self-enhancement. *Journal of Personality and Social Psychology, 59,* 19-38.

Raskin, R., Novacek, J., & Hogan, R. (1991b). Narcissistic self-esteem management. *Journal of Personality and Social Psychology, 60,* 911-918.

Rawlins, W. K. (1992). *Friendship matters: Communication, dialectics, and the life course.* New York: Aldine.

Read, S. J. (1992). Constructing accounts: The role of explanatory coherence. In M. L. McLaughlin, M. J. Cody, & S. J. Read (Eds.), *Explaining one's self to others: Reason-giving in a social context* (pp. 3-19). Hillsdale, NJ: Lawrence Erlbaum.

Reber, A. S. (1992). The conscious unconscious: An evolutionary perspective. *Consciousness and Cognition, 1,* 93-133.

Reid, W. J. (1985). *Family problem solving.* New York: Columbia University Press.

Reis, H. T. (1994). Domains of experience: Investigating relationship processes from three perspectives. In R. Erber & R. Gilmour (Eds.), *Theoretical frameworks for personal relationships* (pp. 87-110). Hillsdale, NJ: Lawrence Erlbaum.

Reis, H. T., & Shaver, P. (1988). Intimacy as interpersonal process. In S. Duck (Ed.), *Handbook of personal relationships: Theory, research, and interventions* (pp. 367-389). New York: John Wiley.

Reiss, D. (1981). *The family's construction of reality.* Boston: Harvard University Press.

Reynolds, V., Falger, V., & Vine, I. (Eds.). (1987). *The sociobiology of ethnocentrism: Evolutionary dimensions of xenophobia, discrimination, racism, and nationalism.* London: Croom Helm.

Richards, I. A. (1925). *Principles of literary criticism.* New York: Harvest/HBJ.

Richards, I. A. (1965). *The philosophy of rhetoric.* New York: Oxford University Press.

Richardson, J. (1991). *Existential epistemology: A Heideggerian critique of the cartesian project.* Oxford: Clarendon.

Riggio, R. E., Tucker, J., & Throckmorton, B. (1987). Social skills and deception ability. *Personality and Social Psychology Bulletin, 13,* 568-577.

Roberts, L. J., & Krokoff, L. J. (1990). A time-series analysis of withdrawal, hostility, and displeasure in satisfied and dissatisfied marriages. *Journal of Marriage and the Family, 52,* 95-105.

Robinson, W. P. (1993). Lying in the public domain. *American Behavioral Scientist, 36,* 359-382.

Rodin, M. J. (1982). Non-engagement, failure to engage, and disengagement. In S. Duck (Ed.), *Personal relationships: Vol. 4. Dissolving personal relationships* (pp. 31-49). New York: Academic Press.

Roiger, J. F. (1993). Power in friendship and use of influence strategies. In P. J. Kalbfleisch (Ed.), *Interpersonal communication: Evolving interpersonal relationships* (pp. 133-145). Hillsdale, NJ: Lawrence Erlbaum.

Rommetveit, R. (1980). On 'meanings' of acts and what is meant and made known by what is said in a pluralist social world. In M. Brenner (Ed.), *The structure of action* (pp. 108-149). Oxford: Blackwell.

Rommetveit, R. (1988). Meaning, context, and control: Convergent trends and controversial issues in social-scientific research on human cognition and communication. *Inquiry, 30,* 77-99.

Ross, L., & Nisbett, R. E. (1990). *The person and the situation.* New York: McGraw-Hill.

Roth, D. L., Snyder, C. R., & Pace, L. M. (1986). Dimensions of favorable self-presentation. *Journal of Personality and Social Psychology, 51,* 867-874.

Rothbart, M., & Park, B. (1986). On the confirmability and disconfirmability of trait concepts. *Journal of Personality and Social Psychology, 50,* 131-142.

Rowland, D. L., Crisler, L. J., & Cox, D. J. (1982). Flirting between college students and faculty. *Journal of Sex Research, 18,* 346-359.

Ruble, T. L., & Thomas, K. W. (1976). Support for a two-dimensional model of conflict behavior. *Organizational Behavior and Human Performance, 16,* 143-155.

Ruehlman, L. S., & Wolchik, S. A. (1988). Personal goals and interpersonal support and hindrance as factors in psychological distress and well-being. *Journal of Personality and Social Psychology, 55,* 293-301.

Ruesch, J. (1973). *Therapeutic communication.* New York: Norton.

Ruesch, J., & Bateson, G. (1968). *Communication: The social matrix of psychiatry.* New York: Norton.

Rummelhart, M. A. (1983). When in doubt: Strategies used in response to interactional uncertainty. *Discourse Processes, 6,* 377-402.

Rusbult, C. E., Onizuka, R. K., & Lipkus, I. (1993). What do we really want? Mental models of ideal romantic involvement explored through multidimensional scaling. *Journal of Experimental Social Psychology, 29,* 493-527.

Rusbult, C. E., & Zembrody, I. M. (1983). Responses to dissatisfaction in romantic involvements: A multidimensional scaling analysis. *Journal of Experimental Social Psychology, 19,* 274-293.

Ruscher, J. B., & Hammer, E. D. (1994). Revising disrupted impressions through conversation. *Journal of Personality and Social Psychology, 66,* 530-541.

Russell, J. A. (1994). Is there universal recognition of emotion from facial expression? A review of the cross-cultural studies. *Psychological Bulletin, 115,* 102-141.

Sabine, J., & Silver, M. (1982). *Moralities of everyday life.* Oxford: Oxford University Press.

Sabourin, T. C., & Stamp, G. H. (1995). Communication and the experience of dialectical tensions in family life: An examination of abusive and nonabusive families. *Communication Monographs, 62,* 213-242.

Saidla, D. D. (1990). The construct validity of individual and interpersonal correlates of roommate relationship quality. *Journal of Social and Personal Relationships, 7,* 311-330.

Samter, W. (1994). Unsupportive relationships: Deficiencies in the support-giving skills of the lonely person's friends. In B. R. Burleson, T. L. Albrecht, & I. G. Sarason (Eds.), *Communication of social support: Messages, interactions, relationships, and community* (pp. 175-214). Thousand Oaks, CA: Sage.

Samter, W., Burleson, B. R., & Basden-Murphy, L. (1989). Behavioral complexity is in the eye of the beholder: Effects of cognitive complexity and message complexity on impressions of the source of comforting messages. *Human Communication Research, 15,* 612-629.

Sarason, B. R., Pierce, G. R., Bannerman, A., & Sarason, I. G. (1993). Investigating the antecedents of perceived social support: Parents' views of and behavior toward their children. *Journal of Personality and Social Psychology, 65,* 1071-1085.

Sarason, I. G., Pierce, G. R., & Sarason, B. R. (1990). Social support and interactional processes: A triadic hypothesis. *Journal of Social and Personal Relationships, 7,* 495-506.

Saxe, L. (1991). Lying: Thoughts of an applied social psychologist. *American Psychologist, 46,* 409-415.

Scharfstein, B. (1993). *Ineffability: The failure of words in philosophy and religion.* Albany: State University of New York.

246   MISCOMMUNICATION

Scheff, T. J. (1990). *Microsociology: Discourse, emotion, and social structure.* Chicago: University of Chicago Press.
Schneider, W. (1985). Training high-performance skills: Fallacies and guidelines. *Human Factors, 27,* 285-300.
Schul, Y., & Burnstein, E. (1985). When discounting fails: Conditions under which individuals use discredited information in making a judgment. *Journal of Personality and Social Psychology, 49,* 894-903.
Schwarzer, R., & Leppin, A. (1991). Social support and health: A theoretical and empirical overview. *Journal of Social and Personal Relationships, 8,* 99-127.
Scott, M. B., & Lyman, S. M. (1968). Accounts. *American Sociological Review, 33,* 46-62.
Sears, D. O. (1983). The person-positivity bias. *Journal of Personality and Social Psychology, 44,* 233-249.
Seger, C. A. (1994). Implicit learning. *Psychological Bulletin, 115,* 163-196.
Semin, G. R., & Gergen, K. J. (Eds.). (1990). *Everyday understanding: Social and scientific implications.* Newbury Park, CA: Sage.
Semin, G. R., & Marsman, J. G. (1994). "Multiple inference-inviting properties" of interpersonal verbs: Event instigation, dispositional inference, and implicit causality. *Journal of Personality and Social Psychology, 67,* 836-849.
Sharpe, D., Adair, G., & Roese, N. (1992). Twenty years of *deception* research: A decline in subjects' trust? *Personality and Social Psychology Bulletin, 18,* 585-590.
Shean, G. D. (1993). Delusions, self-deception, and intentionality. *Journal of Humanistic Psychology, 33,* 45-66.
Sheppard, B. H., Blumenfield-Jones, K., & Roth, J. (1989). Informal third-partyship: Studies of everyday conflict intervention. In K. Kressel & D. G. Pruitt (Eds.), *Mediation research* (pp. 166-189). San Francisco: Jossey-Bass.
Sherman, J. W., & Klein, S. B. (1994). Development and representations of personality impressions. *Journal of Personality and Social Psychology, 67,* 972-983.
Shotter, J. (1993). *Conversational realities: Constructing life through language.* London: Sage.
Showers, C. (1988). The effects of how and why thinking on perception of future negative events. *Cognitive Therapy and Research, 12,* 225-240.
Showers, C. (1992). The motivational and emotional consequences of considering positive or negative possibilities for an upcoming event. *Journal of Personality and Social Psychology, 63,* 474-484.
Sillars, A. L. (1985). Interpersonal perception in relationships. In W. Ickes (Ed.), *Compatible and incompatible relationships* (pp. 277-305). New York: Springer-Verlag.
Sillars, A. L., & Wilmot, W. W. (1994). Communication strategies in conflict and mediation. In J. A. Daly & J. M. Wiemann (Eds.), *Strategic interpersonal communication* (pp. 163-190). Hillsdale, NJ: Lawrence Erlbaum.
Skowronski, J. J., & Carlston, D. E. (1989). Negativity and extremity biases in impression formation: A review of explanation. *Psychological Bulletin, 105,* 131-142.
Smith, E. R., & Zarate, M. A. (1992). Exemplar-based model of social judgment. *Psychological Review, 99,* 3-21.
Smith, S. H., & Whitehead, G. I. (1993). The manipulation of publicness: The role of audience information. *Contemporary Social Psychology, 17,* 8-13.
Smith, W. P. (1987). Conflict and negotiation: Trends and emerging issues. *Journal of Applied Social Psychology, 17,* 641-677.
Snyder, C. R. (1989). Reality negotiation: From excuses to hope and beyond. *Journal of Social Psychology, 8,* 130-157.
Snyder, C. R., & Higgins, R. L. (1988). From making to being the excuse: An analysis of deception and verbal/nonverbal issues. *Journal of Nonverbal Behavior, 12,* 237-251.

Spitzberg, B. H. (1993). The dialectics of (in)competence. *Journal of Social and Personal Relationships, 10,* 137-158.

Stafford, L., & Canary, D. J. (1991). Maintenance strategies and romantic relationship type, gender and relational characteristics. *Journal of Social and Personal Relationships, 8,* 217-242.

Staw, B. (1981). The escalation of commitment to a course of action. *Academy of Management Review, 6,* 577-587.

Sternberg, R. J., & Dobson, D. M. (1987). Resolving interpersonal conflicts: An analysis of stylistic consistency. *Journal of Personality and Social Psychology, 52,* 794-812.

Sternberg, R. J., & Kolligian, J., Jr. (Eds.). (1990). *Competence considered.* New Haven, CT: Yale University Press.

Sternberg, R. J., & Soriano, L. J. (1984). Styles of conflict resolution. *Journal of Personality and Social Psychology, 47,* 115-126.

Stewart, A. J. (1982). The course of individual adaptation to life changes. *Journal of Personality and Social Psychology, 42,* 1100-1113.

Stiff, J. B., Kim, H. J., & Ramesh, C. N. (1992). Truth-bias and aroused suspicion in relational deception. *Communication Research, 19,* 326-345.

Sumner, W. G. (1906). *Folkways: A study of the sociological importance of usages, manners, customs, mores and morals.* Boston: Ginn.

Surra, C. A., & Longstreth, M. (1990). Similarity of outcomes, interdependence, and conflict in dating relationships. *Journal of Personality and Social Psychology, 59,* 501-516.

Svenson, O. (1981). Are we all less risky and more skillful than our fellow driver? *Acta Psychologica, 47,* 143-148.

Tardy, C. H. (1994). Counteracting task-induced stress: Studies of instrumental and emotional support in problem-solving contexts. In B. R. Burleson, T. K. Albrecht, & I. G. Sarason (Eds.), *Communication of social support: Messages, interactions, relationships, and community* (pp. 71-87). Thousand Oaks, CA: Sage.

Taylor, D., & Altman, F. (1987). Communication in interpersonal relationships: Social penetration processes. In M. Roloff & G. Miller (Eds.), *Interpersonal processes: New directions in communication research* (pp. 237-277). Newbury Park, CA: Sage.

Taylor, L., Gittes, M., O'Neal, E. C., & Brown, S. (1994). The reluctance to expose dangerous lies. *Journal of Applied Social Psychology, 24,* 301-315.

Taylor, S. E. (1989). *Positive illusions: Creative self-deception and the healthy mind.* New York: Basic Books.

Taylor, S. E. (1991). Asymmetrical effects of positive and negative events: The mobilization-minimization hypothesis. *Psychological Bulletin, 110,* 67-85.

Taylor, S. E., & Brown, J. D. (1988). Illusion and well-being: A social psychological perspective on mental health. *Psychological Bulletin, 103,* 193-210.

Taylor, S. E., & Brown, J. D. (1994). Positive illusions and well-being revisited: Separating fact from fiction. *Psychological Bulletin, 116,* 21-27.

Taylor, S. E., Wood, J. V., & Lichtman, R. R. (1983). It could be worse: Selective evaluation as a response to victimization. *Journal of Social Issues, 39,* 19-40.

Taylor T. J. (1992). *Mutual misunderstanding: Scepticism and the theorizing of language and interpretation.* Durham, NC: Duke University Press.

Thomas, E. J. (1977). *Marital communication and decision making: Analysis, assessment and change.* New York: Free Press.

Thompson, E. P., Roman, R. J., Moskowitz, G. B., Chaiken, S., & Bargh, J. A. (1994). Accuracy motivation attenuates covert priming: The systematic reprocessing of social information. *Journal of Personality and Social Psychology, 66,* 474-489.

Thompson, J. B. (1987). Language and ideology: A framework for analysis. *Sociological Review, 35,* 516-536.

Thompson, N. S. (1986). Deception and the concept of behavioral design. In R. W. Mitchell & N. S. Thompson (Eds.), *Deception: Perspectives on human and nonhuman deceit* (pp. 53-65). Albany: State University of New York Press.

Toolan, M. (1991). Perspectives on literal meaning. *Language & Communication, 11,* 333-351.

Toulmin, S. (1972). *Human understanding: The collective use and evolution of concepts.* Princeton, NY: Princeton University Press.

Touval, S., & Zartman, W. (1989). Mediation in international conflicts. In K. Kressel & D. G. Pruitt (Eds.), *Mediation research* (pp. 115-137). San Francisco: Jossey-Bass.

Tracey, T. J. (1994). An examination of the complementarity of interpersonal behavior. *Journal of Personality and Social Psychology, 67,* 864-878.

Trope, Y. (1986). Identification and inferential processes in dispositional attribution. *Psychological Review, 93,* 239-257.

Trope, Y. (1989). Levels of inference in dispositional judgment. *Social Cognition, 7,* 296-314.

Trope, Y., Cohen, O., & Alfieri, T. (1991). Behavior identification as a mediator of dispositional inference. *Journal of Personality and Social Psychology, 61,* 873-883.

Uleman, J. S., & Moskowitz, G. B. (1994). Unintended effects of goals on unintended inferences. *Journal of Personality and Social Psychology, 66,* 490-501.

Valentiner, D. P., Holahan, C. J., & Moos, R. H. (1994). Social support, appraisals of event controllability, and coping: An integrative model. *Journal of Personality and Social Psychology, 66,* 1094-1102.

Vallacher, R. R., Nowak, A., & Kaufman, J. (1994). Intrinsic dynamics of social judgment. *Journal of Personality and Social Psychology, 67,* 20-34.

Van der Dennen, J. M. (1987). Ethnocentrism and in-group/out-group differentiation: A review and interpretation of the literature. In V. Reynolds, V. Falger, & E. Vine (Eds.), *The sociobiology of ethnocentrism: Evolutionary dimensions of xenophobia, discrimination, racism and nationalism* (pp. 1-47). London: Croom Helm.

van Geert, P. (1991). A dynamic systems model of cognitive and language growth. *Psychological Review, 98,* 3-53.

Vangelisti, A. L. (1994). Messages that hurt. In W. R. Cupach & B. H. Spitzberg (Eds.), *The dark side of interpersonal communication* (pp. 53-82). Hillsdale, NJ: Lawrence Erlbaum.

Vangelisti, A. L., Knapp, M. L., & Daly, J. A. (1990). Conversational narcissism. *Communication Monographs, 57,* 251-274.

VanLear, C. A. (1987). The formation of social relationships: A longitudinal study of social penetration. *Human Communication Research, 13,* 299-322.

VanLear, C. A. (1991). Testing a cyclical model of communicative openness in relationship development: Two longitudinal studies. *Communication Monographs, 58,* 337-361.

Vaux, A. (1988). *Social support: Theory, research, and intervention.* New York: Praeger.

Vaux, A. (1990). An ecological approach to understanding and facilitating social support. *Journal of Social and Personal Relationships, 7,* 507-518.

Vine, I. (1987). Inclusive fitness and the self-system: The roles of human nature and sociocultural processes in intergroup discrimination. In V. Reynolds, V. Falger, & I. Vine (Eds.), *The sociobiology of ethnocentrism* (pp. 60-80). London: Croom Helm.

Vuchinich, S. (1986). On attenuation in verbal family conflict. *Social Psychology Quarterly, 49,* 281-293.

Vuchinich, S. (1990). The sequential organization of closing in verbal family conflict. In A. D. Grimshaw (Ed.), *Conflict talk: Sociolinguistic investigations of arguments in conversations* (pp. 118-138). New York: Cambridge University Press.

Wall, J. A., Jr., & Lynn, A. (1993). Mediation: A current review. *Journal of Conflict Resolution, 37,* 160-194.

Wall, V. D., & Nolan, L. L. (1987). Small group conflict: A look at equity, satisfaction, and styles of conflict management. *Small Group Behavior, 18,* 188-211.

Walton, D. N. (1990). *Practical reasoning: Goal-driven, knowledge-based action-guiding argumentation.* Savage, MD: Rowman & Littlefield.

Washburn, C. (1969). Retortmanship: How to avoid answering questions. *Etc, 26,* 69-75.

Watson, D. (1989). Strangers' ratings of the five robust personality factors: Evidence of a surprising convergence with self-report. *Journal of Personality and Social Psychology, 57,* 120-128.

Watzlawick, P., Beavin, J., & Jackson, D. (1967). *Pragmatics of human communication.* New York: Norton.

Watzlawick, P., Weakland, J., & Fisch, R. (1974). *Change: Principles of problem formation and problem resolution.* New York: Norton.

Weary, G., & Edwards, J. A. (1994). Individual differences in causal uncertainty. *Journal of Personality and Social Psychology, 67,* 308-318.

Weber, A. L., & Harvey, J. H. (1994). *Perspectives on close relationships.* Boston: Allyn & Bacon.

Weber, A. L., Harvey, J. H., & Orbuch, T. L. (1992). What went wrong: Communicating accounts of relationship conflict. In M. L. McLaughlin, M. J. Cody, & S. J. Read (Eds.), *Explaining one's self to others: Reason-giving in a social context* (pp. 261-280). Hillsdale, NJ: Lawrence Erlbaum.

Weesie, J. (1994). Incomplete information and timing in the volunteer's dilemma: A comparison of four models. *Journal of Conflict Resolution, 38,* 557-585.

Wegner, D. M. (1992). You can't always think what you want: Problems in the suppression of unwanted thoughts. In M. P. Zanna (Ed.), *Advances in experimental social psychology* (Vol. 25, pp. 193-225). San Diego, CA: Academic Press.

Weiner, B. (1992). Excuses in everyday interaction. In M. L. McLaughlin, M. J. Cody, & S. J. Read (Eds.), *Explaining one's self to others: Reason-giving in a social context* (pp. 131-146). Hillsdale, NJ: Lawrence Erlbaum.

Weinstein, N. D. (1980). Unrealistic optimism about future life events. *Journal of Personality and Social Psychology, 39,* 806-820.

Weinstein, N. D. (1982). Unrealistic optimism about susceptibility to health problems. *Journal of Behavioral Medicine, 5,* 441-460.

Weisenberg, M., Wolf, Y., Mittwoch, T., & Mikulincer, M. (1990). Learned resourcefulness and perceived control of pain: A preliminary examination of construct validity. *Journal of Research in Personality, 24,* 101-110.

Wells, G. L., & Turtle, J. W. (1987). What is the best way to encode faces? In M. M. Gruneberg, P. E. Morris, & R. N. Sykes (Eds.), *Practical aspects of memory: Current research and issues* (Vol. 1, pp. 163-168). New York: John Wiley.

Werth, L. F., & Flaherty, J. (1986). A phenomenological approach to human deception. In R. W. Mitchell & N. S. Thompson (Eds.), *Deception: Perspectives on human and nonhuman deceit* (pp. 293-311). Albany: State University of New York Press.

Wiemann, J. M., & Krueger, D. L. (1980). The language of relationships: I. Deception. In H. Giles, W. P. Robinson, & P. M. Smith (Eds.), *Language: Social psychological perspectives* (pp. 55-62). Oxford: Pergamon.

Wilder, C., & Collins, S. (1994). Patterns of interactional paradoxes. In W. R. Cupach & B. H. Spitzberg (Eds.), *The dark side of interpersonal communication* (pp. 83-103). Hillsdale, NJ: Lawrence Erlbaum.

Wilkes-Gibbs, D., & Clark, H. H. (1992). Coordinating beliefs in conversation. *Journal of Memory and Language, 31,* 183-194.

Wilmot, W. W. (1987). *Dyadic communication*. New York: Random House.

Wilson, T. D., & Brekke, N. (1994). Mental contamination and mental correction: Unwanted influences on judgments and evaluations. *Psychological Bulletin, 116,* 117-142.

Woike, B. A. (1994). The use of differentiation and integration processes: Empirical studies of "separate" and "connected" ways of thinking. *Journal of Personality and Social Psychology, 67,* 142-150.

Woike, B. A., Aronoff, J., Stollak, G. E., & Loraas, J. (1994). Links between intrapsychic and interpersonal defenses in dyadic interaction. *Journal of Research in Personality, 28,* 101-113.

Wojciszke, B. (1994). Multiple meanings of behavior: Construing actions in terms of competence or morality. *Journal of Personality and Social Psychology, 67,* 222-232.

Wold, A. H. (Ed.). (1992). *The dialogical alternative: Towards a theory of language and mind.* Oslo, Norway: Scandinavian University Press.

Wortman, C. B., & Conway, T. L. (1985). The role of social support in adaption and recovery from physical illness. In S. Cohen & S. L. Syme (Eds.), *Social support and health* (pp. 281-302). San Diego, CA: Academic Press.

Wynne, L., Ryckhoff, I., Day, J., & Hirsch, S. (1958). Pseudo-mutuality in the family relations of schizophrenics. *Psychiatry, 21,* 205-220.

Yaffe, M. (1981). Disordered sexual relationships. In S. Duck & R. Gilmour (Eds.), *Personal relationships: Vol. 3. Personal relationships in disorder* (pp. 111-122). New York: Academic Press.

Zautra, A. J., & Wrabetz, A. B. (1991). Coping success and its relationship to psychological distress in older adults. *Journal of Personality and Social Psychology, 61,* 801-810.

Zimmerman, M. A. (1990). Toward a theory of learned hopefulness: A structural model analysis of participation and empowerment. *Journal of Research in Personality, 24,* 71-86.

Zimmermann, S., & Applegate, J. L. (1994). Communicating social support in organizations: A message-centered approach. In B. R. Burleson, T. L. Albrecht, & I. G. Sarason (Eds.), *Communication of social support: Messages, interactions, relationships, and community* (pp. 50-70). Thousand Oaks, CA: Sage.

Zuckerman, M., DePaulo, B. M., & Rosenthal, R. (1981). Verbal and nonverbal communication of deception. In L. Berkowitz (Ed.), *Advances in experimental social psychology* (Vol. 14, pp. 1-59). New York: Academic Press.

Zuckerman, M., Koestner, R., & Alton, A. O. (1984). Learning to detect deception. *Journal of Personality and Social Psychology, 46,* 519-528.

Index

About the Authors

C. David Mortensen is Professor of Communication Science in the Department of Communication Arts at the University of Wisconsin—Madison. He is the author of many books on communication and conflict, including *Communication: The Study of Human Interaction; Violence and Communication: Public Reactions to an Attempted Presidential Assassination;* and *Problematic Communication: The Construction of Invisible Walls.* He is currently writing *Misunderstanding Other People* and *The Search for Common Ground.*

Carter M. Ayres is a psychologist for the Sun Prairie, Wisconsin, school system. He is interested in the application of humanistic psychology to problematic circumstance in adult-child interaction.